Born in 1953

The story about a post-war Swedish cohort, and a longitudinal research project

Sten-Åke Stenberg

STOCKHOLM
UNIVERSITY PRESS

Published by
Stockholm University Press
Stockholm University
SE-106 91 Stockholm, Sweden
www.stockholmuniversitypress.se

ORCID: https://orcid.org/0000-0002-7118-2724

Supporting Agency (funding): Åke Wibergs stiftelse

First published 2018
Cover Image: Photographer Unknown/DN/TT Nyhetsbyrån
Cover Copyright: DN/TT Nyhetsbyrån, License: CC-BY-NC-ND
Cover Design: Karl Edqvist, SUP
Translator: David Shannon (from Swedish to English)
Original version in Swedish: Stenberg, Sten-Åke (2013). *Född 1953: folkhemsbarn i forskarfokus*. Umeå: Boréa Bokförlag

ISBN (Paperback): 978-91-7635-087-4
ISBN (PDF): 978-91-7635-084-3
ISBN (EPUB): 978-91-7635-085-0
ISBN (MOBI): 978-91-7635-086-7

DOI: https://doi.org/10.16993/bav

To read the free, open access version of this book online, visit https://doi.org/10.16993/bav or scan this QR code with your mobile device.

Peer Review Policies

Stockholm University Press ensures that all book publications are peer-reviewed in two stages. Each book proposal submitted to the Press will be sent to a dedicated Editorial Board of experts in the subject area as well as two independent experts. The full manuscript will be peer reviewed by chapter or as a whole by two independent experts.

A full description of Stockholm University Press' peer-review policies can be found on the website: http://www.stockholmuniversitypress. se/site/peer-review-policies/

Editorial Board (Interim) of Social Sciences

Recognition for reviewers

The Editorial Board (Interim) of Social Sciences has applied single-blind review for proposal and manuscript assessment.

Martin Diewald, Professor of Social Structure, Bielefeldt University (Universität Bielefeldt), Germany. ORCID: https://orcid.org/0000-0002-9101-1586 (review of manuscript)

Amanda Sacker, Professor of Lifecourse Studies, ESRC International Centre for Lifecourse Studies in Society and Health (ICLS), UCL, United Kingdom. ORCID: https://orcid.org/0000-0001-8796-5398 (review of proposal)

Contents

PART III. ON THE FREEDOM, UTILITY AND RESPONSIBILITIES OF RESEARCH

Foreword

I am a child of the Swedish Folkhem,[1] born at Sabbatsberg Hospital in Stockholm on May 6, 1953. Twelve days later, my mother carried me home to her modest one-room apartment on Bråvallagatan on the other side of Vasaparken – a park in northwest central Stockholm. As she passed the children playing in the park, she may have thought for a moment about whether she would actually be able to cope with me. If so, her uncertainty would have been justified. At that time, it was still considered shameful to give birth to an "illegitimate" child. Abortion was illegal and for thousands of single mothers, the only alternative was to give the child up for adoption. But my unmarried mother had decided to keep her child. She passed Sankt Eriksplan with its trams and trolley buses and the metro station that had opened a little over six months earlier. In the neighbourhood around Bråvallagatan there were a large number of shops and several cinemas. Cooling water ran down the window of the butcher's shop, the fishmonger sold dried cod, and the haberdashery on Rörstrandsgatan had everything from fabric to needles and sewing patterns. On the corner of our block there was a radio store, which would start to sell television sets three years later, and further along the street there was a photo shop where my mother used to have her films developed.

No father was waiting for us at home, but my mother's sister, who was four years younger, stood ready with all the equipment deemed necessary for a newborn of the day. Together they would raise me.

Little could my mother have suspected that her newborn baby would become a Metropolitan child, that I would come to be included in a uniquely researched and statistically recorded group of 15,117 individuals, who had all been born in 1953 and were living in Greater Stockholm ten years later. This controversial sociological research project, known as Project Metropolitan, and its history, is what this book is about.

Sten-Åke Stenberg,
Stockholm, August 29, 2018.

PART I
PROJECT METROPOLITAN

The dream of a Nordic collaboration

Project Metropolitan was designed to follow people from childhood until adulthood. The overarching question was "Why do some get on better than others in life?" The project was questioned by the mass media and became the subject of considerable national and scientific debate. This debate concerned the freedom of research, the integrity of the individual and the task and role of the media vis-à-vis the research community.

Since 1964, all those who were living in Greater Stockholm in 1963 and who had been born in 1953, have been part of a Swedish sociological research project.[2] At the start, the project included 15,117 individuals, of whom over 1,000 have since died. It was called Project Metropolitan, but when it was updated at the beginning of the 2000s, it was rechristened *The Stockholm Birth Cohort*.[3]

Project Metropolitan was initiated during a period of optimism. After two devastating wars, the world was to become more peaceful; the economy was booming, unemployment was low and economic growth appeared to be limitless. This faith in the future was reflected in among other things the optimistic idea of beginning a large-scale joint Nordic research project. The man behind this idea was the Norwegian historian, and later sociologist, Kaare Svalastoga. Svalastoga's interest in sociology had been aroused during the Nazi occupation of Norway. Between April 1944 and the end of the war he had been interned in Grini, a notorious prison camp located outside

Image 1. The Norwegian historian and sociologist Kaare Svalastoga, who took the initiative for Project Metropolitan. Photographer: W. Månsson/ Nordfoto/NTB/TT Nyhetsbyrån. Copyright: Photographer: W. Månsson/ Nordfoto/NTB/TT Nyhetsbyrån, License: CC-BY-NC-ND.

How to cite this book chapter:
Stenberg, Sten-Åke. 2018. The dream of a Nordic collaboration. In: Stenberg, Sten-Åke. *Born in 1953: The story about a post-war Swedish cohort, and a longitudinal research project.* Pp. 3–24. Stockholm: Stockholm University Press. DOI: https://doi.org/10.16993/bav.a. License: CC-BY

Image 2. Professor Gösta Carlsson. Photographer: Unknown/ Sydsvenskan. Copyright: Sydsvenskan, Sydsvenskan, License: CC-BY-NC-ND.

Oslo. His internment was a result of an opinion survey that he had conducted during the occupation without the Germans' knowledge. The survey concerned the Norwegians' view of democracy and the reforms they wanted to be effected after the war.

Two years after the end of the war and his release from Grini, Kaare Svalastoga published his study: "Sosial ulikhet i en fangeleir" (Social Inequality in a Prison Camp).[4] The historian Svalastoga had quite simply conducted a sociological study based on his co-inmates, and he presented a systematic overview of the camp's social stratification. Who was at the top of the social hierarchy, and who was lower down? How was work, food and tobacco distributed? Everything was presented systematically, often in tables. By this time, Svalastoga had moved from Norway to the USA, where he continued along the sociological path. In 1950 he became a doctor of sociology. Kaare Svalastoga was first and foremost interested in what is usually referred to as the class society, i.e. how people in society can be organised into social groups. He was among the first to point to the need for social data that could capture changes across generations. He was naturally not alone in this field, and he had a number of sources of inspiration.[5]

At the end of the 1950s, he raised the idea of a Nordic study that would follow people from childhood until adulthood. He used the concept sequential, which involved following people's lives over a long period and in sequences.[6] This can be done in two ways, either retrospectively – starting in adulthood and collecting information based on memories, together with register data, for example – or prospectively – starting in childhood and describing people's lives successively, as they live them. By adopting a retrospective approach, researchers save time and the costs of the research are reduced. The disadvantage is that those who are included in the study may have difficulty remembering incidents and attitudes from earlier periods of their lives. Memories are also filtered as we move through life, which means, for example, that things that may once have been perceived as disagreeable are forgotten. Instead, the major advantage of following people's lives as they live them is that data are collected at the same time as the incidents occur. Prospective research is both expensive and time consuming. Mature researchers who initiate work of this kind know that their careers, or indeed their lives, may be over before it is time to analyse the results.

The project emerges

Kaare Svalastoga, who had by this time left the USA and was working in Copenhagen, raised the issue of his Nordic research project when he met other Nordic sociologists in various contexts. In 1960, he succeeded in organising a private meeting with the two Swedish Professors of Sociology, Gunnar Boalt from Stockholm and Gösta Carlsson from Lund. Boalt raised the issue of the difficulties faced by the sociological studies of the time in distinguishing cause from effect. Svalastoga argued that this problem could be resolved by following people over the course of their lives. The difficulty was that studies of this kind would be far too expensive to conduct, since as a result of migration into and out of smaller study areas they would have to be conducted at the national level. Gunnar Boalt argued that this need not to be a problem, since his own research had shown that 94 percent of all the boys in Stockholm who had graduated from the fourth grade of elementary school in 1936 were still living in the city at the age of 24. The same ought to be true of the other Nordic capitals.[7]

Kaare Svalastoga's view then changed and he started to argue seriously for what would subsequently become Project Metropolitan. He received support for the idea from both of the Swedish professors at the meeting, but since only two of the Nordic capitals were represented, he then also made contact with the other Nordic capitals and succeeded in engaging Professors Erik Allart and Sverre Holm from Helsinki and Oslo respectively. In Oslo, the project would subsequently be led by Ørjar Øyen and Natalie Rogoff Ramsøy, while in Stockholm the project would be led by Carl-Gunnar Janson.

Image 3. Professor Gunnar Boalt. Photographer: Unknown/ Department of Sociology at Stockholm University. Copyright: Department of Sociology at Stockholm Universit, License: CC-BY-NC-ND.

Image 4. Professor Carl-Gunnar Janson. Photographer: Bo Präntare. Copyright: Bo Präntare, License: CC-BY-NC-ND.

In March 1961, Kaare Svalastoga formulated a research programme. He also established informal contacts with possible sources of research funding in the USA, but without success. In the programme, he identified four main areas of research. The first was social mobility over the life course and between generations, and in particular the significance of education for this mobility. An individual's level of education was largely determined by the individual's social position, which was in turn also affected by education.

The second area was membership of groups and formal organisations. Today this is sometimes referred to as social capital, something which has been found to be of considerable significance in relation to social position and influence. The third was social adjustment and deviant behaviour. Deviant behaviour was not exclusively viewed as something negative, but could also take the form of a positive deviation if an individual achieved more than was expected, e.g. in the case of successful athletes or artists. Finally, Svalastoga emphasised the choice of peers and family formation as a fourth important area. Even today, these areas remain central to social research and research in the field of social medicine, and are of major significance for our understanding of social mobility between generations.

Two years later, a conference was held in Oslo with participants from Norway, Sweden and Denmark. Finland did not have a representative at the meeting, and for various reasons never got started on the project. The participants at the meeting agreed on a research plan, and they also agreed that the project would be initiated in 1964. In addition, the meeting decided that it would be pointless to plan for more than three to four years at a time. The study would concentrate its focus on the interactions between personality, family, school and the local community among a generation of boys. This would be achieved by means of four studies that would in part be chronologically overlapping: An ecological/geographical study of the cities, a descriptive study of the boys' development, particularly from birth to age eleven, a questionnaire survey in school when the boys were aged twelve, and a questionnaire survey among the mothers when the boys were aged thirteen. The overarching objective of the project could be simply summarised in the question "Why do some get on better than others in life?"

Organising the project

Following the Oslo meeting, a series of additional meetings ensued at which the project was organised. Since the children would be followed into adulthood, and since the focus of the research would be directed towards the significance of childhood conditions for outcomes later in life, the optimal approach would have been to study the boys from birth. Since the boys were to be followed prospectively, however, this would mean waiting a very long time before the data could be analysed. It is not until people are in their thirties that their position on the labour market becomes more or less stable. The researchers would thus have hardly any time to analyse the data during their own careers. The sample was therefore specified so that the children were aged ten at the time the project started. The twenty years that the researchers would have to wait before being able to conduct more detailed analyses of the data was still a very long time, but it was not so long as to make the project unworkable.

When it came to the contents of the research, Svalastoga's original research programme from 1961 was still in place, but it was decided to allow a certain level of variation between the different countries due to differences in the special interests of the various research groups involved. Funding would be organised nationally and periodically. Svalastoga motivated the size of the study – an entire birth cohort of boys – by stating that it created better opportunities to study rare phenomena. In studies based on samples, the most uncommon phenomena are only found in a very small number of individuals. This is true not only of unusual social problems, such as criminality, but also of factors such as extreme changes in social status between parents and children.

Image 5. Kaare Svalastoga was interned in the Grini prison camp between 1944 and the end of the war. Here we see the prisoners lined up for the final time in May 1945, waiting to be taken home on the buses that can be seen in the background. Photographer: Unknown/Nordfoto/NTB/TT Nyhetsbyrån. Copyright: Nordfoto/NTB/TT Nyhetsbyrån, License: CC-BY-NC-ND.

Today it would probably be regarded as professional misconduct only to include boys in a study of this kind, but in the 1960s researchers thought differently. Kaare Svalastoga's motivation for only focusing on boys was that men constituted a more "variable gender", and this provided better opportunities for testing the results. He argued that women were not socially mobile in the same way as men, and were therefore not as interesting to study. He also wrote that in a number of areas such as ill-health, mortality and deviant behaviour, men could be regarded as the "weaker sex" in the sense that their methods of adapting to their environment created greater social problems. For this reason, boys were more interesting than girls from a research perspective.[8]

In Stockholm, girls came to be included anyway when the time came to conduct the first questionnaire survey in 1966, both for practical reasons and as a matter of principle. Since the questionnaire was to be distributed in the classroom, it would have been both complicated and a little absurd only to allow the boys to complete it. Despite the fact that gender studies perspectives and gender equality at the time received little attention in the context of either public debate or research, Carl-Gunnar Janson also argued that it was important to include the girls in the study. By comparison with Kaare Svalastoga, Carl-Gunnar Janson was a pioneer in this respect.

It very quickly became clear that it would be difficult to complete a project that included the whole of Scandinavia. There was nobody in Finland who was prepared to work with the study. In Norway, the newspaper *Aftenposten* initiated a public debate on personal integrity when the project's researchers requested information from the Oslo school card index register in 1964. This debate eventually led to the project being discontinued. It was thus only in Denmark and Sweden that the project was implemented, and even these two countries would subsequently experience serious crises in connection with the research.

Project Metropolitan in Norway

On September 24, 1964, the Board of Education in Oslo decided to give permission for the project to use the card index registers of the city's school children. Although several of the centre-right board members were sceptical, only one board member from the Høyre (Conservative) Party voted against the decision. Those who were positive towards the proposal were members of the Arbeiderpartiet (Labour) and the communists. One of the Education Board's sceptics told *Aftenposten* that she had spoken to a number of concerned parents: "We don't have any guarantees that the material perhaps, or possibly, in some distant future [won't] become some kind of

Kinsey report."[9] Other board members from the Conservative party wondered whether the project ought to contact the boys' parents directly.

The chairman of the Oslo Board of Education, who represented the Labour Party, himself had a son who had been born in 1953, and he said he was happy to be able to follow the research project so closely over the coming years. The Communist Party representative wanted to go even further, and emphasised that the project was motivated not only on educational but also on social policy grounds. He argued that "The school system should have collected this information themselves ... We discuss disciplinary problems in schools – without having the material to evaluate what schools in a metropolitan community should be giving children in order to prepare them for life in such a demanding environment."

The school inspector Oddvar Vormeland spoke of sociology as a support science for teaching:

> Previously we saw the child only in the school situation. Now we must see the child in the home, the neighbourhood, and the region in connection with the school situation – for the benefit of school work.[10]

Aftenposten attacked the project in an editorial. The newspaper was disappointed that only one member of the Board of Education had experienced doubts, and called for a broader debate among elected politicians. The editorial also raised many of the criticisms that would later reappear in relation to Project Metropolitan in Sweden. The project was described as superficial. "They believe that with the help of schedules and index cards they can produce a true picture of today's eleven-year-olds." At the same time, the study threatened the sanctity of individual privacy by going "far beyond the boundaries that should be drawn to safeguard private life". In addition, the newspaper felt that the long-term time frame employed in the project was worrying: "Nobody knows today what people in twenty years' time will 'have on register' concerning the boys who are eleven years old today."

Finally, the newspaper underlined that it was naturally not a question of obstructing or expressing doubts about the research. It did not wish to disenfranchise the experts in this field, but it was about "the right of ordinary people to be able to say no when research wishes to enter the area of their private lives, about being able to say no to being 'an event'".[11] When *Aftenposten's* political editor considered the possible benefits and harms of the project in this way, he was to all intents and purposes conducting an ethical review of the research project. The research violated personal integrity, but did not go far enough in this violation to be able to provide interesting results.

Reactions to the decision of the Board of Education and *Aftenposten's* editorial came without delay. A fierce debate raged in the newspaper from October to December of 1964. Parents were worried that their children would be asked inappropriate questions that might harm both them and their families, and they felt that their responsibility as parents was under threat. Lawyers, senior civil servants and researchers also took sides. The Supreme Court attorney Knut Tvedt characterised the research plan as "macabre"[12], but Professor Sverre Holm, who was head of the Department of Sociology, defended it as "an important precondition in the defence of individual and human rights."[13] Johannes Andenæs, one of Norway's leading lawyers, also expressed his support for the project. "My impression is that the concern that has been expressed in relation to Project Metropolitan is somewhat excessive. The whole thing is intended to be used for research that will serve the best interests of mankind."[14]

There were also researchers who distanced themselves from the Norwegian Metropolitan project in various ways. These included a university lecturer who had caused something of a stir one year earlier when he spoke in a radio debate and advocated that school children should be given information about sex and provided with contraceptives by school doctors. He now distanced himself from Project Metropolitan in an open letter to *Aftenposten*, stating that he was "not in any way" linked to the project.

"All I know is that if I had been born during a year close to this year, I would have made sure to find out whether the boy who wanted to dance with me at the school dances had been born in 1953. If he had been, it would have been no thank you, both to the dance and to a later trip to the cinema. I wouldn't want to be investigated together with him ..."

Letter to the editor published in the morning edition of Aftenposten, December 1, 1964.

The issue of the project was also discussed in the Norwegian Parliament (Stortinget). In a Parliamentary Question, Per Lønning of the Conservatives argued that "it ought to be in the interests of both the home and research, for schools that are going to make information on pupils and their family conditions available to scientific studies, to first inform the parents about this and obtain their consent."[15]

The Norwegian debate was largely about the issue of how "voluntary" it would be to participate. The Board of Education in Oslo noted in December that the decision they had taken three months earlier had only been about providing the researchers with access to information from the school system's card index register. The remainder of the study required asking the parents for their permission.[16] This view was the same as that of the researchers. A further concrete issue was that of whether the researchers would be given access to intelligence tests that were conducted by the school system during the first school years. This permission was never granted.

Svalastoga commented in writing on the debate, and among other things raised the question of the meaning of individual liberty. He argued that individual liberty was a socially produced societal resource and not an innate property, and went on to say that arguing that the study was a violation of individual liberty was based on a misunderstanding of the objectives and methods of sociology. The objective of sociology is to formulate laws about the structure, function and change of social groups and sociology can thus contribute to illuminating the social conditions required for individual liberty. At the same time, he admitted that increases in knowledge could be used by "both humanists and fascists", but that this problem was not specific to sociology. "Physicists and biologists have given us sufficient knowledge to both extend and shorten human life."

Svalastoga emphasised that the methods of sociology involve all participation being voluntary and all use of documented information being based on public acceptance. As regards studies focused on children, he argued that it ought to "be reasonable that the parents or

"We remember five long, bitter years of denunciation and the consequences of this. We remember something else, something about card indexes that could be useful to the enemy. They had to be destroyed. Our boys risked their lives for this. We who are parents today want an absolute guarantee from the researchers that the card index on our children is 100 percent secure."

Letter to the editor published in the evening edition of Aftenposten, October 14, 1964.

the parents' public representatives or school authorities determine whether the study can be permitted."[17]

Thus a number of public sector agencies were consulted about starting the project in the different participating countries, but the parents were not given very much information. One of the reasons for this was that at this time – the beginning of the 1960s – parents' rights were not as strictly regulated in legislation as they are today. Even though they could be given the opportunity to decide, argued Svalastoga, decisions made by public representatives and school authorities would be sufficient. This is also what happened subsequently in Stockholm. The parents were not informed, but rather it was the authorities that approved the research. This would turn out to be one of the Swedish Metropolitan project's major problems.

Project Metropolitan in Denmark

Whereas in Norway Project Metropolitan broke down before it had even had the chance to seriously get underway, the Danish version of the project was able to get started in accordance with the plans that had been drawn up at the "professors' meeting" of 1960 under the leadership of Kaare Svalastoga. It was also Svalastoga who led the project until 1976 at the University of Copenhagen's Department of Sociology. The project included just over 11,000 children, all of whom were boys. As would subsequently be the case in Sweden, however, the Danish project was to become the centre of a storm. Only a few years after the project had started, the student revolt of 1968 erupted in Paris, and then spread quickly to other universities in the western world. In Copenhagen, the consequences were particularly serious for sociology, and for the Sociology Department's research they were nothing short of catastrophic.[18]

In 1970, a group of students and recently appointed part-time teachers started publishing a journal named *Kurasje*, which quickly became a forum for a so-called Marxist and capital logic perspective in Danish sociology. "Positivism" was rejected in favour of the motto "Research for the people, not for profit".[19] In the first issue of the journal, the editorial summarised the critique of social science by stating that the practitioners of the prevailing social sciences "have quite specifically defined roles as 'social engineers' and 'adaptive technocrats', whose task is to subdue the conflicts in society." The students did not want to become "willing manipulators for the existing society, where the few exercise power over the many."[20] Kaare Svalastoga and Project Metropolitan found themselves in the line of fire for this critique. The project was a perfect example of the positivism that was being rejected.

The conflict with the older professors and teachers became violent, and was intensified by a battle with an individual staff member. The lecturer Erik Høgh, who would later take over from Kaare Svalastoga as leader of the project, had been accused the previous year of maladministration and of having exploited the work of students for his private consultancy firm. The first issue of *Kurasje* was largely focused on this issue. Høgh was later completely exonerated of all the accusations. The older teachers surrounding Kaare Svalastoga continued with their work, but their teaching and research opportunities became increasingly restricted, and few students applied to take their courses. In the end, this led to Project Metropolitan, along with its leadership and teachers, being banished to the university attic, at the same time as the department itself continued to be beset by conflict.

In 1976, responsibility for the project passed to a research group under the leadership of Preben Wolf, and Svalastoga himself retired eight years later. The chaotic situation at the department,

Image 6. Professor Kaare Svalastoga in 1969, pushing through the student barricades at the Department of Sociology, University of Copenhagen. Photographer: Erik Gleie/ STELLA pictures Stockholm/ Oslo. Copyright: Erik Gleie/ STELLA pictures Stockholm/Oslo, License: CC-BY-NC-ND.

in combination with a lack of resources, meant that conditions for research were poor, and in addition there had been few publications from the project. In the minutes of one project meeting in 1975, Høgh had dramatically summarised the situation by stating that "he was actually opposed to Project Metropolitan, not because he was against the idea and the research design, but because nobody had acknowledged that a project of this kind required a completely different level of resources than had been available up to that point. It was wrong to expect something to come out of nothing."[21]

At the beginning of the 1980s, the project, under Erik Høgh's leadership, moved away from the fading environment of the university to the private Institute for Longitudinal Studies in Copenhagen. When the Swedish Project Metropolitan became the subject of debate in 1986, the Danish project was also mentioned in several Danish newspapers. The headlines were similar to those in Sweden: *You have been recorded in a secret register; We were conned; He's fiddling with 12,000 lives,* and *Storm of protest against the data controllers.* The debate did not have the same major consequences in Denmark as it did in Sweden, however. In part this may have been due to the fact that the Danish Metropolitan data were at this point not at the university, but were rather being administered by researchers in the private sector. Given the legislation of the time, it was therefore difficult for the authorities to regulate the project. Little happened over the following years. There was however some agitation from the Danish equivalent of the Swedish Data Protection Authority, which on at least one occasion threatened the project with police intervention. At the same time, the situation at the Department of Sociology had become so chaotic that the Ministry of Education decided in 1988 to close the department down.

In the mid-1990s, the situation for the Danish Project Metropolitan became increasingly desperate. The project had not received any funding since 1978. The project's academic ties were weak following its banishment from the university, its leadership was not getting any younger, and nothing was being published. But there was glint of light in the midst of all the darkness. At the beginning of May 1995, Erik Høgh wrote to Carl-Gunnar Janson that he was in touch with the university once again, and that the re-opened Department of Sociology wanted to take over responsibility for the data. At the same time, he recalled that the University of Copenhagen had at one point wanted to burn the project data, and those working in the project had been ridiculed and persecuted. The project had been saved by the Institute for Longitudinal Studies, which had "brought the Metropolitan material through the spiritual wilderness, protected like the Ark of the Covenant, until times became less fascist at the University of Copenhagen. Times improved, the Department of Sociology was closed, and then a new one was opened."[22]

Five years later, the researchers in social medicine Merete Osler and Björn Holstein of the National Institute of Public Health at Copenhagen University contacted Erik Høgh. Following a series of meetings between the three, the project was returned to the university in 2001. When the Danish Data Protection Authority subsequently gave permission, it became possible to update the material and today the research has taken off again and has produced a series of publications. Since the Danish Metropolitan data, unlike the Swedish, were never anonymised, the researchers were able to send out a new questionnaire in 2004 to the approximately 11,000 men from the original study population. Almost 70 percent of them completed the questionnaire.[23]

Project Metropolitan in Sweden

In Sweden, the study population was defined as all children born in 1953 and living in the Greater Stockholm area on November 1, 1963 – a total of 15,117 individuals. Thus the population also included children who were born outside Stockholm, either in another part of the country or abroad. Of the total, 7,719 were boys and 7,398 girls.[24] Today more than 1,000 of them are no longer living.

"Here are some questions about how you enjoy your schoolwork and some other things. The questions should be answered yes or no by placing a cross (x) in either the yes-box or the no-box. You are to answer the questions as correctly as you can, and you should give us your exact thoughts. Nobody either at school or at home will get to see your answers, and they will only be read by a person who does not know you."

Instructions from the School Survey questionnaire 1966.

"I have a few momentary images. I remember that I thought it was fun. It was fun to answer questions about friends and a class party and what you wanted to be when you grew up. Nobody reacted negatively. Quite the reverse. And it was completely silent in the classroom, I remember. That didn't happen very often. I remember that Mum was also interviewed later on. Someone came to our home and I think Mum was proud of being asked to answer questions. I was there in the background, and sometimes Mum turned to me to help with an answer."

(Jan Andersson)

The collection of data was initiated in the late spring of 1966 with a questionnaire distributed to all the children. This survey was labelled the *School Study* because it was completed in the classroom during school hours. The next major questionnaire survey, the *Family Study*, was conducted two years later. It was not until 1985 that a third questionnaire survey was conducted, in collaboration with Radio Sweden's audience surveys. Since this questionnaire focused largely on leisure time habits, it was labelled the *Culture and Leisure Time Study*. There were also plans for further surveys. These did not make it past the planning stage, however, as a result of difficulties obtaining permission from the Data Protection Authority, which was established in 1973.

The School Survey

More or less all of the affected Swedish agencies and organisations supported the School Study, but unlike in Norway, the mass media showed no major interest in the research. The daily broadsheet *Dagens Nyheter* noted however, on April 30, 1966, under the headline "15,000 Stockholm residents having their future charted in research project", that the project had been given research funding, and an editorial comment published on May 2, 1966, referred to the project as an example of good research.

As was noted earlier, no approach was made to the parents when the schools were contacted. At the same time, Statistics Sweden (SCB) and the Swedish Council for Social Science Research wrote a letter to "school managers, head teachers and certain teachers in Greater Stockholm" in which the latter were encouraged to participate in the survey of pupils born in 1953. The letter noted that the plans were to follow the students "prospectively during their education", and that those responsible for the survey had consulted with the National Board of Education, the National Association of Legal Guardians, and with teachers' and school directors' organisations. The letter stated

Image 7. Stockholm schoolchildren born in 1953. Photographer:
Unknown Copyright: Unknown, License: CC-BY-NC-ND.

"To be honest I can't remember any-thing about the Metropolitan study. As a twin, you were constantly being stud-ied every which way. Metropolitan was probably just one among all the other studies. They blend into each other. The only thing I remember a bit more is that we once had to go from the Gärdes school to the school of arts, crafts and design, where we were to listen to voices and say whether the voices sounded kind or happy or angry! And that wasn't the Metropolitan study."

(Ulla Abelin)

"I remember that they wanted to know a great deal about the family. Among other things they wanted to know how many books you had at home. And I remember thinking HOW do you count books? We had so many. And there were questions about how much your parents earned. I didn't know. And which social class you belonged to. I think I wrote upper-middle class. Some of the ques-tions were quite difficult for a school-child. Then I remember that someone came to our house later and interviewed Mum. She agreed to it of course. When society demanded something of you, you agreed to do it, that's how it was. OK, please answer these questions!"

(Lotta Samuelsson Aschberg)

that: "Agencies and organisations have recommended teachers and school directors to cooperate in the collection of the material." There was also consultation with the Board of Education for the City and County of Stockholm, the Local Education Authority in Stockholm and with representatives of school managers and teachers in Greater Stockholm.[25]

Just prior to the start of the survey, the publication *News from the National Board of Education*, stated that: "The National Board of Education wishes, with reference to the significance of such a material as a basis for scientific research in the service of school and society, to recommend that school principals and teachers cooperate in ensuring that the intended information is added to the school sta-tistics to as great an extent as possible."[26] In addition, the Association of Teachers in Colleges and Departments of Education, the National Union of Teachers, the National Association of Legal Guardians, the Association of School Principals and Directors of Education, the Association of Specialist and Technical Teachers, the Swedish Association for Remedial Teaching and the Swedish Teachers' Union wrote a letter encouraging all school directors, head teachers and teachers to participate in the survey.[27] Against this background of complete agreement, it was not surprising that participation in the survey was more or less universal at the classroom level. Project Metropolitan was at this time not the only school survey. Since the beginning of the 1960s, Statistics Sweden had conducted a number of follow-up surveys within the school system in collaboration with a range of research institutions.[28]

The 1966 School Survey consisted of two questionnaires.[29] The first contained a cognitive test and questions on interests and attitudes towards school, leisure time and educational plans.[30] The second con-tained, among other things, sociometric questions. The children were asked to name three classmates as best friends, which classmates they would like to arrange a class party with, and which classmates they would most prefer to work together with in school. The second questionnaire also asked about their career plans.

The Family Survey

The Family Survey was conducted two years later. The sample for this survey comprised a total of 4,021 guardians, primarily mothers, who completed a questionnaire about, among other things, their views on child-rearing, occupational choices and social conditions. The sample was stratified. This meant that all the mothers of the children who had the best and the worst results on the cognitive tests included in the School Survey were included, along with the mothers of every fifth child between these two extremes. The reason for this was that the researchers were particularly interested in social mobility, and in order to conduct statistically reliable calculations, it was important to include a sufficient number of the children with the best and worst results.

The survey was divided into five sections. The first contained questions about the mothers' family situation and their relationship with the child; the second focused on the work and occupations of maternal and paternal grandparents, parents and children; and the third included questions about the child's educational and occupational plans, the parents' involvement in school work and their attitudes to school and different occupations. The fourth section dealt with norms and the child's behaviour and relationships with family members, while the fifth section focused on more general questions about child-rearing, society and the future.

When the project was called into question in 1986, it was partly because the information presented to the mothers had not been sufficiently clear. Nor was it felt that the link to the School Survey in which the mothers' children had participated two years earlier had been made clear. When one reads the letter sent to the parents today, this link does not appear to have been made so unclear. The letter

"As I remember, I was interviewed and questioned a number of times about different things. Not so strange, maybe. There was no doubt a lot to look into when it came to an odd boy with dyslexia, difficulties in school and a stammer. But all those studies meant that I felt like I'd been chosen, a bit special. I thought that there must quite simply be someone or some people who knew better and who understood things better than the teachers at school. Those who understood better knew that there was something special about me, and wanted to find out more about me and what it was that made me that way."
(Bo Östlund)

"There was something with an incredible number of questions that we sat there and were supposed to answer. None of us asked why and nobody wondered what it was about. Our teacher had said that we were to fill in the answers and so we did it nicely and obediently. At the French School you always did what the teacher told you to, nicely and obediently."
(Margareta Kempe Allansson)

"I don't have any particular memories of the Metropolitan study. There were often surveys in school and there was never any question about not answering. You were twelve years old and you didn't question things. We also had a very strict teacher, and she was someone that you didn't oppose."

(Agneta Wolffelt)

"The project is an attempt to improve our knowledge of how people's lives take form in one way or the other. It has no immediate practical objectives other than the quest for knowledge. It is thus a question of so-called pure research. But like all research of this kind, the project is useful over the longer term, since the knowledge it provides will put us in a position to improve the conditions in which people live."

(Instructions to Statistics Sweden's interviewers: Project Metropolitan 1968, P 0763, Instruction of LOKO, Project Metropolitan archive)

stated that the survey was part of the Metropolitan study, and that the children were being followed in a large study which had included questionnaires and interviews. Unfortunately, no specific mention was made of the School Survey of 1966.

The information contained in the instructions to the interviewers was more detailed, and the link to the School Survey was described clearly. For some reason, however, the study's leadership wrote that this information was primarily intended for the interviewers themselves. Thereafter, the interviewers received the following instruction: "Certain ips (interview persons) may conceivably be worried by the project's 'longitudinal character', i.e. that children are followed over a long period of time and data on them are collected in a register, for example as a result of the debate about the Swedish Security Service. It would therefore be appropriate to present the survey quite truthfully as a sociological family survey, in which we want to know about the families' composition, background, habits and opinions. If an ip asks a direct question about whether the survey has anything to do with the school questionnaire from the spring of 1966, he/she should be informed that this is part of the same project, but that the Family Survey is self-contained within this project, and that it has nothing to do with school or the school authorities. By conducting several small studies within the same project, they can in part support one another. The spouses' intimate marital life or sexual relations in general are not touched upon."[31]

It would of course have been better if the project had clarified the links between the two surveys. But the contemporary debate made the researchers hesitant about doing so. Carl-Gunnar Janson would also come to regret this when the entire project was called into question eighteen years later: "Now, after the event, I unreservedly regret this misjudgement. I can only say that a great deal has changed since 1968. At that time, interview subjects viewed questions about sex and marital life as offensive, but were generally not worried about registers and computers. It was in fact an argument in favour of the study that the data would be handled completely impersonally using computers."[32]

Documentation

The project's records document the work conducted to regularly collect additional data. When the study population had been identified with the help of the residency registration system, data were collected from a range of administrative registers such as birth journals, population and housing records, national service enrolment information, social services registers, county council data and crime registers. It is very likely that collecting the data required more work than the researchers had imagined. Even at this stage there were aspirations to work on theory development and to conduct preliminary analyses of the data that had been collected. In the project report for the period 1967–1969, however, Janson wrote that "for the time being, the work to process the data has been interrupted pending the arrival of the delayed data", but that the intention had been to report preliminary results following the long data collection period, ..., something which had thus not been possible."[33] In spite of the stress of the data collection work, Janson nonetheless succeeded in publishing an article in the journal *Youth and Society* in 1970, in which he discussed the project's future analyses of youth crime.[34]

Prior to the introduction of the Data Act, all that was required to collect data from the relevant registers was the permission of those who maintained the registers. At the end of the 1960s and the beginning of the 1970s, however, growing concern was noted among the public and in the media regarding how the so-called supercomputers might be used. One sign of this concern was that from June 1972, as a result of earlier changes in practice, Statistics Sweden would no longer release information on crime at the individual level. Since Statistics Sweden received their crime data from the Swedish Police Authority, however, Janson made a direct application for the data to the Police

"There are of course no restrictions for LOKO (the interviewer) to mention or talk about Project Metropolitan with the ip (interview person). The ip's possible questions must obviously be answered truthfully. Referring to the project may also conceivably increase certain ips' willingness to be interviewed. But the project may not be described in such a way that the ip is given the completely erroneous impression that the family is constantly being secretly monitored, with observations being recorded in a register."

(Project Metropolitan 1968, P 0763, supplementary instruction for LOKO [Local representative], Project Metropolitan archive)

Board, which was granted.[35] In spite of this success, new problems emerged: "Since that time, a series of data-technical, almost farcical complications have meant that it has not been possible to transfer the information to the project's own tapes."[36]

The reason was that the university and the Swedish Police Authority had different computer systems. In May 1973, the project applied for information from the 1965 population and housing census. "Following a written exchange, the application was rejected on May 28, 1973. I was informed of the decision on July 10, following repeated enquiries. It had been , the reason being made out of 'consideration for the affected individuals' integrity'."[37] The difficulties were linked to the fact that a new agency, The Swedish Data Protection Authority was to be established on July 1, 1973, and that the following year, Sweden would become the first country in the world to introduce data protection legislation.

The Swedish Data Protection Authority, the Data Act, and the Social Scientists

The sociologists and social science faculties find themselves in open conflict with the Data Protection Authority. What should the researchers inform the Project Metropolitan children about? The first decision is made to anonymise the data.

The Swedish Data Protection Authority and the Data Act caused a great deal of concern among empirically focused social scientists in Sweden. Prior to the Act's introduction in 1974, their work had only been regulated by the Secrecy Act and by ethical guidelines. The period between the mid-1970s and 1986, when Project Metropolitan became the subject of a major social debate, was characterised by more or less open conflict between social researchers and the Data Protection Authority. The researchers argued that the new Act represented a threat to the freedom of research. The Data Protection Authority argued that the research risked violating individuals' personal integrity.

When the Data Act came into force, Project Metropolitan made an application to maintain a personal data register.[38] Just over a year later, in November 1975, the Data Protection Authority investigated the project, and noted that the individuals included in the register had not been informed that information on them had been collected from various authorities.[39] A permit to maintain a personal data register was issued the following June, but with reservations: "When it comes to the supplementation of existing registers with information from registers maintained by other agencies, this will as a rule be

Image 8. The Data Protection Authority's Director General, Jan Freese, 1985. Photographer: Kent Hult/Sydsvenskan. Copyright: Kent Hult/Sydsvenskan, License: CC-BY-NC-ND.

How to cite this book chapter:
Stenberg, Sten-Åke. 2018. The Swedish Data Protection Authority, the Data Act, and the Social Scientists. In: Stenberg, Sten-Åke. *Born in 1953: The story about a post-war Swedish cohort, and a longitudinal research project*. Pp. 27–41. Stockholm: Stockholm University Press. DOI: https://doi.org/10.16993/bav.b. License: CC-BY

"... more than one social scientist – both young and old – [has] been heard to express the suspicion that the Data Protection Authority's reviews of social research instruments in questionnaire surveys may constitute a means of diverting attention from more serious and intractable integrity problems linked to the administrative personal data registers that are maintained by public sector agencies and commercial organs. A less sinister interpretation is that the Data Protection Austhority and its board of directors have never properly thought through the special situatio n occupied by research, nor its needs and its both critical and innovative role."

Letter to the Data Protection Authority from the Swedish Sociological Association, March 1975, signed by Professors Ulf Himmelstrand, Hans Berglind and Robert Erikson.

conditional upon acquiring the consent of those registered."[40] In the project's Work Report for 1975/1976, Janson briefly discussed the new requirements resulting from the Data Protection Authority's decision. He stated that the project would be able to retain the data that had been collected to date, but that the Authority's "instructions" meant that it would be difficult and in "some cases impossible" to collect new data since, as Janson noted, "remarkably, this relates not only to questionnaire surveys but also to register studies."

However, the Data Protection Authority's decision was more a matter of making a point than of issuing an instruction, which could be discerned from the Authority's use of the term "as a rule". But Janson and his colleagues interpreted the Authority's statement as a demand, and they responded by intensifying the conflict.

The Swedish Sociological Association takes a stand

A little over a year earlier, the Swedish Sociological Association had written to the Data Protection Authority and insisted that social research should be exempted from the regulations. The Association also wanted to meet with the Authority for talks. In its letter, the Association divided the registers into three categories: administrative, membership, and statistical and research registers. The objectives of the latter category were exclusively to provide knowledge concerning groups, not individuals. Thus, research could not pose a threat to individuals' personal integrity. The Association argued further that the "personal data in social research, even prior to the introduction of the Data Act, have been both more inaccessible and less interesting for unauthorised exploitation than the data in the majority of other personal data registers." This was due to the fact that research registers were based on samples. At the same time, the letter's authors accepted that large data sets, of the kind maintained by Statistics Sweden, could be used for research, but noted that these data were protected by the Secrecy Act.

The Sociological Association also objected to the new requirement for research institutions to provide information to registered individuals detailing the information that the registers contained about them. This requirement would in effect run counter to the intention of the legislation. The reason for this was that "one as a rule does not know who is included in a certain sample", and that it would therefore be "difficult and expensive, if not impossible, to find out in which surveys of this kind a given individual had participated." The new Act would change this situation, making it necessary to establish new registers in order to have a record of the samples people had participated in. Since the Act was already in effect, the Association proposed a number of "practical solutions that would, in a way that would satisfy the Data Protection Authority, separate personal identity numbers, or other information that made it possible to identify people, from other factual information in the personal data registers used in social science, except in cases where personal identity numbers were required for the administration of panel studies or to combine data from different registers."

The formulation chosen by the Association gives an intimation of the problems associated with studies that follow the same individuals over a long period of time in the way that Project Metropolitan did. The Sociological Association was therefore worried that the new Act would force researchers to remove personal identity numbers from their data, which would mean that projects of this kind would have to be discontinued.

The Association also claimed to hold a fundamentally positive view of "confidentiality protections and the work of the Data Protection Authority in this respect". However, the Association stated that it felt very concerned at the way the Authority had written that they would examine the "nature and quantity of the personal information that will be included in the register". This concern was linked to criticisms that had been voiced in 1974 in relation to the so-called ULF-surveys.[41] The Data Protection Authority and the Chancellor of

The first annual meeting of the Swedish Sociological Association was held in 1962. At that time, sociology had been a university subject for a little over ten years. The tasks of the Sociological Association were formulated in the following four points:

- To promote the scientific development of sociology and its fields of application
- To safeguard the trade-union interests of its members
- To work for an improved understanding of sociology and social science at the public sector agencies, and among the public
- To strengthen sociology's professionalism and sense of responsibility

Justice, Ingvar Gullnäs, had questioned whether these surveys could be compatible with the protection of personal integrity, and the Data Protection Authority, in collaboration with Statistics Sweden, had wanted to review the survey questionnaire and possibly remove any "sensitive" questions. The Sociological Association argued that there was a risk that not only questions "that are sensitive in some sense" would be removed, but also questions "that could lead to serious social criticism or that are sensitive for organisations and the authorities."

The Sociological Association argued that the Data Protection Authority was in actual fact protecting the interests of the powerful at the expense of individual interests. Since social research in no way constituted a threat to individual integrity, the Data Protection Authority was protecting "the undesirable 'integrity' of the authorities and established interests from critical information." Therefore, the Association claimed that members had "expressed concern that this type of review might become a means of governing the country's social research from the perspective of the authorities and other established interests." One of the Sociological Association's conclusions was that "the Data Protection Authority and its board of directors have never properly thought through the special situation occupied by research, nor its needs or its critical and innovative role."

If the Sociological Association was looking for a confrontation with the Data Protection Authority, it had succeeded. The Authority would later return to the Association's statement that it had not properly thought through the research community's special role.

Further attacks on the social scientists

In May 1975, further criticism of Project Metropolitan was published. This time it was Kerstin Anér, a Member of Parliament representing the Swedish Liberal Party (Folkpartiet), who criticised the project in an article in the national newspaper *Svenska Dagbladet*.[42] She stated that since the introduction of the Data Act a year earlier, there had been very few complaints from the authorities. By contrast, there had been "loud and intense" complaints from the research community. Anér referred to medical registers by name, but argued that the social science registers were the real problem, since in this case the research came so close to the decision-making process at both the public and individual levels "that it was no longer possible to distinguish between them. Access to data then becomes the same as access to power. Neither being able to refuse [access to one's] data, nor being able to gain access to them, becomes a new form of powerlessness."

Anér used Project Metropolitan as an example, arguing that "Sociologists have selected several thousand individuals, all born in Stockholm in 1953, and are subjecting them to a series of interviews over many years. With the help of these, they obtain a good picture of many aspects of these Stockholmers' lives. They then expand on this with information from a large number of public registers – childcare, prison and probation, healthcare etc. Thus, those interviewed are laid bare under the researchers' microscopes to a much greater extent than they can imagine themselves."

She went on to criticise the project's objectives as vague: "To see how the Stockholmers live, are housed, relocate, work, and thus perhaps become the basis for certain measures on the part of politicians." This would increase the power of the politicians. In the same breath, Anér argued that the quality of the data was poor, "full of sources of error" and that it therefore could not result in useful research: "If this kind of manipulation of data concerning individuals is to be permitted, all of it carefully furnished with personal identity numbers, all of it stored for an indefinite period of time, it really ought to be proved for each individual research project that the benefits outweigh the risks for the individuals involved." But this test in itself was not enough: "One must otherwise, by political means, weigh the benefits for a group of **having** this information, against the benefits for another group where this information does **not** exist or where they themselves may exercise direct control over it."[43]

Subsequent critics of the project would also return to Anér's arguments. In hindsight, one might ask why it was that it was only the researchers who were identified as a threat. The information, after all, had originally been recorded in administrative registers. The data taken from these registers by researchers could not be used to make decisions that might affect individuals' lives.

Jan Freese, the computers and the scientists

One year after the publication of Kerstin Anér's article on Project Metropolitan, the book *Data och livskvalitet* (Data and Quality of Life) was published by the appeal court judge and director of the Data Protection Authority, Jan Freese, in which he expressed major concern over developments.[44] He argued that the individual would soon be "living as in an aquarium, where everything could be seen by everyone." Among other things, he mentioned Project Metropolitan. His criticism of the researchers was particularly sharp. The social scientists, and the sociologists in particular, had of course argued that registers should be divided up into administrative and research registers.

Jan Freese agreed that there was a difference, but that this was often limited to the "objectives" and that there was occasionally no difference between the registers, since the statistician and the researcher both used "an exact copy of the administrative register".[45]

From time immemorial, politicians have talked about how they wished to change the world, with emphasis on improvement. But what have been the end results? People were quick to make use of computers, but always clumsily and awkwardly. Just consider all the mistakes that were made when people started to produce sociological models. At the beginning of the digital age, with the help of scientists and planners, models were developed for new societies, with the correct proportions, rationally and economically, between maternity hospitals, nurseries, schools, workplaces, hospitals, geriatric care and crematoria. People were selected with the help of society's central information systems on healthcare, social services and the corrections system, and test data were collected on intelligence, together with workplace information on work capacity and relations among co-workers etc. The correct social structures that were necessary for the models that had been developed were identified, and people were placed into them. While they were unable to program in happiness at this stage, many benefits were produced.

Jan Freese, cited from the Danish Journal *Data* (1976) and the book *Den maktfullkomliga oförmågan* (The Powerful inability) (1987).

It was true that the researchers used information from administrative registers, and this type of research has since become even more common. Today this research is much more sophisticated and has given Swedish social and medical research a unique position in the world. The central difference between the public sector administrative registers and the research registers was – and still is – that the authorities can make decisions about specific individuals based on the information in these registers, whereas researchers cannot and should not affect the lives of specific individuals. Freese noted that research was also conducted by public sector agencies. Research of this kind has expanded in more recent years, and it is of course extremely important that such agencies separate their research from possible measures focused on specific individuals.[46] However, this problem did not arise in relation to Project Metropolitan, which was university based.

Freese raised the same criticism of social research as Anér. He argued that the data contained in the registers were often of such poor quality that the research would also necessarily be poor. He ignored, or was not aware of, the fact that there were methods for dealing with missing or incorrect data.

Protests from the Faculty of Social Sciences

In the project report for 1976/1977, the growing conflict between the project and the Data Protection Authority emerges even more clearly. Janson wanted to collect data on the results of the physical and psychological tests conducted on the children's fathers at the time of their entry into national service, but this was not to be. The permit granted by the Data Protection Authority in 1976 had, as already noted, stated that the permission of those registered would be required in connection with questionnaire surveys and, as a rule, also for the addition of new register data. Janson maintained that there was a particularly important difference between questionnaire surveys and register data. He therefore objected to the idea that all types of data collection should require the consent of those included in the study. The study subjects could not be viewed as "participating" in the collection of data from registers, and consent should therefore not be required.

Unlike questionnaire surveys, the use of information from registers did not lead to the production of new data.[47] These data already existed, and were simply being utilised by the researchers: "The position adopted by the Data Protection Authority that the consent of those registered may in principle be required in connection with register studies, and not only in connection with questionnaire surveys where consent is uncontested, is of major significance as a matter of principle. This may represent a serious threat to the use of the almost unique information source that has to date been available to Swedish researchers in the form of the system of population registers."[48]

Janson sought the support of the Faculty of Social Sciences at Stockholm University. This support manifested itself in April 1977, when the faculty board sent a letter to the Data Protection Authority, signed by Professor Olof Ruin and the faculty board's secretary, Agneta Englund. The faculty noted that the Data Protection Authority had the previous June allowed Project Metropolitan to retain data that had been collected prior to the introduction of the Data Act. The faculty's view of this was positive, but the faculty agreed with the criticism that the Sociological Association had voiced two years earlier with regard to the Data Protection Authority's statement that: "When it comes to the supplementation of existing registers with information from registers maintained by other agencies, this will as a rule be conditional upon acquiring the consent of those registered."

The faculty board also perceived the Data Protection Authority's statement as a directive and argued that in the light of such a rule "it was likely to be more or less impossible, or at least very difficult, to use register data concerning living individuals in social scientific research." The reasons were both practical and financial, and the use of questionnaires as an alternative was often worse, since these could be subject to low response frequencies even if the respondents were positively disposed towards the research. This problem was particularly serious in relation to small and atypical population groups "e.g. persons known in connection with certain types of crime" and because privileged groups would "be able to prevent register studies of social disparities."[49]

On the one side were the researchers, with their ethical guidelines, who were certain that their registers could never be used for anything other than research. On the other side stood the Data Protection Authority, who for the benefit of the individual citizens were to avert any tendencies towards their being controlled with the help of the computer. Moreover, the Authority wanted to serve as a bastion against oppression and the abuse of power. The Data Protection Authority viewed the researchers' statements as a provocation.

The decision to anonymise the data

In May 1977, the Data Protection Authority replied to the faculty's letter: "As can be seen from the decision regarding Project Metropolitan [...] as a rule, the condition will be that consent is obtained from those registered. Thus the issue is examined on a case by case basis, and exceptions are possible and have occurred."[50] This was an important clarification. Thereafter, the Data Protection Authority did not demand that all of those included in Project Metropolitan should be informed. Instead the Authority determined that the data should be anonymised in 1983.[51] Until that time, the researchers would be permitted to continue to collect data from registers as before, but for the planned future interview surveys, the condition was that those affected would be given complete information.

The Data Protection Authority's reply included an appendix, whose contents were intended to illustrate the Authority's train of thought.[52] The appendix took the form of a lecture that the Authority's Director General had held the previous year on the issue of the Data Protection Authority and medical research.[53] The lecture had begun by citing the 1975 letter from the Sociological Association, which stated that the Authority and its board of directors had "never properly thought through the special situation held by research, nor its needs or its critical and innovative role." In response to this criticism, the Director General presented on the one hand a statement from the Swedish Liberals' (Folkpartiet's) data policy program, and on the other a parliamentary bill presented by the Swedish Conservatives (Moderaterna). The Liberals' statement argued, among other things, that the research "should be able to show not only that a given survey had a reasonable objective, but also that this objective would actually be achieved by the survey, that it could not equally be achieved by any other means, and that the survey did not come into conflict with the individual's right to personal integrity." The Conservatives' parliamentary bill argued that citizens could not be "expected to play their part in the future by acting as guinea pigs in research contexts, unless certain minimum requirements were met with regard to the protection of personal integrity."

Catch-22

The Data Protection Authority's decision not only stopped the planned collection of data concerning the fathers at enrolment into national service, but also an interview survey on family formation and entry into the labour market. The latter survey was to have been based on the same sample as the Family Survey, but would focus on those born in 1953 themselves. It had initially been expected that it would be possible to use these survey participants as a means of contacting their fathers in order to obtain consent to use their national service enrolment data. In the end neither data collection took place. In the project report for 1977, Janson noted that: "According to the Data Protection Authority's decision of 22 June 1976, new data may not be added to the project for computer processing without the permission of those registered, in which case they must be informed in detail about all the data that has already been collected. Since it is impossible to obtain such consent from a sufficiently large proportion of the population, and from particularly problematic categories of this population, new data have not been collected for computer processing." It was the interview survey that Janson judged to be impossible to conduct. He was worried that the requirement to provide information would lead to a high level of non-response, which would make the continued collection of register data impossible.

At the end of the 1970s, the project found itself in something of a catch-22 situation. A great deal of work had been invested in collecting data up to the point at which the children of 1953 were just over twenty years old. This would amount to a massive waste of money and effort if it were not possible to continue until they had at least started to establish themselves in the labour market and to start families. The project's research questions were focused on the significance of childhood conditions for, among other things, social mobility, while to date, the project only had data relating to childhood and growing up, whereas data relating to entering adulthood was missing. At the same time, the new regulations meant that the research participants had to be informed about all the data that had been collected every time a new questionnaire or interview survey was conducted. The possibility of obtaining the consent required by the Data Protection Authority in connection with an interview survey was overshadowed by the risk that the participants would not want to continue. The development of computer technology had resulted in fantastic opportunities to process large data sets of the kind produced in Project Metropolitan, but

"The Data Protection Authority has in this regard given particular consideration to the fact that these data will, only to a very limited extent introduce new information to the register concerning those registered, that would change the assessments already made on the issue of integrity in any essential respect. The Data Protection Authority would like to mention once again that the essential issue from the personal integrity perspective is that the register cannot be maintained further than until the end of 1984, unless those included in the register are informed about the registration of their data, and at the same time give their consent to such registration."

Swedish Data Protection Authority, reference no. 574–83.

at the same time, the climate of public opinion had also undergone a shift. Unlike today, computers were not something that everybody owned, but rather only existed as bulky machines controlled by public sector agencies. This raised concerns about their improper use for purposes of monitoring and controlling the public.

As has been noted, the Data Protection Authority had not persisted in its demand that the collection of new register data should require the consent of those registered, and at the beginning of 1979, it also formally modified its decision. A supplementary statement was issued in relation to the earlier pronouncement that the project should inform those registered in connection with the collection of new register data. This supplementary statement noted that the earlier pronouncement "was primarily focused on a so-called follow-up survey in the form of interviews that had been planned for the final phase of the study [...]", and "since the data that are now being collected are exclusively drawn from the registers of the agencies that have previously provided data for the study, the Data Protection Authority finds that it should also be possible to waive the requirement of providing information to those registered in the current instance."[54] It had taken the Data Protection Authority almost three years to clarify its 1976 decision.

In September 1981, the project applied to supplement its register once again, and also to extend the length of the project until 1984. In the application, Janson made a reservation that further data series, which were not specified in the application, might need to be added. The reason given was that there would otherwise be a risk of the study becoming obsolete. "If an important new research question were to arise in the subject area covered by the project during the estimated five years that remain of the project, further additions may be required."[55]

One month later, the Authority responded that it would not willingly grant the project a new permit, unless it was assured that the register would be anonymised:

The Data Protection Authority has previously stated its view in principle on the issue of providing information to those registered concerning, among other things, the extent of the register. For various reasons, the Authority found it possible to refrain from prescribing directives of this kind regarding this register. The basis for the assessment included the fact that the register would be maintained during a limited period of time [...]. The Department [of Sociology] should therefore, as far as possible, provide an account of the possibilities of for example anonymising the register once the described additions have been made, or at the time at which the register's permit expires. The Data Protection Authority feels it is important even now to express its view that if the register is to be maintained for an additional period of time, then the issue of providing information to those registered ought once again to be taken up for consideration.[56]

Carl-Gunnar Janson then specified the variables of interest and wrote in relation to the issue of anonymisation that: "Once all the data relating to the observation period up to and including 1983 have been incorporated, the personal data register may be anonymised if the project's population tape[57] is archived long term, for a suggested period of ten years."[58] In December, the Data Protection Authority decided that the project would be allowed an extension until 1984, as requested. But in order to continue subsequent to that time, those registered should be informed. The Data Protection Authority also wanted clarification concerning which data were to be collected.[59]

The key tapes and the third and final questionnaire

In December 1984, Janson applied once again for an extension of the project. He wanted to finalise all the register data and conduct the Leisure Time Survey during the spring of 1985. This new survey would be conducted using a postal questionnaire and the questions would relate to "radio and TV, reading, other leisure time activities, church attendance, holidays, access to holiday homes and certain other resources. Employment, occupation, the composition of the

"[...] the project involves a very substantial investment in terms of money and work, and the combined project data may be of significant value for studies focused on the living conditions of middle-aged and elderly people, e.g. occupational careers and social mobility, health and mortality, unemployment and assistance needs, family conditions and social adjustment [...] In ten years, it may be deemed possible to inform the individuals included in the register, or certain categories of them, about their inclusion in the register. In twenty years, there may be reason to note which cohort members have died, etc."

Letter from Carl-Gunnar Janson to the Data Protection Authority, 1985-12-16, reference no. 2991–85.

In 2004 the Ethical Review Act was introduced in Sweden, targeting all research
on humans. The implications for the
social sciences were related to collection
and use of so-called sensitive information about identifiable individuals, such
as race or ethnic origin, political opinions, religious beliefs, membership in a
trade union, issues relating to health or
sexuality. Moreover, information about
previous convictions or other coercive
measures are regarded as sensitive. The
researcher must obtain approval from a
regional ethical vetting board in order to
collect and/or use such data. From June
2008 the research must be approved by
the board even though participants have
given their consent.

household, partner's employment and occupation and the respondents' perceptions and evaluations of their current situation."[60]

The application was later supplemented with a detailed description
of the questions and of the introductory information to be included in
the questionnaire: "Most of you, who are now being asked to participate, completed questionnaires in school when you were aged 13. Two
years later the majority of your mothers were interviewed. The project
has since not collected any new data but has only included already existing information from registers."[61] The omission of any reference to the
word Metropolitan was probably due to the fact that almost nobody
who was included in the survey was aware of the word at that time.
Otherwise it was clear that those who were being asked to participate
had been included in earlier surveys. The Data Protection Authority
approved the application and the register permit was therefore extended
until the end of 1985. It was stipulated that those interviewed should be
informed about the register's aim and planned application, what type
of information was included, and where it had been gathered, and that
providing information was to be voluntary. For those who did not wish
to be included in the study, the personal data should "be removed from
automatic data processing media or anonymised as soon as possible."[62]

The questionnaire for the Leisure Time Survey was distributed in
1985, and the final collections of register data were conducted at the
beginning of 1986.[63] This was done in a way which may be viewed
as a forerunner of the methods that have since become completely
dominant. A data tape including the participants' personal identity
numbers and a list of serial numbers was sent to Statistics Sweden.
Statistics Sweden added information on among other things treatment for alcohol abuse, and then returned the data tape with the
serial numbers, but with the personal identity numbers removed.
Meanwhile, the project was anonymised via the destruction of the
"key tape" (which linked the serial numbers to the personal identity
numbers), while the material could nonetheless still be updated with
the help of the serial numbers.

At the end of December 1985, Janson had sent one additional application to the Data Protection Authority. Prior to the delayed, but imminent, anonymisation of the data, he once again posed a question that he had raised five years earlier. He wanted to submit the key tape containing the serial and personal identity numbers to the Swedish National Archive, noting that the information that had been collected might also be valuable for studies of the living conditions of middle-aged and older individuals, with regard to, for example, health and family factors.

A short time later, the Data Protection Authority asked the Swedish National Archive to formulate an opinion. This opinion stated: "The National Archive concurs with the proposal of the Data Protection Authority that the personal data register be submitted to the National Archive for safekeeping, and that an anonymised copy may be retained by the data controller." The National Archive emphasised that "the register's unique character, the size and composition of the population studied, the extent of the registered personal data and the length of the study period to date, indicate that it is important to preserve the opportunity for extended longitudinal studies."[64]

However, on March 5, 1986 the Data Protection Authority rejected Janson's request to submit the key tape to the National Archive.[65] The Authority also determined that the register should be anonymised by May 30. Three Authority members from the Social Democrats and one from the Swedish Confederation of Professional Employees (TCO) felt that the available information was inadequate, and therefore wanted the decision to be postponed. They therefore abstained when the decision went to the vote.

"I felt that the rule of law was endangered. That no one was taking a stand on either the content or the project as a whole in relation to other similar ventures. There was an expectation of a resolution – at any cost. And there was that press conference waiting, where one's heroism was to be narrated."

(Birgitta Frejhagen Social Democrat and member of the board of the Data Protection Authority 1974–1987, Klein 2009)

The Debate on Project Metropolitan

The Project Metropolitan debate is started by the broadsheet Dagens Nyheter, *and soon spreads to other newspapers and to radio and television. Four thousand people request register excerpts. The Supreme Commander of the Swedish armed forces views Project Metropolitan as a national security threat. The integrity debate dies down.*

On February 10, 1986, the Project Metropolitan debate was triggered by the broadsheet *Dagens Nyheter* (DN). The headline on newspaper placards read "Project Metropolitan: 15,000 Swedes in secret data register". Headlines on the inside pages included "Observed in secret for 20 years" and "Researchers know everything about 15,000 Swedes". A short time earlier, Janson had embarked on a long-planned journey to the USA, having been invited as a visiting lecturer. He was therefore forced to deal with the serious situation in which the project suddenly found itself from abroad. In hindsight, there is little doubt that things would have been better if he had been in Stockholm when the controversy erupted.

The DN articles turned out to be the start of an intensive debate with extensive media coverage. From the time of the first DN article on February 10 until the end of March, the four high-circulation Stockholm newspapers *Aftonbladet*, *Dagens Nyheter*, *Expressen* and *Svenska Dagbladet* published 133 headlines on Project Metropolitan.[66] An exhaustive review of the Project Metropolitan controversy would require a book of its own. No such book has been written, but the following year Gunilla Qwerin was commissioned by the Swedish

Image 9. The TV-show "Magasinet", February 1986. Photographer: Jan Wirén/Sydsvenskan. Copyright: Jan Wirén/Sydsvenskan, License: CC-BY-NC-ND.

How to cite this book chapter:
Stenberg, Sten-Åke. 2018. The Debate on Project Metropolitan. In: Stenberg, Sten-Åke. *Born in 1953: The story about a post-war Swedish cohort, and a longitudinal research project.* Pp. 43–60. Stockholm: Stockholm University Press. DOI: https://doi.org/10.16993/bav.c. License: CC-BY

National Council for Crime Prevention to study the media coverage of Project Metropolitan, and conducted a thorough analysis of the debate.[67]

Today, over 25 years later, many have forgotten the Project Metropolitan debate, while others are too young to have any memory of it at all. The debate nonetheless continues to influence the conditions for social research in Sweden. In spite of the harsh media criticism, it would turn out that no formal misconduct had taken place. The media also discovered that the legislation they had used to lash out at the research community could also be turned on them. Many social researchers supported Project Metropolitan, albeit not always publicly. And there was serious concern about the possible long-term consequences of the debate for social research. The year after the media controversy, for example, the Swedish Medical Research Council wrote the following in its consultation response in respect of the governmental inquiry *Protecting integrity in the information society*: "The one-sided and unnuanced debate on this type of research [epidemiological research based on register data (author's note)] in relation to the so-called Metropolitan Project in 1986, has unfortunately had a negative effect on developments. Important projects have been discontinued. In certain cases, the collection of essential new data has been interrupted or discontinued, and in other cases active researchers have stopped accepting students."[68]

In subsequent decades, the memory of the media controversy became a nightmare that the research community largely tried to forget. Many also felt that criticisms might have been avoided if researchers had been more communicative and had played a more active role in the debate. Some also linked Project Metropolitan and similar register-based research to paternalism and social engineering.

Dagens Nyheter's "exposé" employed formulations and a terminology that discredited the researchers and that came to dominate the agenda of this debate for a long period of time. Although many of the project's participants were not aware of their involvement in the

"We have not charted the lives of those born in 1953 in the most minute detail. The data we have were never intended for anything of this kind. We are statistically oriented sociologists, and our data are intended for statistical analysis. We have relatively superficial (but in part sensitive) and sparse information, which is sufficient for our purposes, but not to describe the lives of specific individuals. Anyone who believes differently has been misled."

Carl-Gunnar Janson, handwritten document, Project Metropolitan archive.

study, they had not been "observed in secret", and of course Project Metropolitan did not know "everything about 15,000 Swedes". The project had previously been the subject of both positive and negative newspaper articles on a number of occasions and, as has already been mentioned, the Data Protection Authority's Director General, Jan Freese, had written about it in his books.[69]

In the first DN article, the Family Survey was described as being based on "in depth interviews", when it had in fact been a questionnaire survey, and Jan Freese was quoted, saying: "It's like turning people into caged rabbits." In addition, the article quoted Carl-Gunnar Janson's fateful (as it would turn out) statement on research subjects' being able to apply to have the information relating to them removed from the register: "It is grotesque that those interviewed should subsequently be able to deprive me of the material that I have been working on for over twenty years. My having collected information about them from various registers doesn't mean that they have participated. It is quite fantastic that they believe they can own the information that relates to them. Research should not be subject to the Data Act."

Both at the time and today, there is no legal right to be removed from a research register. If a person is included in a research project, and for example has been interviewed, it is not possible to subsequently request that this information be removed. In formal terms, the data constitute public information. It is of course possible to discontinue one's participation in the research, but researchers may continue to use any existing data. Thus, we citizens do not own any personal information that is contained in administrative registers.[70] Some authorities remove data from their registers at various intervals, but those included in these registers cannot themselves decide to be removed.[71] This was what Janson was referring to when he stated that the study participants did not own the information relating to them. The DN article also stated that the cover letter linked to the questionnaire survey that was conducted in 1985 in collaboration with Radio Sweden's listener surveys, did not include the information "that the

"I can still remember the shock I felt when the reporter from Expressen *rang and said that I and 15,000 others were among the most scrutinised people in Sweden. I got my next shock when I opened the envelope containing my data excerpt from the register. It scared me that they had found out so much about me. [...] Since then I have never answered any questionnaires of any kind. Either orally or in writing. I don't want to have my whole life charted."*
(Manni Thofte)

researchers had been studying the recipients for many years." This was not really the case (see the section entitled *The key tapes and the third and final questionnaire*).

The day after the publication of its first article, *Dagens Nyheter* published the front-page headline "Storm breaks on secret data register". Below the headline, the introduction read: "Shock, bitterness, fury. There has been a violent reaction to DN's revelation that 15,000 people have had their lives charted for over twenty years by a secret study." On the inside pages, the project was described as "record-breakingly expensive", since it had cost "over seven million in research grants". Given that the project had been ongoing for over 20 years, this was not a particularly large sum of money. The annual cost of the project to that point had been approximately 300,000 SEK. The newspaper also published statements in which the Liberal Party Member of Parliament Ylva Annerstedt, and the Secretary of the Liberal Party expressed criticism of the project, whereas Birgitta Frejhagen, one of the Social Democrat members of the Data Protection Authority, expressed support: "My assessment is that the project is very important and that the researchers have handled the information they have been given very well."

The evening tabloids followed up the story on the same day that *Dagens Nyheter* published its first article. The headline in *Aftonbladet* read "15,000 Swedes in secret register – Stockholmers' lives charted in great detail for over twenty years".[72] The *Expressen* front-page headline was "15,000 Stockholmers secretly monitored for 20 years. Find out what the computer knows about you – use the form provided in Expressen".[73] The article's text took a more personal turn: "Professor Carl-Gunnar Janson and his wife Ann-Marie at Stockholm University have been investigating and registering all Stockholmers born in 1953 for over 20 years. Virtually every piece of information that exists on an individual has been included in Janson's register." The front page showed a photograph of the downhill skier Manni Thofte with a clenched fist, who was quoted as saying that he did not want to be monitored. *Expressen* also published the Jansons' passport photographs and personal identity numbers. The article concluded with Ann-Marie Janson having to answer a number of questions that were similar to those posed by the project in the 1985 questionnaire. Unlike *Aftonbladet*, *Expressen* spoke only to Stockholmers born in 1953 who held negative views about the project, and a column of text was devoted to a summary of interviews conducted with Jan Freese, with Justice Minister Sten Wickbom and with Gunnar Hökmark, the Conservative board member at the Data Protection Authority. Freese used his caged-rabbits' metaphor, Wickbom said that he would convene his experts on data legislation to examine whether the register could be allowed to exist, while Hökmark wanted the register to be discontinued: "If the research project is to continue, the Professor will just have to contact all the 15,000 he wants to study."

The debate continued at a high level of intensity for almost a month, with headlines such as "When researchers peep through the keyhole", "They stole the whole of my private life", "Professor paid from the USA", "How the Professor tricked his 'guinea pigs'", "Burn all the computer data about us", "I refuse to give my correct personal identity number", "Pointless computer research", "Secret boxes disappear from Project Metropolitan". When Prime Minister Olof Palme was murdered on February 28, the intensity of the debate waned. At the beginning of March, *Dagens Nyheter* published a proclamation by ten prominent researchers[74] under the headline "Proclamation in support of computer-aided empirical research". The authors stated that "the mass media campaign against the use of computers in social, behavioural and medical research" was based on ignorance and misunderstanding, and that it could have damaging consequences. They emphasised that the goal of "computer-based research" was to improve the knowledge on, among other things disease, the functioning of schools and social exclusion. Today, when every home has a computer and virtually everyone has his own smartphone, few would question the use of the computer as a research tool. Nonetheless, there

"I was mentioned in the newspaper because I worked in the marketing division at Dagens Nyheter *at the time, and the journalists must have found out that I was born in '53. I don't think that it was OK to have ended up in a register from which one's information could not be removed. But I wasn't particularly upset, and I didn't get involved in the debate. I was working with surveys myself, and I could understand why it can be a good thing to see the broader context and to be able to make improvements."*

(Agneta Wolffelt)

remains concern about how personal data is dealt with in the context of research. The proclamation was criticised because it was financed by Statistics Sweden, and it probably did little to mollify those who were critical of Project Metropolitan.

As the authors of the proclamation had feared, the debate produced lasting effects. Response frequencies declined across a range of surveys, and some have argued that the debate was probably the "reason that the Population and Housing censuses were scrapped."[75]

4,000 register excerpt requests

The massive amount of attention that was focused on Project Metropolitan as a result of the media debate gave rise to a great deal of curiosity concerning the contents of the register. Approximately 4,000 individuals requested excerpts detailing the information that the register contained on them. This need not be interpreted as indicating that all these people were opposed to the research as such. Many were quite simply curious to know what the data said about them.

The stack of requests for register excerpts rapidly produced a critical workload for the few individuals working on the project. Errors appeared both in printouts of the excerpts and in the personal data stored in the register. Also, a number of ethical problems arose. Was it in fact right to send these individuals all the information contained in the register? Did the register contain information that they were not themselves aware of, and that might be damaging, for example that they had been adopted but had never been informed of this fact?

One of those whose register excerpt contained incorrect personal information was the author Niklas Rådström, who wrote a debate article about this in *Dagens Nyheter* on May 25, 1986. His excerpt had been affected by a dislocation in the data set, so that the information in his excerpt belonged to a completely different person. The errors provided rewarding opportunities for sardonic observations

"I didn't get particularly involved. Nothing more than that I probably spoke with some other people about it. Then I requested a data excerpt in order to see what it said about me. But I didn't go to Radiohuset [the offices of Radio Sweden] to demonstrate. It took a long time for the papers to come, and it didn't make for very good reading. I'd had a tough time in school, a working-class kid with a single mum and bad grades. Also, there were a number of things that were quite simply factually incorrect."
(Bo Östlund)

and Rådström concluded that Project Metropolitan was "a thoroughly meaningless, crap study". His conclusion was understandable, given the contents of his register excerpt. And it should be noted that the errors that had affected Rådström's data (and that of a number of others) were corrected.

As early as two weeks after the first *Dagens Nyheter* article, the Data Protection Authority held a meeting with the project's staff. The objective was to clarify how the requests for information from the register should be dealt with.[76] According to the minutes of this meeting, no excerpts were to be dispatched prior to the Data Protection Authority's scheduled meeting on the future of the project. Incomplete requests (which lacked personal identity numbers etc.) were to be returned to those who had sent them with an invitation to submit a new request. Information could only be sent if it directly related to the individual making the request; excerpts would not, for example, be sent to mothers requesting information on deceased offspring. Nor would information from public agency records that was assessed to be inappropriate, be released. The same was the case for the responses made by mothers in the 1968 questionnaire survey. This was "to be communicated in a way that causes as little concern as possible."

On April 17, the Data Protection Authority conducted an inspection of the project, motivated by complaints and questions from the public "due to their having requested register excerpts over two months ago, without as yet having received a response."

Ann-Marie Janson, who represented the project at the inspection, explained the problems associated with the large number of requests, and the inadequacy of the resources available to carry out the programming required for computerised register excerpts. A great deal of work had also been devoted to translating the coded data into comprehensible text. But additional manpower had been called in, and in spite of the problems, the project expected to be able to respond to all the requests. Information from police and crime registers was not released, due to confidentiality regulations. Nor was information relating to hospital admissions, discharges and diagnoses. The quality of these data was assessed to be too poor, and the project staff were concerned that the release of incorrect information could be harmful to those concerned. However, there were no legal grounds to support this course of action in the Secrecy Act. The project also intended not to release data to project participants that was based on information provided by their mothers in 1968 "in confidence and long prior to the introduction of the Data Act [...]. The data controller is of the view that the ethical duty towards the mother carries greater weight than the Data Act's rule on releasing information." The mothers would of course be provided with excerpts about themselves if these were requested.

The Data Protection Authority noted immediately in its inspection report that there was no legal basis for refusing to release either healthcare data or the information provided by the mothers, but promised to get back to the project with further clarification. Their decision was published on April 24.[77] All requests that had been received prior to May 1, one month prior to the date on which the register was to be anonymised, were to be effectuated. The Data Protection Authority understood the problems associated with responding to 4,000 requests, and did not wish to criticise the fact that doing so had taken a long time. As already noted, however, the Authority found no legal basis for the project's decision not to release healthcare data or the mothers' questionnaire responses from 1968. But because of the risk of harm, the Authority nonetheless accepted that the project did not intend to release the information about the mothers: "The Data Protection Authority understands that the data controller feels he has landed in a dilemma with regard to such information. The information in question was provided in confidence and on the condition that the recipient would be bound to professional secrecy long before the introduction of the Data Act." Following the Data Protection Authority's meeting of May 21, acting director G. A. Westman sent the minutes to Ann-Marie Janson together with a handwritten message:

"The Authority expressed that the excerpts must of course represent the contents of the register, irrespective of whether these are correct or incorrect. If you wish to provide additional comments, for example about diagnostic information, this is entirely up to you."[78]

A national security risk?

When the Project Metropolitan controversy had been going on for three months, the Supreme Commander of the Swedish armed forces also chose to make his views known. In a letter to the Data Protection Authority, the armed forces command presented an assessment of the security risk associated with the project, stating that "a register of the Metropolitan type, with all the combined information it contains, constitutes an unnecessary and non-negligible security risk." The Supreme Commander was concerned that a foreign power would be able to exploit the registered information if one of those included in the register were to be employed by the armed forces or given a war posting involving highly classified work. There would also be a risk that a foreign power, with the help of the registered information, would attempt to identify "individuals whom it would be possible to influence in order to exploit them for intelligence purposes." A further reason was that so-called "illegalists" would be able to obtain identities by exploiting the data of deceased persons. In addition, the Supreme Commander felt that ...

... the way the Metropolitan register has been handled has not been adequate from a security perspective. Among other things it has been stated that

- Data have been sold abroad;
- The destruction of large amounts of register data has been conducted without supervision from the relevant supervisory authority (the Swedish National Archive); and
- There have been threats of burglary.

"The Supreme Commander feels it is important that all details of the dissemination of the registered information should be compiled and requests that the Data Protection Authority should attend to this and initiate possible supplementary measures, at the latest when the notification of anonymisation is made to the Authority in accordance with the above. It is proposed that a special security assessment should then be conducted by the responsible authority (the Swedish Police Authority)."

Supreme Commander, operational command 21-05-1986, Säk 903:61977.

The Supreme Commander was not satisfied with the fact that the register had been anonymised, and argued that consideration should always be given to "whether registers of the Metropolitan type should be regarded as being of significance to national defence or national security in some other way." Further, the Supreme Commander wanted the staff who handled such registers to be assessed "from a security perspective" and on the basis the National Security Vetting Directive." Finally, he wished to "note the risks that are always present with regard to extensive knowledge about personal information. The threat to the individual and the risks associated with compiled information must be taken into consideration in our efforts to protect national security, for which reason the Supreme Commander views the information that has emerged about Project Metropolitan register very seriously."[79]

Paper documents are destroyed

In addition to the data tapes, the Project Metropolitan data comprised a large amount of paper documentation. In February, when the debate was at its most intense, a number of threats were directed at Sociology Department staff. The university feared that the documents were in danger, and the administrative director decided that they should be moved to a safe place away from the department. On February 24, 47 boxes were packed and transported to the archive at the university's administrative offices. A short time later, 21 boxes were transferred to the Swedish National Archive. Of the remaining boxes, some were returned to the Sociology Department and the rest were destroyed, including the questionnaire material from the School Survey. In April, the National Archive requested an explanation for the destruction of the School Survey; according to the archive, the survey constituted a "public document" that should be archived.

While all this was going on, Carl-Gunnar Janson was in the USA, from where he kept in contact with the university. He was resolute in his desire that the material should be destroyed, because the researchers had promised the study participants that the questionnaires would not be preserved for any longer than the work required. The university supported Janson's view and argued that the questionnaires were working material and not public documents. Furthermore, according to the university, it was illogical to save the paper documents that would make it possible to reconstruct the project. The Data Protection Authority had after all ordered the data to be anonymised. The National Archive argued that even if they were not public documents, the questionnaires could be defined as archival documents that should be retained.[80] The university argued that this was unreasonable. If this was the case, no working material at the university could ever be disposed of without the approval of the National Archive.

The Chancellor of Justice examined the issue of the questionnaires' destruction and concluded in October 1986 "that the measures taken by the university without the required contact with the National Archive had been in breach of the regulations."[81] The Chancellor also stated that there was no legal basis for promising those who completed the questionnaires that they would be destroyed.[82] At the same time, the Chancellor could see extenuating circumstances: "The criticism I have directed at the university does not preclude the fact that I am aware of the problems associated with the question of public confidence in the researchers, and in sensitive information not being passed on. Considering that the debate about Project Metropolitan largely focused on the fears of those born in 1953 that the information collected would find its way into the wrong hands, the measures taken to destroy the questionnaire material were in line with earlier promises intended to safeguard the integrity of the surveyed individuals." The Chancellor then made a call for "legislative measures to safeguard the pursuit of important research", and for better cooperation between the National Archive and the research community. In this way, the Chancellor of Justice dismissed the Metropolitan case.

"I still have a problem with the Metropolitan business. There is something shady about this surreptitious registration of me and fifteen thousand others. I felt this as early as 1965, when it started and I was in the fifth grade. Our teacher handed out a form that we were expected to fill in without any explanation at all. To begin with it was fairly harmless stuff, but after a while you came to questions about who you would invite if you had a party, and who you liked and didn't like. I felt instinctively that this was my own business. Why should I tell someone else about this, when I don't know who they are or what they are going to do with the information? My first act of public protest was probably to write Donald Duck and Mickey Mouse as answers to the question of who I would invite to a party."

Summary of discussion by Olsson, Anders R., in Kajsa Klein (2008)

Bad data and dangerous researchers

Another voice in the Metropolitan debate was heard from the southern Swedish university city of Lund. In March 1986, the law professor Anna Christensen wrote a debate article in *Dagens Nyheter*.[83] Her criticism summarised the views that a number of academics held about research based on large data sets, the roles of the researcher and on society and democracy.

Anna Christensen claimed that the researchers had good intentions, but that there was a form of oppression inherent in the knowledge that was produced as a result of a blurring of the boundaries between administrative research and the administration conducting the research. The researchers were driven by a shared passion to improve the world, in the hope that an effective administration based on scientific methods would produce some form of "righteous and all-embracing order". They wanted to chart "people's ideas and actions" and trace covert alcoholics and anyone else who was trying to hide, in order to identify those "who are trying to wriggle out of this righteous order by, for example, reporting in sick in order to avoid going to work. Above all, the goal is to identify those 'at risk' at an early stage and take appropriate measures before they cause any harm to themselves and others."

The argument was linked to Václav Havel's discussion of the "fanatic of the abstract project", which claimed that utopias like communism that were motivated by benevolence and rationality were at risk of overreaching and becoming totalitarian. According to Christensen, Sweden had already reached this point, and the public should be on their guard: "The first ill-fated moment of destruction has already occurred, and people understand this. It is this insight that is manifesting itself in the protests against data registers and administrative research." The public, and particularly the "at-risk cases", would increasingly "keep quiet about what it is that puts them at risk, i.e. exactly what the administration wants to know." As a result, it

"The archival problems are extremely expensive. Nonetheless, in the final analysis one always apparently submits to the tired, but constantly cited argument that there may be a young sociology student in 50 years' time, who will need every conceivable piece of information in order to write a 20-page undergraduate dissertation. At the same time, it may be noted that every other comparable country is able to manage both its examination of the past and its development, without these "rabbit cages" of information about people, among other things."

Freese, Jan. (1987) *Den maktfullkomliga oförmågan* (The Powerful Inability), p. 94.

would also become more difficult to conduct "charting and detection work" (questionnaire surveys). But since the administration would never understand that the public were not afraid of the information leaking to neighbours etc., but rather of the administration itself and, by extension, of totalitarian society, it was incapable of doing anything about this. This was the "blind spot" of science.

Christensen assumed that Sweden was on the way to becoming a totalitarian "Folkhem"[84]. The sociology professor Joakim Israel also criticised the project, but expressed fears of a different kind. What Israel envisioned was instead a kind of capitalist dictatorship. Another difference between the two was that Christensen viewed politicians as saviours. They would legislate to prevent the conspiracy between researchers and advocates of the folkhem. In reality, however, developments took quite a different turn to those feared by both Christensen and Israel. What in fact happened was that the market expanded at the expense of the politicians, and the opportunities for social research have since been restricted by an extensive system of regulation.

A little over a year after the publication of the first *Dagens Nyheter* article on Project Metropolitan, Gunnar Fredriksson wrote about the relationship between journalists and researchers under the headline: "Do we want to know why some people get cancer?" He maintained that there was a baffling cultural divide between the two professions and "a deep disdain for the media among researchers", that was more than "the same old banal grumbling." He concluded the article by stating rhetorically that he could not answer "questions about this cultural divide particularly well, not least because journalists were usually not even aware that they do in fact often have a hostile approach to research, as part of a fashionable wave of anti-intellectualism that is sweeping the entire western world."[85]

Later the same year, Jan Freese wrote a debate article in *Aftonbladet* in which he remarked that the Data Act had become outdated. The government had instructed the Data Protection Authority to publish directives that would in effect require newspapers to obtain the consent of everyone from dictators to terrorists in order to include their names in the newspapers' digitalised archives. "Unfortunately, they contain information that is at times of no better quality than that proffered by the Oracle of Delphi." Freese felt that this was unreasonable but that "this absurd situation is likely to continue until we have an earnest debate on press ethics, and legislation in 1991 that is at least suited to the 1980s."[86]

For several years after the debate there was confusion about what the Data Act actually meant. As Jan Freese had noted, it would turn out that the journalists' own computer-based registers did not fit the legislation. The journalist Anders R. Olsson, who had been active in the Metropolitan debate, later described developments as a growing and increasingly striking conflict between "rules to protect the individual on the one hand and freedom of speech on the other."[87]

Anders R. Olsson described a number of incidents that today appear ludicrous. In 1987, for example, the government and the Chancellor of Justice maintained that people named in Radio Sweden's published descriptions of broadcast news stories had to "be informed of this and of their right to be removed from the register." This was even the case for individuals such as Ronald Reagan and Madonna.[88] At the beginning of the 1990s, Anders R. Olsson brought the conflict before the courts in a case in which the Data Act and the Press Freedom Act were contrasted with one other. According to Olsson, the Data Protection Authority argued that their remit was not limited by the Press Freedom Act, although their powers in this regard had never been used in practice. In principle, this meant that the Authority could enter the editorial offices of a newspaper and "with the support of the Data Act demand to read, delete and edit articles that had not yet been published."

A few years later, the Swedish Union of Journalists commissioned Anders R. Olsson to write a handbook on freedom of speech and freedom of the press. The legal situation was unclear, and Olsson therefore applied to the Data Protection Authority for permission to write the manuscript on a computer. He planned for the most part to provide "references to/quotations from authorities in the field of press freedom law, but also a small amount of information of a sensitive nature in [the form of] defamation cases that illustrated important principles."[89] The question was whether the Data Protection Authority would refrain from applying the Data Act to a sphere that was regulated by the Press Freedom Act. Anders R. Olsson's book was published in May 1992, before the Data Protection Authority had time to reach a decision. It was not until the following year, when the Parliamentary Ombudsman had criticised the Data Protection Authority for the time it had taken to process the case, that the Authority reached a decision: "The Data Protection Authority rejects the application."[90] Thus, in arriving at this decision, the Data Protection Authority had determined that Olsson's book broke the law. This was of course an absurd situation, and the decision was appealed to the government. After eight months the government stated that the Press Freedom Act, since it constituted part of the Swedish constitution, took precedence in the context of a norm conflict.[91] By this time, however, Anders R. Olsson's book had been in the bookshops for fourteen months. Since this time, journalists, authors and artists have been exempt from the legislation that regulates personal data registers and research ethics.

The high levels of commitment and aggression that characterised the debate considerably diminished the significance of integrity-related issues for a long time; few could find the energy to engage with the new threats. Not many people in 1986 could imagine that virtually every household would have a computer of its own just twenty years later, and that it would be possible to read newspapers from all over the world at the kitchen table, conduct one's banking business in bed, or engage in e-mail or chat conversations with people from New Zealand to Greenland. Project Metropolitan was quite harmless in relation to what was to come. But the debate had a negative effect on Swedish research for a long time. More than 25 years after the

"There probably wasn't so much to get upset about. Think about how things are today, when there is so much information about everyone everywhere. I talked a lot about this with others who were born in 1953. Of course, you'd been subject to an interrogation, where they found out things that maybe not everyone would want other people to know. Then I sent for my papers. I was really curious about my answers. In the papers it said that I and my twin brother had been adopted when we were one-month old. I had known about this for a few years. But imagine if this had been the first time I'd got to learn about my birth. That wouldn't have been good."

(Gerd Svensson)

data set had been anonymised, Project Metropolitan was still being referred to as an example of problematic research, and some of those included in the project's data set still feel that they have been the objects of abuse.[92]

Statements about project Metropolitan – then

"*This type of survey is important. Metropolitan was also important, but it was the clumsy way in which it was done that I reacted to. I still think it was wrong.*

(Lotta Samuelsson Aschberg)

"*I thought that the debate was exaggerated. I didn't feel abused. I thought that I was already probably registered, since I was so politically active on the left wing.*

(Weje Sandén)

"*An acquaintance who was also born in 1953 was extremely upset about what she read in the papers. She knew how old I was and said that I was probably in the project as well. She found it difficult to understand that I wasn't so angry. She felt she was being watched by "big brother" and was almost fanatical in her indignation. But I didn't actually care very much. I didn't feel I was being watched at all. I didn't apply to see the information they had on me either. If I felt anything about the whole thing, it was rather that it sounded quite exciting and interesting.*

(Margareta Kempe Allansson)

"*It was an intense debate, and it even attracted attention outside Sweden. The Economist wrote a thoroughly negative article on Project Metropolitan. Their point of view was the Swedish big brother society, which was mapping its citizens.*

I have a strong memory of the debate on the Evening Show, with Gary Engman, where I was a participant. We were at a hopeless disadvantage. The atmosphere was very aggressive. It wasn't the sort of debate that we were used to. We needed some kind of media training, but of course that sort of thing didn't exist at the time.

Nonetheless, it wasn't that I was unused to TV. I'd been on a number of shows as a criminologist. But then I'd had a different role, I was the expert. On the Evening Show, it was tough. But we were probably naïve too. We thought there would be a willingness to balance the debate a little, but that just didn't happen. Everyone who represented the project in some way was hung out to dry.

(Jan Andersson)

"*I don't remember too much about the debate in the newspapers, and I can't remember that I felt abused or manipulated as many of those who were quoted in the papers described it.*

I have a vague memory of the demonstration at Radiohuset, but I would never have considered participating. I had so much to do at home during those years, with a five-year-old and a two-year-old. Spontaneous demonstrations weren't at the top of my agenda. But I filled in the form in Expressen *and sent it in. It felt like it was something you should do. And I really wanted to see what it said about me. Although I don't know what I was actually expecting.*

(Ulla Abelin)

Statements about project Metropolitan – now

"*In hindsight, I think it might have been fun to send in for the papers and to read what I'd answered to all the questions on that occasion. But I still don't think it was anything to get upset about. From my little treadmill of everyday life I've maybe made a contribution to research on things that are important. I feel a little bit of pride about that!*

(Margareta Kempe Allansson)

"*I wasn't particularly upset then, and I'm not upset today either, about the Metropolitan researchers collecting so many facts about me. Everything was anonymised after all, and perhaps the research may be of use to society in some way. Today you probably take it for granted that the authorities know a great deal about you. And today, of course, it's as easy as anything for everyone to find information on people on the Internet.*

(Ulla Abelin)

"*I'm as much opposed to secrecy today as I was then. It was as wrong as it could be, that the people involved weren't informed what project they were part of, and it was just as wrong that it was possible to identify these people. That's why it was so important that the demand for anonymisation was actually complied with. At the same time, I can understand that there may have been good intentions behind the whole project and that it could be useful. But all participation in that type of project should be voluntary.*

(Manni Thofte)

"*When I received my register excerpt I was angry, because the researchers had found out a load of things about me, and collected information for many years without my having any idea about it. I didn't understand what it could be good for. Today I look at it differently. I have a greater understanding of the importance of that kind of information if you want to improve society.*

(Bo Östlund)

Metropolitan 2018

Project Metropolitan has been updated and renamed The Stockholm Birth Cohort. The law has been changed and the project has once again become a personal data register.

Carl-Gunnar Janson died in 2007. A few years earlier, the Metropolitan study had been transferred to the Swedish Institute for Social Research (SOFI) at Stockholm University. There remained a large number of social research questions that could be analysed with the help of the material, but since no new data had been added after 1986, the possibilities were nonetheless limited. At the beginning of the 2000s, the idea was broached that it might actually be possible to update the old Metropolitan material with the help of register data. Denny Vågerö, at Stockholm University's Centre for Health Equity Studies (CHESS)[93], and I discussed the possibility of doing this, and in 2003 we applied to the Research Ethics Committee at the Karolinska Institute for permission to update the Metropolitan study. The committee approved our application.[94] One critical condition was that both data sets were to be anonymised.[95] Personal identity numbers would not be accessible at any point in the process or at any of the agencies involved in the update process. If we or anyone else were able to identify the individuals in the study, the update would be unethical. Since the promise that was given in 1986 remains in force – the data are anonymous and will remain so – we were able to begin the work to update the material.

Image 10. Sten-Åke Stenberg and Denny Vågerö applied for permission to update the old Metropolitan data set in 2003. When the update process had been completed, the project was given a new name. It is now known as "The Stockholm Birth Cohort.". Photographer: Reidar Österman. Copyright: Reidar Österman, License: CC-BY-NC-ND.

How to cite this book chapter:
Stenberg, Sten-Åke. 2018. Metropolitan 2018. In: Stenberg, Sten-Åke. *Born in 1953: The story about a post-war Swedish cohort, and a longitudinal research project.* Pp. 63–69. Stockholm: Stockholm University Press. DOI: https://doi.org/10.16993/bav.d. License: CC-BY

How could it be possible to update the material?[96] To begin with, we had the anonymised data from Project Metropolitan. Each row in the data set corresponds to an individual, while the columns contain a number of variables such as age, number of children etc. At CHESS there were other anonymised data relating to almost the whole population, including all those born in 1953 who were still alive in 1980. These data relate to the individuals' health and social conditions from the 1960s until the early years of the 2000s, and are known as the HSIA database.[97] Both the Metropolitan and HSIA data sets include identical information from the Population and Housing censuses conducted in 1960 and 1980. It would therefore be possible to match data between the two projects. In order to do so, however, it would first be necessary to create a sufficient number of unique anonymous observations in each data set to make the matching process worthwhile. The problem was greatest, of course, in relation to the HSIA data, which contained almost 115,000 observations. This meant that the matching process would be difficult, but not impossible.

To begin with, all those who were not born in 1953 were removed, and the remainder were divided into two groups according to gender. With the help of eleven variables from the Population and Housing censuses, such as the number of flats in a given building, year of construction, and the marital status and occupation of the individuals' parents, it was possible to produce unique anonymous observations. The same procedure was then applied to the Metropolitan data. This was easier, of course, because the Metropolitan data included somewhat fewer than 15,000 observations.[98] In practice, however, it turned out that matching the two data sets was easier said than done. Although the variables in the two data sets came from the same source, the figures had often been rounded off or recoded so that they did not correspond. Intensive work to reconstruct the original variables produced results, however, so it was possible to match the data.

We refer to the process as "probability matching" because even though we are convinced that the matches between the two data sets are correct in virtually all cases, we can never be entirely certain for each individual observation. There are errors, but we are unable to identify them. In spite of these problems, we have matched 96 percent of the Metropolitan data with new data from the HSIA. It must also be emphasised that we have matched anonymised data, and have thus not identified any of the individuals.

Once the data had been updated, we renamed the project. It is now called *The Stockholm Birth Cohort*.

Nobody was identified

Although it would have been of great value to have been able to re-interview those included in the study, it would have been both illegal and unethical to attempt to identify anyone. The researchers know nothing more about the identity of the observations than they did prior to the matching process, i.e. nothing at all. Linking two anonymised data sets to one another does not increase the possibility of anyone being identified. Statistics Sweden would be able to identify the individuals included in the HSIA, but they have no idea which of these individuals are included in the Metropolitan data. It would furthermore be a criminal offence if the staff at Statistics Sweden were to attempt to find out which individuals were included in the Metropolitan study. The researcher thus has no identifiable information whatsoever. The data are anonymous and any attempts to identify individual observations are illegal.[99]

A changed situation with the introduction of the Personal Data Act

Once the Metropolitan data had been anonymised in 1986, when all personal identity numbers were destroyed, making it impossible to add new data from, for example Statistics Sweden, the project was no longer of any interest for the Data Protection Authority. The researchers could continue their work, and there were no restrictions on how the data could be processed. There was, after all, no longer any personal integrity to protect.[100] In 1998, Sweden introduced the Personal Data Act (Personuppgiftslagen), which was based on the EU's Data Protection Directive.[101] During a transitional period lasting until 2001, the existing Data Act remained in force, but it was then completely replaced by the Personal Data Act. All permits issued by the Data Protection Authority then became invalid.

According to the Personal Data Act, personal information includes "all kinds of information that may directly or indirectly be attributable to a living natural person." Since the Metropolitan data cannot be *directly* linked to any individuals, from 1998 onwards the question became whether it was possible to link the data to individuals *indirectly*. The researchers argued that this was not possible. Nor did the probability matching and the data update process conducted in 2004 increase the possibility of doing so. However, the Metropolitan study had been the subject of controversy, and a large number of people had been affected. The researchers therefore chose to apply for ethical approval.

Following the update process, the work was scrutinised by the Swedish Research Council in connection with an application for research funding. The Council conducted a thorough examination of the work, which was examined by among others the Council's expert group on ethics. The Council's conclusion was that the project could continue and would be given financial assistance.[102] In 2010, the Data Protection Authority also decided to examine the project. In September of the following year, the Authority stated that the project's data consisted of personal data and that the project should once again apply for ethical approval.[103] While the researchers found it difficult to understand how the data could be viewed as personal data according to the definition employed by the Personal Data Act, they decided not to appeal the Authority's decision, and instead once more applied for ethical approval. This application was approved on December 15, 2011.[104]

Thus the project had identifiable data until 1986. Thereafter, the data were anonymised, but with the introduction of the Personal Data Act in 1988, they once again became defined as personal data. The Data Protection Authority believed that it would be possible to *indirectly* link these data to living persons in the sense described in the Act. Project Metropolitan had been revived, and the data resurrected from the dead, so to speak, and they had once again become sensitive personal data. In actual fact, nothing had happened. The Data Protection Authority's interpretation of the Act is that the individuals included in the study could in theory be indirectly identified. The fact that this would in practice be impossible is of no interest in this context.

The HSIA data was indirectly identifiable, since Statistics Sweden retained a "key" to the relevant personal identity numbers. At Statistics Sweden, each of the individuals in the data set had a serial number. These serial numbers provided the key for accessing the individuals' personal identity numbers. The researchers were given the serial numbers but not the personal identity numbers. Providing the personal identity numbers to the researchers is prohibited. Furthermore, the researchers have absolutely no interest in them. The matching of the Metropolitan data with the HSIA database has also introduced a degree of uncertainty. The researchers know that the fit between the two data sets is very good, but there are incorrect matches and nobody knows which observations these relate to. The staff at Statistics Sweden do not know – and will never know – which observations have been matched. The researchers do not know – and will never know – which individuals are included in the HSIA database.

But would it be possible to "reverse-identify" the individuals in the data set? Is it possible to identify a person exclusively on the basis of the variables included in a data set? The Data Protection Authority appears to believe that the greater the number of variables, the greater the likelihood that it will be possible to identify individuals.[105] This is only partly true, however. In order to be able to identify a person, you have to know that person's values on a sufficiently large number of precisely specified variables in order for the individual to emerge as a unique observation in the data set. If, for example, a data set has a text-based variable for occupation, and the value for a given observation is Prime Minister, then it is fairly clear whom the data relate to. Less extreme examples may be found in individuals with rare medical conditions, or who come from very small minority groups. In summary, the issue of reverse identification is not about the number of variables in the data set, but rather two other things: firstly, anyone wishing to obtain improper access to an individual's data must already have sufficient knowledge of the individual whom they wish to identify; then there must also be variables that correspond to this pre-existing knowledge, and these must have values that are so unusual that it is possible to uniquely identify a specific individual in the register. But this is also prohibited by law, and furthermore, it is extremely difficult.[106]

Is it reasonable for a data set to be defined as a personal data register if it is possible to *indirectly* link the data to living individuals? Would it not be better to call things what they are, rather than what they might possibly become? A letter opener is a letter opener. It only becomes a murder weapon if and when it is used to stab someone.

In its 2011 decision, the Data Protection Authority stated that the researchers had to have a research question in order to be permitted to use the data. The data from Project Metropolitan may not be destroyed, yet they may not be used in the absence of a specified research question. According to Paragraph 9 of the Personal Data Act, personal data may only be collected for specific, explicitly stated and legitimate purposes. The Act does not state the level of detail at which these purposes must be specified, but according to the Act's legislative history, they may not be of a nature that is too general. Paragraph 6 of the Ethical Review Act contains a similar provision. Applications to the review board must "relate to a specific project or part of a project or in a similar way to specified research". The project has received such approval, but as soon as a researcher wishes to examine a question that is not covered by an existing review board decision, a new application for ethical approval must be made. This is the case despite the fact that nothing has changed in the project's data. In the 1970s and 1980s, it was identifiable data that were regarded as constituting a threat to individual integrity. In today's Ethical Review Act, it is the researcher's ideas that must be controlled.

Social Research Then, Now and in the Future

Would it be possible to initiate a Project Metropolitan today? Perhaps, but for better or for worse, conditions today are very different from those of the 1960s.

What kind of process would be required to start a Project Metropolitan today? For a number of reasons, a project of this kind would look very different with regard to both its content and how it would be conducted. Today research is controlled much more strictly by legislation and regulations than was the case in the 1960s. Today's researchers cannot ask questions and collect data as freely as those of yesterday. Current regulations would also make the work much more arduous, and would require repeated applications to the regional Research Ethics Review Board. Another difference relates to the questions. They would be answered by children living in a completely different society to that inhabited by the children of the Metropolitan study.

The childhood of the Metropolitan children differed in many ways from the conditions experienced by children today. They lived in more crowded housing. During their primary school years, they attended school on Saturdays, and their parents were given four weeks' annual holiday for the first time in 1963. When they were born, there was no television in Sweden, but before they started school, they experienced the excitement of television sets starting to appear in some homes. It was not until they were adults that they would become acquainted with digital technologies in the form of mobile phones and the Internet. Today's children socialise online with friends from near and far, whereas the Metropolitan children had pen-pals whose names they had probably found in children's magazines. The range

Image 11. Sergels torg, Stockholm. Photographer: Sten-Åke Stenberg. Copyright: Sten-Åke Stenberg, License: CC-BY-NC-ND.

How to cite this book chapter:
Stenberg, Sten-Åke. 2018. Social Research Then, Now and in the Future. In: Stenberg, Sten-Åke. *Born in 1953: The story about a post-war Swedish cohort, and a longitudinal research project.* Pp. 71–84. Stockholm: Stockholm University Press. DOI: https://doi.org/10.16993/bav.e. License: CC-BY

of foods, fizzy drinks and sweets on sale in shops was nowhere near what it is today, and overweight schoolchildren were a rarity. The list of differences could be made very much longer.

A new Project Metropolitan would of course have to be adapted to all these things. In the 1966 School Survey, the Metropolitan researchers asked the children how much time they usually spent watching television. The same question could be asked today, but an equally natural question would be how much time they spent at their computers. And children today could certainly also be asked the question: Do you think pupils should be allowed to smoke in school? But it is unlikely that almost one-quarter of them would answer in the affirmative, which was the case in 1966. At the same time, there are many questions that are just as important to ask today: How often do you spend time together with one or more of your school friends during your leisure time? How often do you go to the cinema? How long do you usually spend doing homework? How often do you usually read newspapers? Have you been sent out of the classroom for something you've done? Some of these questions would need to be re-specified based on the realities of contemporary life, however. Do children get together both in real life and online? Do they read newspapers in paper form or on the Internet? Do they watch films at the cinema, on television, on their computers or on smartphones?

Project Metropolitan is of value from both a historical and a social policy perspective. The childhoods and lives of a generation have been documented for the future. In a hundred years, when we are all dead and gone, future generations will be able to understand their historical background with the help of the Metropolitan data. This is of value in itself, and it will undoubtedly be of interest to many people. But the project's objective was not only that of describing the living conditions of people born in the mid-20th century. Svalastoga, Janson and the other researchers who worked on the project wanted to arrive at conclusions that would contribute to creating better living conditions for today's children. Can Project Metropolitan help us to assess the future opportunities for today's children, given the fact that conditions have changed so much during the half century since the project was started? This is a difficult question to answer. I believe that it is possible in a number of ways. But readers will have to make up their own minds on the basis of the research results that are presented in the second part of this book.

As has been described, a 2018 version of Project Metropolitan would be much more highly regulated than the original study. Before the project could even start, an application would have to be sent to, and approved by, the regional Ethical Review Board. This is due to the fact that since 2004 there has been a legal requirement that all research on sensitive personal data must be examined by such a board. If the data a researcher wishes to collect are not sensitive, no approval is required from an ethics review board. Such non-sensitive data may include information on substance abuse, social welfare recipiency, divorce and debt, or eviction cases registered at the Enforcement Authority. It is not entirely easy to comprehend why the legislation has determined that some types of information should be regarded as sensitive and others not.

In the application, a clear research question must be formulated. It is not possible today, as in the 1960s, to collect data from different registers more or less unconditionally. On the other hand, researchers would not have to collect the data from a range of different agencies' authorities' registers, since much of the data from these registers has been compiled and retained at Statistics Sweden. The researchers could therefore delay requesting data for research questions that might become relevant at some point in the future. However, there are still some forms of register data that are retained by other agencies, such as the Enforcement Authority. These data are removed from the register after a few years, which means that if the researchers wanted to make use of them, they would have to be included in an application to the Research Ethics Review Board.

To simplify the work involved, the focus should be directed towards the School Survey. An important reason for this is that questionnaires and interviews provide researchers with an opportunity to collect data that are not included in registers, and they also make it possible to measure attitudes and opinions in real time. But how should the all-important research question be formulated? The research programme presented in 1961, with its four central themes focused on social mobility within and across generations, membership in groups and formal organisations, social adjustment and deviant behaviour, and choice of friends and family formation, would not have sufficed as research questions. The simple question of why life turns out better for some people than for others would in no way be regarded as sufficiently specific. It is questionable whether it would even have been possible to formulate a research question that would have been accepted by the Data Protection Authority and the Research Ethics Review Board.

By restricting the research question, the researchers should be able to obtain approval for their application. Applications may also be made successively, by beginning with one research question and subsequently adding more research questions to the project. This may sound like a good idea, but to obtain results, researchers probably need to spend more time conducting research than writing applications to the Ethics Review Board. Furthermore, it would be impossible to conduct the entire School Survey at the same time, which would mean that the researchers would be unable to analyse all of the pupils' answers in the same context.

Thus if the work were to continue, it would have to be on the basis of a well-defined research question and a more limited school survey. Once the approval of the ethics review board has been received, work may begin on the survey and contact can be made with the interview subjects. Of course, it would be necessary for these individuals to provide "informed consent" to participate in the study. Informed consent means that the children must understand both the study's objective and the data that are to be used. Since the School Survey was focused on children under the age of thirteen, a similar survey today would require the consent of both parents.

For the 1966 School Survey it was sufficient to obtain consent from the education authorities, teachers' organisations and the national parents' and school association. Nowadays, researchers would face the complicated task of obtaining consent from the parents of over 15,000 children. The level of non-participation would probably be high, particularly among children from families experiencing social problems. When data are collected, they must also be analysed. The research question must be answered, and is often reformulated into a number of more concrete questions. By definition, the goal of research is often unclear, which means that problems and new questions may arise in the course of the work. It may turn out that the data needed to answer a certain question are missing, and that some unnecessary information has been collected along the way. If the missing data are available at Statistics Sweden or in other registers, the research material may be supplemented, but if these data are sensitive, a supplementary application must also be sent to the ethics review board. If this applies to data that should have been collected in the questionnaire, it is practically impossible to repair the damage.

New questions – new ethical review

Research subjects may also decline to continue participating in a project, although data that have already been collected may not be destroyed. After a time, a project may therefore include a great deal of data. Since register data can always be added and updated for as long as the project data are identifiable, these data are not as important as the information that the researchers themselves collect from questionnaires and interviews. However, as soon as a new research question emerges, which is not covered by a decision of the ethics review board, a new application must be submitted.

If the Family Survey were also to be conducted, the process would have to be repeated. For this survey too, a research question would have to be formulated and approved. If it were possible to carry out some form of family survey, the information collected could be added to the project data. But since new research questions require new applications for ethical approval, the information cannot be used for research indiscriminately.

In this way, it might be possible to conduct a new Project Metropolitan today. The requirement of a well-defined research question would cause the project to be less comprehensive, and it would be problematic to ask questions that the researchers believed might produce opportunities for future research. Regardless, the project would be much more complicated to administer, and the level of non-response would be much greater today than it was in the 1960s.

The requirement of a specified research question does not apply to everyone who wishes to carry out a survey. If a journalist were to carry out a questionnaire survey, permission would only be required from parents and schools. The conditions in such a case would be determined by Sweden's constitutional protections for freedom of speech and of the press, and not by the Ethical Review Act. The journalist would, however, face greater problems than a researcher in supplementing the study with register data from, for example, Statistics Sweden. But it would not be impossible. There would probably be a requirement that the journalist should provide the relevant personal identity numbers to Statistics Sweden, and that this information should simultaneously be destroyed at the journalist's editorial offices. It would also be possible, however, to have Statistics Sweden retain the personal identity numbers to allow for a possible follow-up survey in the future.

A researcher working at a market research company or polling organisation would not have to write an application for research ethics approval either. The polling firm SIFO, for example, conducts large-scale surveys of the Swedish public's consumption patterns, which also include questions on political views, trade union membership and personal health. These surveys could just as easily have been formulated at universities, and are of course based on, among other things, statistical sampling theory and psychological theories.

To be ethically justifiable, these surveys must follow "existing legislation and the joint voluntary rules that have been adopted by the
ERM" (the ethical council for market research surveys).[107] This means
that SIFO and other market research companies are not subject to
review prior to conducting their surveys, but that their work may
be reviewed subsequently – if someone makes a complaint. Further,
this review process is not regulated by law, but is rather based on
voluntary participation.

The surveys conducted by pharmaceutical companies are similar to
those conducted by market research firms. The Swedish Association of
the Pharmaceutical Industry (LIF) is an association of 80 companies
that account for 80 percent of pharmaceutical sales in Sweden. The
document *Rules for Non-Intervention Studies and Financial Support
for Quality Registers* contains the organisation's rules for when applications must be submitted to research ethics review boards.[108] The
organisation distinguishes between surveys that include sensitive personal data and those that do not, and states that market research
surveys do not include such data, and that they do not constitute scientific research. It is only if the market researcher plans to publish the
results in a scientific context that an application for ethical approval
becomes necessary. The concept of what constitutes scientific research
is also unclear for the government and the Central Ethical Review
Board.[109] The Swedish Association of the Pharmaceutical Industry
has adopted the makeshift solution that is currently practised by the
ethical review boards: If the applicant states that the results will be
published in scientific journals, the work is regarded as research.

Defining scientific research

It was not the legislator's intention that a statement that research
results would be published in a scientific publication would be sufficient reason for ethical review. But what, then, constitutes scientific
research?

The Ethical Review Act of 2004 stated that the legislation applied to "scientific research and developmental work based on scientific grounds". Following a revision of the Act in 2008, it has since applied to "scientifically experimental or theoretical work to collect new knowledge and developmental work based on scientific grounds, although not work of this kind conducted within the framework of higher education at the undergraduate or post-graduate level." The Central Ethical Review Board noted that neither of these definitions was particularly clear. Stated briefly, the Board has interpreted the Act as meaning that all work that has a scientific purpose, with the exception of student work, and that is intended for publication in scientific journals, is regarded as scientific research.[110]

One way of defining scientific research would be to determine who is conducting it. For example, it is difficult to exactly define what constitutes teaching, but easier to define who is a teacher. In the government bill outlining the 2004 Act, the government notes that a majority of Sweden's public sector research is carried out at universities, although it is also carried out at public sector agencies such as the National Board of Health and Welfare (Socialstyrelsen). Research is also carried out at private legal entities such as firms, foundations and associations, and even by private individuals. Thus, research can be conducted by almost anyone. Perhaps private individuals engaged in genealogical research should also apply for permission when they contact living relatives?

These developments have resulted in medical journals always requiring researchers to obtain ethical approval before publication. For researchers in the social sciences ethical approval is rarely a requirement for publication. Other professional groups, such as journalists and market researchers, do not need to apply for ethical approval. Since they do not work with "scientific research", they are able to work under completely different conditions. Ethical review has become comparable to the eco-labelling of products. Approval simultaneously becomes an affirmation of the quality of a survey, and may lead to a higher response frequency.

I am myself a member of the Stockholm Regional Research Ethical Review Board for "other research", i.e. cases involving non-medical research. When the board is uncertain of whether an application relates to scientific research, the applicant's commitment to publish in a scientific journal is usually the basis on which the issue is decided. At the same time, the board should be generous in its interpretation, and should treat cases as research if the issue is not entirely clear. A large majority of the applications are for the most part approved without any problem. Possible questions often relate merely to formalities, such as whether the applicant has completed the application form correctly, or has forgotten to inform the research subjects that they have the right to withdraw their participation at any time.

Journalists can protect their data using the principles that enable them to protect their sources. Scientists and market researchers can refer to Paragraph 8 of the Secrecy Act, which states that: "In public sector agency activities that involve the production of statistics, confidentiality applies to information relating to an individual's personal or financial situation that may be traced to the individual."

Journalism would be almost impossible if interviews were subject to advance ethical review. A journalist can interview people who are sick or who are in prison. If the interview subject consents, the results can be published with the subject's name and photograph. The work is of course governed by the ethical rules of the media industry relating to respect of personal integrity. Reviews are only conducted after the event, if someone reports an article to the Press Ombudsman (PO), the Swedish Press and Broadcasting Authority, or the professional ethics council of the Swedish Union of Journalists (YEN). As has already been noted, market research is also subject to review only after the event.

The Ethical Review Act was not introduced because researchers had previously been ethically unaware. The research councils and universities had ethical review committees and groups. Yet there was a good deal more scope for creativity and curiosity in research than is currently the case. In 1981, Janson applied for the project to be extended in order to collect certain data series, for the following reason: "If some important new research question should arise within the project's subject area over the course of the estimated five years that remain of the project, further additions [of data] may be required."[111] A motive of this kind would be in direct violation of today's legislation. New and as yet unknown, research questions may not be used as a justification for the collection of data.

There is, of course, a limit to how much data research projects should collect. The large register databanks maintained by Statistics Sweden have also reduced the need for universities to collect data. Instead, the surveys conducted by researchers themselves are of principal importance. These are subject to logical limits, since questionnaires cannot be excessively long. Researchers must therefore focus on questions related to the research topic in question. Nevertheless, in the absence of the legal requirement for well-specified research questions there would be much greater scope for the type of creativity that is often required in order for research to produce results that are not already known.

Restrictions that cause complications

Governmental documents relating to research often begin with a few lines about freedom of research. The government bill on the research ethics review process 2002/03:50 states, for example, that the researcher's "free quest for knowledge is fundamental." In the description of the background to the legislation, Project Metropolitan is mentioned, along with the fact that the government of the time was of the view "that it would be unfortunate if the discussion should lead to longitudinal research becoming more difficult, since there is, for example, a very great need for research of this kind that can clarify the relationships between environmental factors and health, or between the significance of heredity and environmental factors in society."

The question is whether the legislation has in fact made it more difficult to conduct this type of research? Research based exclusively on register data has in fact become easier, since Statistics Sweden and the National Board of Health and Welfare today store large quantities of data that may be accessed relatively easily. If researchers wish to collect new data themselves by means of questionnaires and interviews, however, the situation has become much more difficult since the mid-1960s. The requirement for a well-specified research question risks putting a stop to the researcher's curiosity.

The Ethical Review Act makes no distinctions between different fields of research. It is of course important to ethically review medical, psychological and other types of research that affect the individual's physical or emotional life in some way. In such cases, there is a clear risk of people being harmed. With the introduction of the Ethical Review Act, the social sciences became subject to the same requirements as medical research.[112]

But why should social science research that is exclusively based on questions and/or register data be subject to the same type of review process? The chairpersons of the ethics review boards are lawyers. The boards are comprised of ten members with scientific expertise and five who represent the public interest. When the board members are divided on a decision, the chairperson has the casting vote. Thus, in the final analysis it may be a lawyer who decides whether social science research is appropriate.

Medical research often has a direct effect on individuals' physical and psychological wellbeing. The social sciences involve asking people questions or conducting statistical analyses of existing register data. There is thus a big difference between medical research and the social sciences. However, certain questions posed in a social science questionnaire or interview could produce a subsequent psychological reaction, e.g. questions about the death of a loved one. The government discussed this problem in the parliamentary bill that introduced the Ethical Review Act. "The government's view is that ethical review should apply to research methods that in themselves are likely to expose the research subject to some form of influence. The interview method does not involve this type of situation; interviews only involve the collection of information. If a research area is in itself so sensitive that reactions may ensue, this is a circumstance that the research subject can take into consideration when he or she is asked to participate."[113] When the Act was revised, this was changed, and now interview studies must also undergo ethical review.

The fundamental principle in the ethical review process is that the benefits produced by the research should be weighed against possible harms. It should follow from this that ethically unproblematic research should always be approved. The former scientific secretary of the Central Ethical Review Board, the professor of paediatrics Gisela Dahlquist, has argued that "Dishonest and bad research is unethical, not only because it deceives the research community or the individual researcher, but primarily because it may produce negative consequences for future patients."[114] Dishonest research is of course disastrous, but the question of "bad" research is less clear. The first problem is that of who should determine what constitutes bad research. And how should this determination be made?

Social science is a heterogeneous field, not least when it comes to methodology. It is much more difficult to judge what constitutes good and bad research in the social sciences than it is in the field of medicine. Researchers with a qualitative focus (who study small amounts of data in archives or by using interviews) often argue that quantitative research (which uses statistical methods to analyse large data sets) is of little worth, and vice versa. If ethical review boards were to dismiss research that the board members regarded as poor, they would be engaging in an unfortunate quality review of social science. Further, experience tells us that what we think of as important today, may well be viewed as relatively uninteresting before too long. Conversely, we also find that questions posed in earlier surveys are given new life as a result of improved statistical methods, new research findings and theoretical developments, even if they did not result in much research at the time. We simply cannot know for certain what will turn out to constitute valuable social science research over the long term.

So why do people need such stringent protections against the curious social scientist? One typical argument is that the ethical review process gives research greater legitimacy. Citizens feel safer when research is subject to a strict system of controls. But could the opposite not be true? An activity that requires such extensive control might be perceived as being particularly dangerous.[115]

Regarding the issue of personal integrity, there are currently many areas outside the field of research where the threat to personal integrity is greater, but which are subject to little or no control. Every time customers swipe their supermarket store cards, information is registered about what they are buying. Data on everything from porridge to headache pills and condoms are recorded in the corporate registers. The data are retained for two years, and are used to collect and analyse information on purchases for the purposes of marketing and formulating special offers and discounts. These businesses may, by combining data from other registers, update and add further personal data in order to develop and maintain high quality registers and good customer care. Information may be provided to consumer associations or legal entities affiliated with the store card programme.[116] The data are, and are intended to be, identifiable. By contrast, the data in social researchers' registers are almost always anonymised, and if they are drawn from the registers maintained by Statistics Sweden, there is no possibility for the researchers to see whom the information relates to.

Since the Data Protection Authority was formed 40 years ago, the issue of the balance between personal integrity and the benefits of research has been a matter of debate. To begin with, the debate also included the balance between personal integrity and the benefits of journalism, defined as the "public interest", and the harm journalism causes to personal integrity. When it became clear at the beginning of the 1990s that journalism was protected by the Press Freedom Act, research found itself alone on the other side of the scales.

This book may serve as an illustration of the lack of clarity that characterises the legislation. Ulla Kindenberg, a journalist, has interviewed a number of individuals born in 1953. Their answers include what the law defines as sensitive personal data, for example criminal offences. As the author of this book, I am an academic researcher. To avoid breaking the law, I would need ethical approval to ask the same questions, and to report the answers. But if I had written the same things in my free time, or as a novel, I would not have required the same approval. As a novelist I would have been able to interview the same people, use their real names, and describe their religious affiliations, alcohol problems and psychoses, as the author Karl Ove Knausgård does, for example, in the *My Struggle* series of novels. Why can a researcher not ask the same questions as a journalist, and why does a researcher, despite ensuring that nobody is identifiable, not enjoy the same publishing freedom as the author of a novel?

PART II
THE CHILDREN OF 1953

Progress and a Belief in the Future

To date over 160 reports have been published, which illustrate in various ways how life turned out for the children born in 1953, from their childhood years until they were approaching retirement. Many of the reports focus on crime, substance abuse and marginalisation, while others look at school, child rearing, choice of friends and health issues.[117]

The children of 1953 were born at a time characterised by optimism and the building of the Swedish "folkhem". Sweden was a country in which everything seemed to be changing for the better, a country on its way to becoming modern. Migration to the cities was increasing steadily, while at the same time agriculture was on the decline. The statutory three weeks of annual holiday had been in place since 1950. An increasing number of families were able to travel on holiday by car in the Saab, Volvo or Volkswagen they had recently purchased. If gasoline costs threatened to consume too much of the holiday budget, two families were crammed into the car. Wines and spirits were still rationed, and would remain so for a further two years. Child benefit, in the sum of 260 SEK annually per child, was paid to the mother on a quarterly basis. Those who could afford to purchased the clothes that the textile firm Algots marketed in advertisements and catalogues timed to coincide with the child benefit payments. Housewives were the norm, and nursery schools were almost unknown, although many six-year-olds went to kindergarten or playschool. The issue of married women going out to work was still controversial, and those married women who did work outside the home had to accept the fact that the joint taxation of married couples took away a large part of

Image 12. Photographer: Arne Sohlström. Copyright: Arne Sohlström, License: CC-BY-NC-ND.

How to cite this book chapter:
Stenberg, Sten-Åke. 2018. Progress and a Belief in the Future. In: Stenberg, Sten-Åke. *Born in 1953: The story about a post-war Swedish cohort, and a longitudinal research project.* Pp. 87–96. Stockholm: Stockholm University Press. DOI: https://doi.org/10.16993/bav.f. License: CC-BY

"We've seen major changes. You have to be prepared to change in order to keep up. When I look around at friends of the same age and old schoolmates, I think they are capable and loyal. Their lives are all in order, they seem to be doing well."

(Agneta Wolffelt)

their income. The decline of the newspaper industry was still a long way off, and there were eleven daily newspapers in Stockholm. IKEA opened its first furniture display in Älmhult, and Sweden won gold at the ice hockey world championships. Television sets had not yet begun to appear in Swedish homes, where people still listened to radio shows such as Carousel, the news from TT and Children's Letterbox. Clubs and associations flourished, and ambitious fathers took correspondence courses given by the educational firm Hermods in order to improve themselves.

In Europe, the rebuilding process was still underway in the countries devastated by World War II. In the USA, where Eisenhower had been inaugurated as president, McCarthy was persecuting communists. In Russia, Stalin died. The UN appointed Dag Hammarskjöld to the post of Secretary General, and Winston Churchill won the Nobel Prize for literature. Tito became President of Yugoslavia, and in the UK a future Prime Minister was born – Tony Blair.

At the same time as the march of progress moved rapidly on and the reforms came thick and fast, many lived in cramped and destitute conditions. Children grew up in poverty, with parents who found it difficult to raise them. Substance abuse and crime had similarly devastating consequences as they do today. In the Stockholm area at the beginning of the 1950s, many of the poorest children were born in the cramped and outdated apartments of the city centre. However, modern homes were being built in new suburbs, and the overcrowded families from the central districts of the city were increasingly able to move to new apartments with bathrooms, balconies and other comforts. In spite of this, however, there was an acute housing shortage that would not start to improve until the so-called Million Programme was initiated in the mid-1960s.[118]

The children born in 1953 started school in 1960, three years after the Swedish Parliament had ruled on nine years of compulsory unitary schooling, which would be renamed "grundskolan" in 1962. Their teenage years, in the 1970s, coincided with the period when access to drugs suddenly exploded. Only a decade earlier, drugs had not been a social problem of any magnitude at all.

Irrespective of whether or not the children of 1953 were themselves politically active, the public debate during their teenage years was influenced by the growing left-wing radicalism that characterised the 1960s and 1970s. Then came the spirit of the 1980s. The great Swedish social project was called into question and individualism became a more powerful force. By the time the children of 1953 celebrated their 40th birthdays, in 1993, Sweden had been hit by an economic crisis and mass unemployment.

During the decades that have passed since the birth of the children of 1953, so much has happened in Sweden and the outside world, that the society of 1953 feels like a different universe. The cold war is now history. The Berlin Wall fell a long time ago, and with it the Soviet state. Nuclear weapons continue to constitute a threat, however, as do acts of terrorism and global environmental degradation. The list of phenomena that did not exist in the world of everyday Swedish concepts in 1953 can be made as long you like – from pizza, garlic, thermos flasks and door codes via interrailing, telephone answering machines, platform shoes and charter holidays, to walkmans, tsunamis, Swedish for immigrants courses, independent schools, "helicopter parents", "bonus children"[119], smartphone, "latte-mums"[120], childcare days[121], internet and Facebook.

At the same time, life goes on. Now, as then, our days are spent going to school, working, raising and spending time with our children and grandchildren, and hoping for a decent life in our autumn years.

160 publications from Project Metropolitan

The first reports from Project Metropolitan were published in the mid-1970s and were primarily descriptive or theoretical. Subsequent reports, which took up the effects of conditions during childhood and youth, had a more analytical focus. The Swedish Metropolitan

"We grew up with the pill and with freedom. Everything was possible. We were OK. When we left school there were jobs, and it was still possible for young people to find somewhere to live."
(Jan Andersson)

study had an emphasis on criminality and social marginalisation, and this is reflected in many of the more than 160 publications that have been produced to date, which often focus on crime, drugs and mental health problems. Almost 70 of these publications have been produced since the material was updated in 2004.[122]

Studies that follow people's lives over a long period of time are called longitudinal. If they are forward-looking and based on data collected at the same time as, or at least close to, the events of interest, they are labelled *prospective*. If they instead look back on the events in question, they are labelled *retrospective*. Project Metropolitan is predominantly a prospective longitudinal study. This creates good opportunities for keeping tabs on the chronological ordering of different events, which in turn improves our ability to draw conclusions about cause and effect.

The results produced by social science research are tentative and are constantly being questioned. The results from Project Metropolitan are no exception. There are many different statistical methods to choose from, and results can vary depending on the choices made. Sometimes results may be contradictory. Social phenomena such as poverty and loneliness also need to be defined in some way. This may be done on the basis of information from registers of income and social welfare benefits, or by posing questions in interviews or questionnaires. Are social welfare recipients poor? Below what level of income is a household poor? Are children who answer that they are mostly by themselves lonely? Researchers have to choose a measure to capture the phenomenon that is to be studied, and there are often many different variables to choose from. When I move on to present

Image 13. When the Project Metropolitan children were born, there were only test broadcasts of Swedish television. When the radio stores showed these broadcasts, spectators flocked around. Photographer: Tore Falk/TT Nyhetsbyrån. Copyright: Tore Falk/TT Nyhetsbyrån, License: CC-BY-NC-ND.

various studies that were based on the project, I do so in order to describe interesting findings, not in order to question these studies. My objective is to answer the question: What conclusions have these studies arrived at? Despite the fact that the project has been ongoing for a very long time, there are still a large number of questions that could be examined with the help of the project data.[123] In the future, Project Metropolitan will also create possibilities to study aging in a life perspective.

Cohorts, Generations and Other Concepts

Everyone born in the same year is part of what is called a "birth cohort". The Metropolitan study is therefore referred to as a cohort study. Another, more common, concept is that of a generation. This may be used to refer to different generations within families, as in the expression "generations come and go", or to people who experience a given phase of life, such as youth, during the same historical period. This latter sense of the term is often associated with musical or literary phenomena or with particularly turbulent periods of history. It may refer to artists or writers who are active during a specific period, such as the "Beat generation" in New York and San Francisco, who were active at around the time that the children of Project Metropolitan were born. It may also refer to people who together experienced a war or other more or less turbulent events. On the basis of this definition, the children born in 1953 may be considered part of the same generation as the children born at the end of the 1940s. They have grown up under similar childhood circumstances in post-war Sweden. Nonetheless, it is perhaps more common to group them together with others born during the 1950s, and to link them to phenomena such as the Swedish "folkhem", fluoride and the Beatles.

The Metropolitan cohort originally comprised 15,117 individuals, but the Metropolitan research studies are almost always focused on groups. If a single observation or a very small group is of particular interest, the results are presented in a way that ensures that nobody can be identified. This means that facts are altered in order to ensure that the identification of individuals will be impossible. One may, for example, change an individual's place of residence, if this is not important for the discussion at hand. Descriptions of groups may, for example, focus on how many girls continued to upper-secondary education, or the risk that the children of divorced parents would experience economic problems as adults.

When involvement in crime is described in terms of group proportions, such as the percentage of boys who have committed offences, it is taken for granted that the others have not committed offences. But when the results are presented in terms of the risk for involvement in crime, it is easy to make the mistake of thinking in terms of individuals rather than the group. If 30 percent of the boys and 10 percent of the girls in a given age group have committed offences, the risk for boys is three times as high as the risk for girls. This may also be expressed by saying that the relative risk for boys compared to girls is three. However, the fact that the risk for boys of becoming offenders is three times as high as the risk for girls does not mean that the risk for every boy is three times as great as the risk for girls. The risk relates to the group of boys, not to one's neighbour's son. This example also illustrates that even if the risks may be perceived as being substantial, the actual numbers involved need not be a matter for concern.

If we instead focus on those who do *not* engage in crime, then in our example we are looking at seven of every ten boys, and nine out of ten girls. This undoubtedly sounds less alarming than saying that the risk for boys is three times as high as that for girls. But as front-page news, this is not a headline that is likely to grab your attention.

Cause and effect

What came first – the chicken or the egg? What is due to what? In the social sciences, where it is rarely seldom possible to conduct experiments, it is difficult to definitively establish cause and effect. It is relatively easy to show that different phenomena are correlated, but it is not as easy to explain why. There are large numbers of studies showing that the unemployed have poorer health than others, and that criminal offenders have grown up under worse childhood conditions. But why is this the case?

When interpreting results, it is important to be aware of the possibility that what appears to be a correlation between two different phenomena may in fact be due to a third phenomenon. This third phenomenon is often something we are not aware of. This is called selection. For example, the poorer health found among the unemployed might be due to people with poor health also being at greater risk of unemployment. Perhaps their health was worse than that of others even before they became unemployed. It is also possible that their health becomes even worse as a result of their unemployment. In this case, their higher levels of ill-health will be due both to their being less healthy prior to becoming unemployed, and to their health having worsened further as a result of their unemployment. It is thus difficult to distinguish between cause and effect.

For this reason, the chronological order of events is important when making comparisons. For example, many adults who receive welfare benefits may have lived under difficult childhood conditions, growing up in families that were also often on welfare. Does this mean that their problems are the result of some form of social heritability? This is of course not entirely unlikely, but in order to be certain, the comparison must also be made in the opposite direction: How large a proportion of the children who grew up in families that received social welfare benefits themselves went on to receive welfare benefits as adults? In the Metropolitan study, 44 percent of those who received social welfare benefits in 1982 (when they were aged 29) came from families who had received welfare benefits at some point during the participants' childhood years. But of *all* those who grew up in families that received social welfare benefits, only twelve percent went on to receive welfare benefits as adults.[124] If individuals are followed back in time, the level of social heritability appears to be four times as high as it does when one instead follows the individuals from childhood into the future. The social physician Gustav Jonsson minted the concept of "social inheritance". He saw that the boys from the Skå children's home, at which he worked, often came from difficult conditions, which could be seen for several generations into the past. But if he had been able to study *all* the boys who had grown up in so-called problem families, the results would have been less alarming, as can be seen from the example involving welfare benefits.

Other surveys

Longitudinal studies were initiated in a number of different countries during the post-war period. The UK was among the first, with the National Survey of Health & Development (NSHD), which was initiated in 1946. In 1958 came the National Child Development Study (NCDS), in 1970 the 1970 Birth Cohort (BCS70), at the beginning of the 1990s, the 1991–2 Avon Longitudinal Study of Parents and Children (ALSPAC) and ten years later the 2000–1 Millennium Cohort Study. In Scotland, the University of Aberdeen has conducted three cohort studies, the first from 1921, the second from 1936 and finally a study focused on children born between 1950 and 1956. These cohort studies are in many ways similar to the Swedish Metropolitan Project. The number of observations lies at around 15,000 and the information included in the studies is largely the same.

One of the world's largest, and still ongoing, longitudinal projects is Project Talent, from the USA, which was initiated in 1960 with a survey of over 440,000 American high school students.

Important Swedish studies include the Malmö Study, which followed all 1,542 children who were in the third grade in schools in greater Malmö in 1938, and the IDA school research project (Individual Development and Adaptation), which was initiated in

1964 and which has followed the development of the children enrolled in schools in the city of Örebro in 1965.

Longitudinal studies need not be based on cohorts of course. The Swedish Level of Living Survey (LNU) from 1968, which has played an important role in the social debate in Sweden, is based on a simple random sample of approximately 6,000 observations. The survey includes a panel of individuals who have been interviewed repeatedly. To date the survey has been conducted in 1968, 1974, 1981, 1991, 2000 and 2010.

In the international context, the American Panel Study of Income Dynamics (PSID) is one of the most widely-used longitudinal data sets. Like the LNU in Sweden, the PSID was initiated in 1968, but has a sample of over 18,000 individuals.

In addition to the data sets described above, there are also a wide range of other studies. These are often focused on specific problems, such as drug abuse and crime, but the number of observations is rarely particularly large. By comparison with the data available to studies conducted in other countries, the public register data that are available in Sweden provide major advantages. Sweden's residential registration system also substantially improves the possibilities of finding individuals in the context of follow-up studies and the country's administrative registers provide a rich and reliable source of data. Despite the differences with the data available in other countries, the Swedish data sets should nonetheless be useful for the purposes of international comparisons. Unfortunately, few if any such studies have been conducted.

Confinement and Being Born in 1953

On infant mortality then and now, on maternity ward routines, feeding and weighing, and on social class and birth weight. The 1950s were a transition period with regard to infant care. The regimentation of the doctors stood in contrast to the spontaneity advocated by psychologists. Abortion was illegal and thousands of Swedish children were put up for adoption.

In the1950s, pregnancy and childbirth were significantly more risky than they are today. As late as 1955, the obstetrician and gynaecologist Mirjam Furuhjelm described pregnancy as similar to being locked in a room with two doors: "The one leads to death, and the other, through agony and suffering, perhaps to a happiness that one hardly dares to dream of – a living child."[125]

The Project Metropolitan data include information from a little over 12,000 birth journals on the delivery process, the child's height and weight, the length of time spent on the maternity ward, and much more. This information shows, for example, that only one percent were born at home, while the rest started life at a maternity clinic or hospital.[126] The majority of the mothers, on the other hand, had themselves been born at home, at a time when mortality rates were high for both mothers and children.[127]

Social class, ill health and life chances

All societies are socially stratified, but the distance between the upper and lower strata varies a great deal between different countries. The

Image 14. Photographer: Björn Henriksson's Malmö collection/ Sydsvenska Medicinhistoriska Sällskapet, Lund. Copyright: Björn Henriksson's Malmö collection/ Sydsvenska Medicinhistoriska Sällskapet, Lund, License: BY-NC-SA

How to cite this book chapter:
Stenberg, Sten-Åke. 2018. Confinement and Being Born in 1953. In: Stenberg, Sten-Åke. *Born in 1953: The story about a post-war Swedish cohort, and a longitudinal research project.* Pp. 99–113. Stockholm: Stockholm University Press. DOI: https://doi.org/10.16993/bav.g. License: CC-BY

When the oldest mothers of the children born in 1953 were themselves born, at some point during the 1910s, one in ten children born in Stockholm died before their first birthday. Among those who were unlucky to enough to be born out of wedlock, the mortality rate was even higher. Thanks to social and medical progress, however, things improved. The youngest mothers in 1953 were only fifteen years old. When they were born, in 1938, infant mortality in Sweden had dropped to 43 per thousand. In Stockholm, the rate was even lower, at 35 per thousand. It was higher, however, among children born out of wedlock, at 54 per thousand.

distribution of society's benefits is not equal. Those at higher levels of society get the most, while those lower down get least. Defining this stratification presents a number of problems. Should definitions be based on power, income, occupation, privileges, or a combination of these? Some additional questions are strongly linked to values: What produces the observed stratification? What significance does the family have, or the individual's own ability or will power? What effects does stratification have on individuals' life chances? There is, of course substantial disagreement about what would constitute an equitable degree of stratification. The literature and views on this question are considerable.

In Project Metropolitan, stratification has been determined on the basis of occupation and income respectively. The origins of this social class model are found in a categorisation developed by Statistics Sweden as early as 1911. At that time, the population was divided into the "higher class", the "middle class" and the "manual working class". This categorisation was then used in the election statistics until 1948, with the categories also being specified as social groups. Within a family, the man's occupation was classified as the principal occupation, and the woman's was classified as the secondary occupation. The different social groups were in turn comprised of different occupations. The most common categorisation system is based on six classes: I. Upper class and upper-middle class; II. Lower-middle class, lower-level officials in private and public service and employees in non-agricultural occupations; III. Lower-middle class, self-employed and professionals in the second social group; IV. Working class, skilled workers; V. Working class, unskilled workers; VI. No occupation or unknown occupation.

Children's life chances are affected by their parents' social situation. When the Project Metropolitan children were born, 14 percent of their families were from the upper class or the upper-middle class, 32 percent were lower-middle class, 6 percent were self-employed, 29 percent were skilled workers and 19 percent were unskilled workers.[128]

Infant mortality declined throughout the 20th century, but one factor that did not change as much was the difference in birthweight between infants from different social classes. Throughout the century there has been a difference in birthweight, based on whether mothers were married or unmarried, and on their class affiliation. (Until 1967 it was possible to see this directly, since the statistics presented the figures separately for married and unmarried mothers. After that point, however, common law unions, and thus unmarried mothers, became so common that it was no longer relevant to measure the difference.)

Women who came from higher social classes and/or were married gave birth to heavier infants. This is also reflected in the birth journals for the children born in 1953. The infants from upper and upper-middle class homes weighed on average 117 grams more than the infants born to unskilled workers. A difference of just over 100 grams may appear small, but in the context of average weights in large groups 100 grams is quite substantial. The differences were also linear, with birthweights declining systematically from the top of the class scale towards the bottom. Those with the lowest birthweights came from families with no social classification. These families were comprised almost exclusively of unmarried or single mothers and families who had migrated to Sweden. On average, the infants born to this group weighed 162 grams less than the infants of married mothers.

Among the children born in 1953, the risk of dying during the first year of life had fallen to 17 per thousand. However, the differences between children born in and out of wedlock remained. In 1953, infants born out of wedlock had a mortality rate of 24 per thousand. These figures can be compared to the situation at the turn of the millennium, at which time no more than four children per thousand died during their first year of life, and the risk of mothers dying in childbirth was virtually non-existent.

Facts Relating to Maternity Hospitals

One-quarter of the children included in the Metropolitan study were born at Stockholm's Southern Hospital (*Södersjukhuset*). Approximately fifteen percent were born at the General Maternity Hospital (*Allmänna BB*) and a similar proportion at Karolinska Hospital, Sabbatsberg Hospital or Southern Maternity Hospital (*Södra BB*). Seventeen percent were born at Danderyd Hospital, the Epidemiological Hospital, Löwenströmska Hospital, St. Erik's Hospital, Södertälje Hospital, the Västerhaninge maternity clinic and "others". In 1954, the Medical Board inspected child healthcare services at the Stockholm City maternity units.[129]

> In 1953, the **Southern Hospital** had only existed for nine years and it was the centre for midwifery training. The unit's 115 places were visited every day by a paediatrician and the children were cared for "both day and night" by paediatric nurses. Almost three of every four mothers from the Södermalm area of Stockholm, and 44 percent of the mothers from Stockholm's southern suburbs, gave birth at the Southern Hospital. Of these mothers, almost 60 percent were of working class background, while 36 percent were from the upper and upper-middle classes.

> The **General Maternity Hospital** was located in Lill-Jansskogen, where it had been since 1913. "Immediately following their delivery, the infants are bathed, but not again. The infants are weighed every day. Their temperature is also taken every day. Every meal is weighed and registered. Several practical details concerning child care were noted, among others that there are heating lamps placed above every nursing station. The equipment includes hand disinfectant for both staff and mothers." As many as 62 percent of the mothers from the southern municipalities, and just over half of the mothers from the nearby Östermalm district gave birth at the General Maternity Hospital. Almost half of the mothers who gave birth at the General Maternity Hospital were from the upper and upper-middle classes, while 44 percent were of working class background.

> The maternity unit at **Sabbatsberg Hospital** was only four years old. Paediatricians visited the unit every day, but at night there was only a single assistant on duty. Almost three of every four children from the

Vasastaden district, and 68 percent of the children from the Norrmalm district were born here. Of the mothers from the western suburbs, 44 percent gave birth at the Sabbatsberg maternity unit. Of those who gave birth at Sabbatsberg, approximately 60 percent were from the upper classes and around one-third had a working class background.

The **Southern Maternity Hospital** had been located on Wollmar Yxkullsgatan since its opening in 1864. The care provided at the unit focused particularly on ensuring that "the children should as far as possible be exclusively breastfed, and the use of breast pumps had been introduced for all first-time mothers and for others with a prior experience of hypogalactia."[130] Just over one-third of the children from the southern suburbs were born at the Southern Maternity Hospital, but only twelve percent of the children from the Södermalm district. The class distribution among those giving birth at the Southern Maternity Hospital was relatively even, with the upper classes accounting for 45 percent, and the working class for 49 percent. When the unit was closed in 1968, the Maria Clinics took over the buildings, and some of the children who were born there in 1953 would subsequently return to the same premises to receive help for substance abuse problems.

At **Karolinska Hospital**, the rooms were "arranged impractically, producing problems for the rational fulfilment of infant care as a consequence". More important, however, was that "the care and monitoring of the children was of a high standard. The paediatrician made a daily round of the wards, examined every newborn infant at least once, and spoke to every mother about child care prior to their leaving the hospital. The infants' food intake, weight and temperature were registered every day." Since Karolinska Hospital was state run, it had no special catchment area, and the mothers who gave birth there came from the whole of the Greater Stockholm area. The largest number came from the northern municipalities, with 29 percent of the Metropolitan children being born at Karolinska. The highest social classes dominated, accounting for 60 percent of the births, while the working class accounted for 34 percent.

Almost half of the children from the Kungsholmen and Gamla Stan districts were born at **St. Erik's Hospital**, and over half of these were from a working class background. A total of 645 children were born at Danderyd Hospital, which at the beginning of the 1950s was known as Mörby Hospital. All the mothers who gave birth here came from the northern and southern municipalities. 329 children were born at the Epidemiological Hospital, Löwenströmska Hospital and Södertälje Hospital, with the mothers here also coming from the municipalities located to the north and south of Stockholm. 72 percent of these came from the working class.

Time spent on the postnatal ward

At the beginning of the 1950s, the recommended period of hospitalisation in connection with a birth was ten days.[131] For the mothers of the children born in 1953, the mean period of postnatal hospital care was nine days. Views changed, however, and over the course of the 1950s, mothers came to be sent home from delivery wards increasingly quickly.

The 1956 *Stockholm Calendar* presents a description of the routines at the Sabbatsberg maternity unit.[132] The rooms were divided into general wards, and semi- and completely private rooms. On the general wards, visiting was allowed for an hour on Sundays at 2 pm, and between 6.30 and 7 pm every day, but only for husbands. In the semi- and completely private rooms, visiting was allowed for one hour on Tuesdays, Thursdays, Saturdays and Sundays at 12 noon. Intimate contact with the newborn infants was not possible, since with the exception of feeding times they were usually placed behind a glass screen in a collective nursery room.[133] Nursery rooms of this kind had been introduced both to reduce the risk of infection and because it was felt that the mothers needed to rest.

At the beginning of the 1950s, there were however some who felt that infants should be with their mothers throughout their time on the maternity ward. This "rooming-in system" had begun in England and the USA, and according to its advocates would do away with the need to maintain such a strict breastfeeding schedule.[134] The idea of doing away with the nursery rooms was linked to new observations in the field of psychology. In 1955, Margareta Embring wrote that it was important to learn to listen to the child in order to understand different types of cries: "hunger cry, sleepy cry, tummy ache cry, companionship cry, etc." This was easiest if the mother was able to have the child next to her from the moment of birth. Embring argued that mothers who gave birth at home were at an advantage over those whose children were delivered on maternity wards, "who virtually

Routines at Southern Hospital maternity unit in the 1950s:

05.15: Wake-up, dressing, breastfeeding, milk collection, temperature taking, nursing and bed making.
8.30: Breakfast, breastfeeding and milk collection, followed possibly by gymnastics.
11–12: Compulsory rest.
12.30: Lunch.
13.00: Breastfeeding, milk collection.
14.00: Temperature taking, afternoon coffee, nursing, bed making and washing.
17.00: Breastfeeding and evening meal.
18.30–19.00: Visiting time.
20.00: Supper.
21.00: Infants put to bed, milk collection.
22:00 Bedtime.

Elisabet Rydh, Stockholm Association of Midwives, *Jordemodern* (Journal of the Swedish Association of Midwives), June 1953

"My mother has saved the journals from my birth. I was born in the afternoon of May 6 at Sabbatsberg Hospital. first days of my life were documented in considerable detail. I was weighed five to six times each day, before and after breast-feeding (and I may also have been given a glucose solution, which they were relatively generous with at the time). During the twelve days I spent on the maternity ward, I was weighed more than 100 times between the hours of six in the morning and ten o'clock at night."
(Sten-Åke Stenberg)

everywhere are immediately parted from the infant, and then have only the regimented, brief feeding periods in which to develop a close relationship." She could see a gratifying change occurring, however. "The past ten years of continuous harping from the psychologists may nonetheless have had a certain effect on rigid hospital regulations. There are actually maternity wards where new mothers can keep their children with them and decide for themselves how regularly the infant should be fed." [135]

Following their time on the maternity ward, almost all the Metropolitan Project children went straight home. Of those who did not go home directly, just over 500 were moved to other hospital wards for continued care, 133 were placed together with their mothers in what were termed "mothers' homes", almost 100 were moved on their own to "infants' homes", and 43 children were adopted. In the vast majority of cases, adoptions were the result of social factors. It was first and foremost unmarried and relatively young mothers who gave up their children for adoption. Of the children born in 1953, just over nine percent were born out of wedlock. [136] Many of these mothers lived together with the baby's father, or were in a steady relationship, and married the father soon after the birth of the child, thereby making the child "legitimate". A great deal of shame could be associated with those mothers who were not able to make the father of their children known, thus causing worries that people would gossip about their "bastards". For many, the only alternative was to put the child up for adoption.

Since the 19th century, doctors had played a dominant role in giving advice and instruction on the care of infants. Following the Second World War, however, educationalists, child welfare staff and child care professionals began to question the authority of the doctors and to speak up and give advice themselves. The emergence of modern psychology during the 1930s and 1940s, together with advances in medicine, would come to have a major influence on Swedish child rearing practices. These changes occurred gradually, and at the beginning of the 1950s society stood on the brink of a period during which the advances made in the fields of psychology and medicine would come to have a decisive impact on children's development. One of the classic books on childrearing was Benjamin Spock's *The Common Sense Book of Baby and Child Care*, which was published in nine Swedish editions between 1950 and 1975.[137] This was incidentally the only book on child care that I know my own mother used. I do not know how much of it she read, but I do know that the leaves of the bound edition that we had at home were no longer uncut.

The foreword to the Swedish edition of Spock's book was written by the paediatrician and child psychiatrist Gunnar Klackenberg, who himself published a number of similar texts. He belonged to a modern generation of paediatricians and the contents of the foreword were in line with the latest advice: "Finally, I would like to earnestly entreat you not to worry or to think that you have made mistakes in the care of your child as a result of anything you may have read in this book (or anywhere else for that matter). Firstly, we do not yet have the answer to every question. Our ideas about how a child should be cared for have changed significantly in the past and will no doubt change in the future." In the beginning of the book, Spock himself writes: "Don't take too seriously all that the neighbours say. Don't be overawed by what the experts say. Don't be afraid to trust your own common sense. Bringing up your child won't be a complicated job if you take it easy, trust your own instincts, and follow the directions that your doctor gives you."[138] There was room for variation and common sense, and also a short recommendation, which might have led to considerable bewilderment if the new parents had taken it too seriously, namely that they should follow the directions of their doctor – at least if they tried to follow the advice of several of the doctors quoted in the fairly extensive child care literature of the time.

In 1956, the journalist and teacher Anna-Lisa Kälvesten wrote an article on *Infant Sociology* in the social democratic journal *Tiden*. During the 1960s and 1970s, Kälvesten would become very active in research that was focused on the Skå children's home.[139] In this article, she

"My mother never married, but instead raised me together with her sister. In order to keep up appearances, she called herself Mrs. Stenberg, and wore my grandmother's wedding ring. My aunt, however, was Miss Stenberg."

(Sten-Åke Stenberg)

primarily analysed publications and pamphlets commissioned by public sector authorities, "that had been disseminated in several hundred thousand copies". She wrote among other things about publications from the Medical Board, the Red Cross, the consumer information agency Active Housekeeping, and two officially recognised organisations: the Swedish Social Welfare Association and the Swedish Association for Mental Health. The publications included both small pamphlets and books published by "doctors and professors" and the "really monumental works on children; enormous, expensive and magnificent collections with the leading experts among their lists of authors".

In the mid-1940s, the "literary mothers" had begun to make their entrance in "newspaper columns, on the radio and in sporadic chapters in the finer handbooks [...] And then a storm started brewing around the clean and healthy little infant in the folkhem." In turn, these mothers drew on the expertise of the child psychologists whose inspiration, according to Kälvesten, came from the west, "primarily from America".

Regimentation, or security and naturalness

In the child care literature some information appeared repeatedly, while there were also frequent contradictions. On the one hand, the paediatricians were dominant, with advice that could be summarised as focusing on regularity, order and cleanliness, while on the other hand the representatives of modern psychology advocated flexibility, security and naturalness. Kälvesten believed that the origins of the regularity message were to be found in a German handbook on child rearing that had first been published in 1906.[140] This handbook recommended that the child should "be given food five times per day and at fixed times: at four-hourly intervals during the day, and with an eight-hour break at night."

She identified three motives underlying these regularity recommendations. The first was that the breastfeeding schedule gave mothers time to do other things, and thereby increased the mother's independence in relation to the infant. The energy gained in this way would enable the mother to function better with regard to breastfeeding. The second was a concern that the infant would be given too much food, and the third was that the child's stomach should be given time both to digest the food and to rest.

Kälvesten also wrote about the advice given by various authorities on subjects such as breastfeeding, thumb sucking and potty training, and about how the underlying motives had shifted from a "natural science hygienic" perspective to an "educational" view. She believed that from the 1920s to the 1940s, the "child professors" had wanted to prevent the "bad habit" of thumb sucking. The advice described would be viewed as little short of barbaric by today's standards. The child's arms were to be bound "so that while the child is able to gesticulate, it cannot raise its fingers to its mouth." Other options involved "putting gloves on the child's hands or smearing its fingertips with a bitter-tasting substance."

The advice on thumb sucking was based on a concern that it would lead to dental deformities. Even nowadays, many parents of young children feel the same concern, and a range of corrective measures are practised. However, if anyone were to follow the advice described by Kälvesten today, it might well lead to the intervention of the child welfare authorities. At the same time, other books contained more modern advice: "The most radical cure for thumb sucking is probably replacing the mother's breast with the mother's embrace, i.e. communicating love, the spiritual nourishment of the soul."[141]

At the end of the 1940s, the experts' advice on potty training was extremely varied, ranging from a very rigid approach: "If you are very careful to ensure that children are placed on the potty at fixed times, when they awake, after mealtimes, just before going to bed etc., the bowels and bladder will adapt themselves to these times, and continence will be learned much more quickly,"[142] to a more cautious view, in the same book: "Holding almost new-born children over the potty,

"At home there was a lot of emotion and love. Both a free rein and toughness. A lot of big arguments at the dinner table. But then I was a spoilt and favoured younger sister. There was a twelve-year gap between my oldest brother and me, and seven years between me and my other brother. The fact that my brothers were so much older also meant that I became like an only child very early.

I never felt any demands on me to keep on studying or to do anything other than dancing. I rarely felt I was forced to do anything at all by my parents during my childhood."

(Margareta Kempe Allansson)

as some more ambitious mothers do, is completely pointless. The child does not understand what is going on. When the child can sit by itself, you may perhaps start to put it on the potty for a moment, just to try it out."[143] The experts agreed, however, that there was no place for toys at potty time. Nor were toys to be allowed in bed.

A time of transition

Thus, according to Kälvesten, the prophets of regularity motivated their message as a means of providing the mother with some peace and quiet. Counter to this, she described the views of mothers of the time, who instead claimed that it was this harsh regimentation that lead to screaming infants and tired mothers. She also showed that attitudes had slowly but surely become more permissive at the end of the 1940s and the beginning of the 1950s. This was apparent not least in the leaflets that were distributed at children's clinics.

Kälvesten summarised the nature of this period of transition with the words: "We can therefore see that two contradictory approaches in the field of infant care both have their advocates, even at the highest level, as the saying goes, and that Swedish officialdom provides the opportunity for both to speak to the public through small, inexpensive pamphlets. By comparison with the uniformity of public guidance prior to 1945, this is probably to be regarded as progress. Now parents have an opportunity, at least in theory, to choose somewhat among the advisers."

Thus in 1953 there was no unequivocal advice regarding how parents should care for their children during the preschool years. These parents lived in a transition period between the old and the new, but it is difficult to judge to what extent they were aware of this, or whether they cared about it at all.

The imposing, illustrated handbooks were not directed towards the public at large. In one handbook, for example, one could read that: "Once the child has arrived, these times characterised by a lack of domestic help provide a thousand opportunities for an enterprising father to show his interest in and love for the child."[144] In another book the author provided advice on table manners, and voiced the thoughts of an imaginary mother: "He eats better in the company of the maid than he does with me."[145] These advisers had the enlightened middle class in view, and such formulations were used when they felt that fathers should assume a greater responsibility for the care and upbringing of young children. Middle class women could no longer count on working class daughters to clean their homes and take care of their children. The post-war labour market provided opportunities for other ways to earn a living.

Half a century later, one might wonder what these enlightened advisers were actually thinking. Didn't they understand that maids also could have children and a family? Were maids by definition uneducated? The families of the middle class could no longer perform their social functions, but what about working class families? They didn't seem to count. In today's society domestics are once again returning to the kitchens and nurseries of the upper classes. This change has been nourished by the high levels of unemployment among immigrants. Today, too, change is inspired by women's liberation and sometimes by economic theories on the rational division of labour. In these contexts, very little is heard of men's work in the home. How much progress has actually been made with regard to gender equality?

Views on child rearing

Although the parents of the children born in 1953 had access to an extensive literature on how to care for and raise their children, there is no doubt that tradition, common sense and the opinions of other parents were at least as important. In the 1968 Family Survey, just over 4,000 mothers were interviewed, among other things about their views on child rearing. The table below presents all the questions, together with the proportions who gave the most positive response alternative. While some of the questions may sound somewhat old

"The deep-rooted prejudices about 'women's work' are now beginning to decline among the well-educated, where one quite often finds a pronounced camaraderie between husband and wife, and parents and children, within the home. However, these prejudices need to be completely destroyed. There will probably come a time very soon when maids become a rarity. The family will then not be able to perform its most essential social functions unless a very cooperative and proficient working relationship is developed within its confines. Our young mothers and fathers must educate themselves so that the work of the home does not become an unbearable burden for the one or the other. They must teach their children at an early age to help in the home and to view this help as a privilege and a joy."

Elofsson, Åke (1945) *On Heredity and the Home Environment* (Om arv och hemmiljö), in Siwe Sture and Folke Borg (eds.) *All about children* (Allt om barn), p. 38.

Table

Questions to the mothers in the Family Survey. Percentage who answered "absolutely right".	Absolutely right (%)
Children should be taught the difference between right and wrong.	94
You have to keep your word.	93
What's most important is that the parents like the child.	91
You have to give yourself time with the child.	85
Children should learn to think before they act.	77
The primary goal of child rearing is to develop the child's personality.	70
You have to be consistent in child rearing.	70
Children have to have firm rules.	67
When children don't understand what's best for them, you have to compel them.	67
Children should learn to be obedient.	61
The main thing is that the child is happy and content.	51
The child should be taught to look after itself.	50
Parents must not quarrel when the children are listening.	47
Parents must ensure that the child likes them.	38
Children should respect their parents.	35
It is not good for the child to be given too much freedom.	33
Children should be taught to control themselves.	29
As long as the child feels loved, nothing else matters.	26
Excitement and variety are more important for children than security.	7
Children should get what they want.	5

fashioned, the majority could still be posed to today's parents. The harmful effects of smoking were not as self-evident at that time. Thus one in three of the mothers answered in 1968 that their fifteen-year-old children were allowed to smoke at home. (I have memories of my own that confirm the irresponsible approach to smoking that was prevalent at the time. When I was involved in orienteering and cross-country skiing at the Hellas athletics club during the 1960s, the coaches encouraged us not to smoke too close to races, because it had a negative effect on our fitness! Nobody mentioned lung cancer.) The table below should be placed on the page near this text.

One of the first reports from Project Metropolitan contained a statistical analysis of the questions in the Family Survey. The objective was to summarise them in terms of more general child rearing patterns.[146] Five different patterns emerged: parent-centred, norm-centred (credibility), child-centred, instrumental (future planning) and authoritarian (rigid).

Parent-centred child rearing attached a great deal of importance to the child learning to obey and respect its parents, and to not being given too much freedom. The norm-centred approach ascribed importance to keeping one's word and differentiating between right and wrong. Child-centred child rearing assigned substantial weight to the children feeling loved and being happy and contented. In the case of instrumental child rearing, the mothers ascribed major importance to what was good for the child's future, which among other things involved the child learning to look after itself and developing its personality. A mother who manifested the authoritarian child rearing pattern declared that firm rules were important and that too much freedom was not good for the child.

Social class and family

The same researchers who identified the different child rearing patterns also attempted to identify explanations for them, and for other attitudes and views held by the mothers. What, for example, could explain the mothers' assessments of the relationships within their own families and their opinions concerning school?[147]

Finding powerful explanatory factors proved difficult. There were some differences, however. The mothers from higher social classes had greater educational ambitions for their children, a more permissive attitude towards their children's alcohol consumption, and a less authoritarian approach to child rearing. Mothers from the higher social classes also described somewhat more often than others that their family life was unusually good, and that their marriages were happy. The small differences in the mothers' responses did not necessarily reflect the actual family conditions. They could also be a result of the mothers from higher social classes having stronger social expectations, for example about having a harmonious family life.

At this time, many more mothers were housewives, and it was natural to attempt to examine the extent to which family relations were affected by whether or not the mother went out to work. The answer was that it did not. Nor did the age of the mother, or the size of the family, have any effect on the relationships within the family.

Adoptive Children and Foster Children

A large number of Swedish children were still being put up for adoption as recently as the 1960s. The most common reason was that the mother could not support herself and her child. Difficult living conditions were also the reason that many children were placed in foster homes or children's homes.

Adoption of Swedish children has now become uncommon,[148] but during the 1950s, between 2,000 and 2,500 children were adopted within the country each year.[149] Of the Metropolitan study children, 140 were adopted between 1953 and 1963. Adoption of children from other countries was very rare.

Difficult living conditions were the primary reason for adoptions. It was difficult for single mothers to support themselves, and the housing shortage in Stockholm also contributed to the difficulties of looking after children as a single parent. At the beginning of the 1950s, single mothers also had low social status. There were even cases where single mothers adopted their own children – so-called stepchild adoptions; 55 of the children in the Metropolitan Study were adopted in this way. This meant that the term "illegitimate" was removed from the national population register. Compared to modern views on single mothers, the difference is striking.

Although children could be adopted directly from the maternity ward, the authorities discouraged this. It was felt that the mother needed time to consider and the recommendations from the General Children's Home (Allmänna barnhuset) and the Medical Board were that adoption should not take place prior to the age of three months.

Image 15. A girl is getting dressed, children's home in Örby/Stockholm. Photographer: Unknown/Pressens bild/TT Nyhetsbyrån. Copyright: Pressens bild/TT Nyhetsbyrån, License: BY-NC-ND.

How to cite this book chapter:
Stenberg, Sten-Åke. 2018. Adoptive Children and Foster Children. In: Stenberg, Sten-Åke. *Born in 1953: The story about a post-war Swedish cohort, and a longitudinal research project.* Pp. 117–125. Stockholm: Stockholm University Press. DOI: https://doi.org/10.16993/bav.h. License: CC-BY

In the meantime, the child was usually placed in an "infants' home". Placements in temporary foster home were discouraged, since neither the adults nor the child would benefit from being moved about between different homes.

Anonymity as a matter of course

"A single woman with a child has a life that is strenuous and demanding in many ways. She does not find it easy to provide the good childhood conditions that she would like to give her child. The opportunities for employment, where she could keep the child with her at work, are entirely restricted to domestic work or certain other forms of work at home. Not all women are in any way suited to, and able to enjoy, work of this kind. As regards employment in domestic service in particular, in practice it is unfortunately the case that those people who say that they are willing to employ a maid with a child often do so with the objective of getting very cheap help, which in practice means that the women will be very greatly exploited on both an economic and a personal level, and will rarely be given the opportunity to spend time outside the walls that constitute their home and their workplace."

Board of Directors, General Children's Home (Direktionen över Allmänna barnhuset), 1955, pp. 13–15

Most adoptions were anonymous. The birth mother was given no information about the adoptive parents and vice versa. Viewed from today's perspective, this may appear strange, and this approach also began to change during the 1950s. Recommendations published by the General Children's Home and the Medical Board in 1955 made a point of stating that adoptive parents should explain to their children that they had been adopted and not allow them to "remain in ignorance of their true origins." The recommendations also noted that the certificate of transfer stated that the child had been adopted and that it would not be possible to keep this a secret indefinitely. It was nonetheless not until the end of the 1960s that people started to be given access to information on adoptions.[150]

The anonymity between the child's biological and adoptive parents was a more complicated issue. The most common scenario was that that they were not given any information about one another. The General Children's Home and the Medical Board noted in their recommendations, however, that this anonymity was illusory: "As a rule, the court's adoption ruling includes the consent of the parents, and thus their names, and often also their address, are given to the adopting parents. The names of the adopting parents are always recorded in the population register, and it is thus a relatively simple matter for parents who wish to find out where their children have ended up to obtain the desired information from the population registry."

Today it is easy to believe that the General Children's Home would have been positive towards the availability of this information. In reality, however, the reverse was true: "It may appear to be a fundamental right for parents to be given this information, but experience has shown that it may often lead to complications and difficulties not only for the adopting parents but also for the child."[151] The General Children's Home set great hopes on a new proposal in the 1954 Inheritance Code that provided greater security with regard to anonymity: "Thus the adoption will as a rule involve the complete severance of the child's biological ties, and its complete incorporation in a new family community".[152]

The idea that the child would be "completely incorporated" in the new family also meant that the parents and the child should not differ too much in their appearance. "If the biological parents are robust individuals with a powerful physique, fair hair and blue eyes, the placement of their child with short, lean individuals, perhaps of southern appearance, should be avoided, and vice versa."[153] This formulation manifests a racial biology perspective, and when abortions and improved social conditions led to Swedish parents instead adopting children from continents other than Europe, these recommendations naturally became impossible to follow.

Most people wonder about their origins at some point in their lives. This is of course particularly true of those who have been adopted or who do not know their parentage for some other reason. The General Children's Home and the Medical Board were aware of this: "There usually comes a period in the adopted child's life, around puberty, when it starts to ask about its birth parents. In the context of an ideal and trusting adoptive relationship, this problem may have been dealt with at an early stage, and the child then has no need for further information or for other parental contacts."[154] The desire to know about one's parentage was viewed as being "natural and completely legitimate", but as a rule it was "more beneficial if the child were to wait with this until it had obtained a certain level of maturity and discretion."[155]

The path to adoption often went via an institution such as the infants' homes that were mentioned earlier. According to the legislation that was in force between 1945 and 1981, the county councils were responsible for ensuring that there were sufficient children's homes and mothers' homes. The latter were primarily intended for unmarried mothers who for financial, "moral" or other reasons had to stay in these institutions prior to and after giving birth, often while they waited until the child was adopted. In 1950, there were approximately 900 places in institutions of this kind. Over time, however, with improved birth control techniques, the expansion of the right to abortion and a shift in the moral climate, the need for such places declined, and in 1980 only thirteen remained. The Social Services Act contains no equivalent regulations. In those cases where the need for such places may exist today, most commonly for mothers with substance abuse problems or other social problems, it is met by using certain residential care homes for children, or via the family welfare system.

Foster children

Between four and five percent of the Swedish population have been in foster care at some point during their childhood, and this was the case for nine percent of the children born in 1953. At the end of 1950, 28,000 children, or one 1.4 percent of all the children in Sweden, were placed either in private foster homes or in residential care. By 1970, this proportion had declined to 0.8 percent.[156] When placement decisions were made for the children born in 1953, there were a large number of children's homes in the city of Stockholm.

In recent years, foster care has been the subject of serious criticism. Research findings suggest that foster care has had negative effects, and has among other things resulted in increased involvement in crime.[157] The 2010 Governmental Neglect and Abuse Inquiry heard testimony from over 400 individuals detailing the neglect and abuse they had been subjected to in foster care. In 2011, the Redress Inquiry proposed that those who had been subject to abuse between 1920 and

1980 should each be awarded 250,000 SEK in compensation.[158] As a result of the strict requirements for compensation awards, however, over half of the applications were rejected, which in turn gave rise to a great deal of criticism.[159]

The Project Metropolitan data provide unique opportunities to study the effects of foster care. As of this writing, there is no other data set that provides an opportunity to follow the lives of foster children for such a long period. To date, the data have been used in four studies focused on how foster care placements affected the children's situation as adults.

Decisions by the social services to place children in foster care were based on either the parents' or the child's behaviour. For young children, parental behaviour was the most common reason for such placements, while for teenagers it was the child's own behaviour. Of the just over 15,000 children born in 1953, 1,166 had been placed in a foster care at some point during the period between their birth and 1972. Of these, 174 had been placed both in foster homes and in residential care, 573 had only been placed in foster homes, and 767 only in residential care. On average, these children had spent 21 months in foster homes and ten months in residential care.

Image 16. A girl draws a picture of her mother, children's home in Örby/Stockholm. Photographer: Unknown/Pressens bild/TT Nyhetsbyrån. Copyright: Pressens bild/TT Nyhetsbyrån, License: BY-NC-ND.

The first of these studies examined the question of whether foster care placements affected the children's risk of becoming involved in crime as adults.[160] In order to assess the effect of foster care placements, the situation of children placed in foster care must be compared with a group of children who had experienced social problems but who had not been placed in care. The researchers therefore selected 2,124 children who had been the subject of social services investigations but who had not been placed in care. Although these children were similar to those who had been placed in foster care, they did not constitute a perfect comparison group. Nonetheless, the comparison was good enough. The assessments of the social services authorities had been correct in the sense that the situation among the comparison group with regard to e.g. financial problems and parental substance abuse was not as bad as it was among those who had been placed in care. The analyses compensated for these differences by using statistical methods to take account of important background factors and by conducting tests to examine how sensitive the analyses were to changes in various conditions.

Among the boys who had been placed with foster families, the risk of conviction as adults was 23 percent greater than for the comparison group.[161] Among the girls, there was no difference between the two groups. More detailed analyses showed that the effect was unevenly distributed: the excess risk found among the boys placed in foster care was exclusively due to the fact that the risk for crime was 58 percent higher among those who were placed as teenagers, between the ages of thirteen and eighteen. Among the younger boys, there was no difference. The results were worse for those children who had been placed in residential care. For boys who had been subject to residential care, the level of excess risk was 67 percent, and for girls 71 percent. Here too, however, the differences in relation to the comparison group disappeared among those children who were under thirteen years of age at the time of their placements. Since the decisions on foster care could be due to either neglect on the part of the parents or the children's own behaviour, it was also possible to examine the effects of foster care placements on the basis of this difference. Here the results showed that boys who were placed as teenagers as a result of their own behaviour were at 25 percent higher risk of committing offences as adults than the comparison group. If they had been placed as a result of parental neglect, the level of risk was 18 percent lower than that found in the comparison group.

The results of the study showed that it was not possible to assess the effects of foster care without taking into consideration who the children were, why they had been placed in care, and the type of care placement they had experienced. Younger children and girls coped better. The worst outcomes were noted for teenage boys, particularly if they had been placed in residential care. The reasons for which the children had been placed were also found to have an important effect on the subsequent outcome. Those who had been placed in order to protect them from parental neglect had better outcomes than the comparison group.

Two other studies have expanded on these results and examined the question of the extent to which children with experience of care placements came to experience lasting marginalisation between the ages of 39 and 55. In one of these studies, marginalisation was defined as social welfare recipiency, unemployment and mental illness,[162] while the other also included the level of education achieved in 2008.[163] The researchers responsible for the first study took the following into account: the biological parents' social class in 1953; the number of years during which the birth family received social welfare payments between 1953 and 1959; and whether the biological parents were married, unmarried or whether the mother had been a single parent at the time of the child's birth in 1953. The second study only included controls for the parents' social class, the child's sex and social welfare recipiency during childhood. The 234 children who had been placed exclusively as a result of their own behaviour were excluded from the analyses.

As expected, the children who had been placed in care came primarily from the lower social classes; their biological families had experienced more years of social welfare recipiency, and approximately three times as many of them had single parents. The results then showed that approximately half the children who had been placed in care had no subsequent problems in their later adult years. However, the group as a whole was nonetheless at approximately twice as great a risk for persistent social marginalisation once the control variables had been taken into account.

The third study focused on mortality rates among the children placed in foster care.[164] The study had three objectives. The first was to examine whether being placed in care between birth and the age of 19 was linked to a greater risk of dying between the ages of 20 and 56. The second was to examine whether the mortality risk varied depending on the child's age at the first placement, the reason for the placement and on whether the child had been placed with a family or in residential care. The third objective was to attempt to improve the opportunities for drawing conclusions about causality. This was done by taking into account various factors in the birth family (social class and the mother's age and marital status) and by using two comparison groups comprised of: 1) children from families who had received social welfare payments but who had not been investigated for placement by the social services, and 2) children who had been the subject of investigations but had not been placed in care. Of the children born in 1953, 789 (just over 5 percent) had died during the years 1973–2009. Just under one-quarter of those who had died had been placed in care during childhood. Even when the researchers controlled for background factors such as social class and the mother's age when the child was born, the children who had been placed in care had a mortality risk that was almost three times as great as that of children who had not been placed in care. If the children had been placed in care during puberty, the risk was just over five times as great. If the placement had been due to neglect in the family of origin, the risk was one and a half times as great, but if the placement had been due to the child's own behaviour, the risk was almost six times as great.

"Our parents gave us a really secure childhood. They were the best parents you could imagine. They were always there, and it feels like they are still with me. I am so glad that it was them we ended up with."

(Gerd Svensson, adoptive child)

The children had variously been placed with a family, in residential care, or had been moved between different placements both in family homes and institutions. It might be natural to think that family placements were preferable to residential care. The study found that the opposite was the case, however, and that children who had been placed in institutions had a mortality risk that was twice as high, while children placed with families had a mortality risk that was three times as high. Those children who had been moved around between different placement forms had a mortality risk that was four times as high.

Finally, the comparison with children who had grown up in families that had received social welfare payments, but who had not been placed in care, and with children who had been the subject of social services investigations but who had instead received other measures, showed that for children who had been placed in care, the mortality risk was between one and a half times and twice as high as it was for these comparison groups.

It is of course difficult to determine which aspects of care placements may have been of significance for the increased mortality risk, or whether there were other factors that both resulted in care placements and in an increased risk of death. Irrespective of these uncertainties, however, it is reasonable to conclude, in line with the researchers who conducted the study, that preventive health care measures and education are particularly important for these children.

An additional study addressed whether this mortality gap may be mitigated by educational success using a time-based risk measure that allows for direct interpretation of the hypothesized associations in terms of years gained or lost. The study showed that children with experience of foster care or residential care died, based on a median survival time, more than a decade before their majority population peers. However, this gap was almost closed among those who performed above average at school, highlighting the important role of educational success in this association.

Housing, Moving and Social Class

In the 1950s and 1960s there was a stream of migration from the outdated apartments of the central city districts to the newly built suburbs, with bathrooms, balconies and plenty of sunlight. It was the beginning of a transformation of the city centre from poor neighbourhoods into a haven for the affluent.

If you could return to the Stockholm of 1953, then besides landmarks such as City Hall, the Royal Palace, church steeples and the Katarina Elevator, you would not recognise much of the city as it is today. While the major transformation of the Klara area and the rest of the city centre had begun with the building of the metro system, most of the old neighbourhoods were still intact at the beginning of the 1950s. There were large numbers of apartments in these neighbourhoods, which have subsequently disappeared to provide space for office buildings, business complexes and multi-storey car parks built in glass and concrete. The inner city was much more densely populated than it is today. Those who lived there and in other neighbourhoods in the city were often housed in crowded and outdated homes, with no hot water or central heating. Many shared a toilet with others on the same stairwell, or used the same outdoor privy as their neighbours.

Another difference was that at that time there were still a large number of factories and workshops in what is now a city almost completely bereft of industry. Outside the city, the expansion of new residential areas that had started during the 1940s continued. To the south and south west, suburbs such as Björkhagen, Kärrtorp, Bagarmossen,

Image 17. Subway station. Photographer: Sten-Åke Stenberg. Copyright: Sten-Åke Stenberg, License: BY-NC-ND.

How to cite this book chapter:
Stenberg, Sten-Åke. 2018. Housing, Moving and Social Class. In: Stenberg, Sten-Åke. *Born in 1953: The story about a post-war Swedish cohort, and a longitudinal research project.* Pp. 127–133. Stockholm: Stockholm University Press. DOI: https://doi.org/10.16993/bav.i. License: CC-BY

In 1953, just over one-fifth of the Project Metropolitan children lived in Stockholm's inner city areas. Almost one-third lived in the southern suburbs, and one in ten in the western suburbs. Almost one-tenth of the children also lived in the southern and eastern suburban municipalities, while a slightly larger proportion lived in Stockholm's northern municipalities. One in ten lived elsewhere in Sweden, and almost three percent lived abroad, the majority in one of the neighbouring Scandinavian countries.

Högdalen, Hagsätra, Västberga, Västertorp and Fruängen were being built.[165] New homes were also being constructed to the west, and in 1954 the Vällingby shopping centre was opened with considerable fanfare. Vällingby symbolised something quite revolutionary – a new type of neighbourhood that combined opportunities for work, housing, shopping and entertainment.

The migration to the suburbs gave families that had been used to poor housing spacious apartments with bathrooms and balconies, and as the depopulation of the inner city continued, the suburban population grew. In 1953, 245,000 people lived in the southern suburbs, a number that had grown to 288,000 in 2006. The corresponding figures for the western suburbs were 104,000 and 203,000 respectively. Over the course of this period, the total population of Stockholm grew by only 10,000, to a total of 783,000.

Migration to the suburbs

The Project Metropolitan families, like many others, followed the stream of migration from the inner city areas out to the suburbs. When the children were born, 3,440 of them were registered as living in the central city districts, the majority in the Södermalm area. Ten years later, half of them had moved. Of the families that left the city, just over half lived to the south of Stockholm in 1963. Almost all of them had moved to the immediate suburbs, and only six percent had moved to the neighbouring municipalities to the south, such as Huddinge and Tyresö. The so-called Million Program,[166] which would lead many to move to the more distant suburbs, was at this time still a few years in the future, and the families that moved to these municipalities at the beginning of the 1960s for the most part moved from apartments to live in houses. The suburbs to the west of Stockholm were often older, and did not expand to the same extent as those to the south of the city, but fifteen percent of those who left the inner city areas moved to the western suburbs of Hässelby and

Vällingby. Six percent moved to the northern suburbs of Danderyd and Täby, and four percent to Lidingö and Solna, which lie to the west of Stockholm.

I am myself a typical example of a move to the suburbs of this kind. During the first six years of my life, my mother and I lived in a two-room apartment with no bath or shower in the Birkastan area of the city. Just prior to starting my first year in school, we moved to a three-room apartment with a bathroom and balcony in the suburb of Björkhagen. This was a big improvement.

During the 1960s, the numbers living in the inner city areas declined a little, but nowhere near as much as they had during the 1950s. The Project Metropolitan children started school in 1960, and as might be expected, many of their families had stayed in the areas where the children had been born a few years earlier.

In the 1970s, the time came for many of the children born in 1953 to leave home. Many moved around for a few years between different forms of accommodation. But by 1981, a large proportion had become established and started families of their own. A large number of them were now once again living in the central city districts, almost 1,000 more than had lived there in 1971.

Social stratification

The update of the Metropolitan data has made it possible not only to study the movement patterns of the Metropolitan families, but also those of the children themselves as adults, until 2009. Almost 60 percent of the children who were born in the Södermalm area were from working class families. In the Östermalm area, the proportions were reversed, and the parents of almost 70 percent of the children were from the two highest social classes. In other areas of the city the class distribution was more uniform. In the city centre, which at the time was largely comprised of the Klara neighbourhood, half of the children were from working class families. Almost half of the children

When the children born in 1953 started their first year at school in 1960, seven of ten lived in rental apartments, and almost five percent shared a toilet with other families, or had an outdoor privy. Almost ten percent had no bathroom or shower room. The same proportion had no refrigerator, and just over seven percent had no hot water. Almost 20 percent lived in crowded conditions.

"I'm a child of the suburbs. My world consisted of Gubbängen and the southern suburbs. There's something interesting in this whole roots business. When my wife and I were looking at houses, we only looked in the area to the south of Stockholm, and we ended up in Örby. The idea of moving to Bromma [to the northwest of Stockholm], where a lot of media people like us live, never crossed our minds."

(Weje Sandén)

"I was born in Solna, outside Stockholm, and moved to Östermalm in the city later on. My family had a good life with travels, dinners, and a summer house in the archipelago. Dad was a charmer and a party-person. It felt as is we could afford to indulge a little although this perhaps wasn't the case. I think I regarded us as somewhat "posh". But it was really a world that was out of our league! I remember a stay at a mountain resort, when everyone changed for dinner. I was only eight years old and had to wear a suit and a bow tie, and I thought I looked really handsome. These were different times. I would never expose my own children to anything like that!"

(Manni Thofte)

from the northern, and one-third of those from the southern, municipalities were born to upper or upper-middle class families.

Did the exodus to the suburbs produce a change in the class composition of the inner city areas? In the Södermalm area, the proportions born in the different social classes were the same in 1953 and 1963. In the Östermalm district there was a small shift, with the proportion of children born to the highest social class increasing, while the proportion of working class children declined from one quarter to just under one fifth. There was a similar trend in the other areas of the city. Of those born in 1953 who lived in the Södermalm area in 2009, almost half had been born into working class families, while the proportion of those born into families from the higher social classes had increased from 40 to almost 50 percent. In the Östermalm area, the concentration of children born into the upper classes had increased a little more, to just over three quarters. In Kungsholmen, the proportion of children born in working class homes had increased from 45 to over 50 percent in 2009.

Substantial differences

The social class into which we are born plays a significant role in relation to where we will live as adults. At the same time, many change their social class affiliation as adults as a result of having climbed up the social ladder and improved their conditions. The differences in the social class composition of the Project Metropolitan children across different areas of Stockholm are substantial when one compares the situation in 1953 with that in 1990 and at the end of the 2000s. In 2009, there were few manual workers living in the central areas of Stockholm.

Approximately 80 percent of the Metropolitan children who were living in inner city areas in 2009 were members of the upper social classes, and in the Östermalm area this proportion was almost 90 percent. It would not be overly bold to say that the central areas of Stockholm have developed into a preserve for high income families over the past 60 years. The increase in the proportion of owner-occupied apartments also illustrates this trend. In 1960, seventeen percent of the homes in apartment blocks in the central areas of Stockholm were owner-occupied. By 2010, this proportion had increased to 64 percent. The majority of the new owner-occupied apartments had previously been rental apartments in the private rental sector. In 1960, private rental apartments comprised 81 percent of the housing stock in the central areas of the city, a proportion that had declined to 30 percent in 2010.

Housing, crime and mental health

Were the children's future prospects affected by where and how they grew up? Why do different neighbourhoods differ with regard to crime? Do housing type and neighbourhood of residence influence the risk of children becoming involved in crime? Is it housing type or neighbourhood that matters? These questions are easily posed, but difficult to answer.

In order to systematically examine the social effects of geographical areas, the researcher first has to decide how these areas should be defined. Administrative divisions, such as municipalities and parishes, do not always correspond with what we ourselves perceive as our neighbourhoods. Even though people live close to one another, their perceptions of the nature of their neighbourhood may vary. Which aspects of a residential neighbourhood affect people? Is it the height of the buildings, or the width of the streets? Is it the area's social composition?

One of the Project Metropolitan studies directed its focus on the significance of housing type for the risk of children committing criminal offences.[167] The housing data were drawn from the Population and Housing Census of 1960, and related to tenure and ownership status, and also to the standard of housing and overcrowding. To begin with,

"We were among the first to move to the [southern] suburb of Hagsätra. It was 1958 and we moved from Hökarängen [also to the south of Stockholm City], where we had lived in an outdated home, and came to a place with a bathroom and a balcony in Hagsätra. I remember that Mum was so happy that she cried. Before Hökarängen we had lived in an even more outdated apartment in Hagalund [to the west of the city] with no hot water and a toilet in the stairwell.

When we moved there, the centre of Hagsätra was still a building site and the metro system hadn't been extended that far. But they finished building the centre quite soon after, and then came the metro. The centre was a lively place, with banks, a library, post office and loads of shops."

(Jan Andersson)

"We moved from the [central] Östermalm district, to Vällingby [to the northwest of Stockholm] when my twin sister and I were aged about ten. I have subsequently come to understand that moving to such a modern home was a big thing for my mum and dad. In Östermalm we had lived in an old building with a gas cooker, a marble sink with a draining board and no bathroom. Mum was afraid of the gas, so Dad always got up early to give the kitchen an airing. She no longer had to be afraid of this in Vällingby.

But when my sister and I had first heard about Vällingby we were very sceptical. This was a few years earlier. Mum and Dad had probably been interested in moving there quite early. The family visited Vällingby in a borrowed car. My sister Åsa and I sat in the back seat and screamed that we hated Vällingby."

(Ulla Abelin)

the study noted that those who lived in public sector rental accommodation engaged in crime to a greater extent than those who lived in other types of housing. Since public sector landlords did not filter out potential tenants in the same way as other landlords, and accepted families with social problems, this finding was not unexpected. The question at issue must instead be examined by weighing together the different factors in an explanatory model that makes it possible to isolate the effect of housing type from the effects of other factors. When the analysis included controls for social class and social welfare recipiency in the family of origin, an unexplained effect associated with housing type still remained. Both the standard of housing and overcrowding were also correlated with the children's involvement in crime. In this respect, housing type was found to be most significant for the lower social classes. However, for families from the upper social classes, it made little difference whether or not they lived in rental accommodation.

Another study analysed the significance of housing type for the risk of experiencing mental illness.[168] The study found that boys who had lived in overcrowded conditions at the age of seven had a 50 percent higher risk of being diagnosed with a mental illness at the time of enlistment for national service than boys who had not lived in overcrowded conditions. The elevated risk for diagnosed mental illness was even higher among boys who had lived in overcrowded conditions both in 1960 and in 1970; here the risk was 1.65 times as high as among boys who had not lived in overcrowded conditions. Since living in overcrowded conditions is correlated with social class, and since social class also affects the risk for experiencing mental illness, the researcher responsible for the study also conducted analyses that eliminated the effects of social class, family income and household size. Despite controlling for the effects of these factors, having lived in overcrowded conditions continued to show an effect, particularly in relation to drug- and alcohol-related diagnoses.

What role, then, did the neighbourhood play in how the children's lives turned out as adults? Certain types of apartments are often concentrated to certain residential areas. Two more recent studies have examined neighbourhood effects. Due to the availability of more advanced statistical tools, possible effects could now be studied more systematically. The results showed that the neighbourhood of residence had virtually no effect on the risk for involvement in crime.[169] Thus during the 1950s and 1960s, the neighbourhood in which children grew up appears not to have had any major effect on their future prospects. What mattered was instead the family's social situation, which has also been noted in other research studies.

The results from earlier and more recent studies point in different directions, which is not uncommon in the social sciences. I will not make any definitive judgement here about these differences, but my own inclination is towards the more recent findings, which suggest that the neighbourhood itself did not play any major role, but that the effects that were observed are primarily due to conditions in the children's families.

Preschool and School Years

Ambitious and engaged parents had a positive effect on the school results of the Project Metropolitan children, and consequently also on how they fared later on in life. Other significant factors included whether they were an only child, their position among their siblings and their level of popularity among their peers.

Most of the Project Metropolitan children grew up with mothers who were housewives and spent their days in the home. Public sector childcare was still rare. In the 1950s, it was therefore primarily single working mothers whose children were given preschool places. There were married women who went out to work, but this was not something that was taken for granted. Instead it was a subject for debate in both the press and on the radio, where headlines included "We want to go out to work too!" It was therefore not strange that only one in ten of the children born in 1953 had full-time preschool places. Demands for "Preschool for all" would not be heard until the early1960s, and it would be a further decade before there was any major expansion in nursery care provision.

Since this time, attitudes towards working women and public sector childcare provision have changed dramatically. In the 1968 Family Survey, the mothers were asked whether they thought that a married woman with children under the age of seven should have a full-time job outside the home. Almost four of ten responded with an unconditional "no" and the same proportion stated that this was acceptable if the mother had to do so for financial reasons. Only half of one percent answered with a firm "yes". At the time of the survey, when the children were aged fifteen, fewer than one-third of the mothers were

"It felt so good to have Mum at home with us, so I also wanted to be at home with my children. It was possible with all four, because I worked nights."
(Gerd Svensson)

How to cite this book chapter:
Stenberg, Sten-Åke. 2018. Preschool and School Years. In: Stenberg, Sten-Åke. *Born in 1953: The story about a post-war Swedish cohort, and a longitudinal research project.* Pp. 135–150. Stockholm: Stockholm University Press. DOI: https://doi.org/10.16993/bav.j. License: CC-BY

Image 18. Child in Stockholm 1954. Photographer: Alma Stenberg. Copyright: Sten-Åke Stenberg, License: BY-NC-ND.

"Mum worked a bit when we were growing up, but never in the summer. She had time off then, and we spent time in the country. She was a dental nurse to begin with, but then she worked in the office at the same place as Dad, Pripps."
(Agneta Wolffelt)

in full-time employment. It would not be presumptuous to guess that the daughters of these mothers would have answered very differently if the same question had been posed to them when their own children had reached fifteen years of age.

Sweden began to introduce the unitary "grundskolan" education system in the same year that the children started in third grade. In this new system, everyone studied the same courses in primary and middle school, while at secondary school, the children were divided into different study programs that had a theoretical or a more practical focus.[170] It took several years to complete the introduction of the school reform throughout the country, and in the Stockholm area the introduction of the new system was not completed until four years later. When the School Survey was conducted, almost all the children who participated were in the sixth grade, just over seven percent had been required to repeat a grade and were thus still in grade four or five, while two percent had started school early and were in grade seven. In the mid-1960s, there were also special teaching forms, which took the form of reading clinics, observation classes, assistance classes and special classes for children with visual or audial impairments. Approximately five percent of the students were in classes of this kind in 1966.

Choice of program and upper-secondary studies

In the same year that the School Survey was conducted, it was time for the majority of the children to choose their study program for the final three years of compulsory education. This also meant that they had to decide whether they wished to continue into upper-secondary education once their nine years of compulsory schooling were completed. In 1966, almost half of the children answered that they intended to continue into upper-secondary education, while four of ten did not know whether they would do so. A methodological study of the Metropolitan data noted that children from the lower social classes were influenced by the social composition of their school class, such that their ambitions to continue on to upper-secondary school increased in line with the proportion of their classmates who came from higher social classes. The level of ambition among children from the upper social classes was not, however, affected in the opposite direction if their classmates included a preponderance of children from lower social classes. This analysis was not actually the central objective of the study, but with this reservation, and the fact that the study had been conducted a quarter of a century earlier, and also that the analysis could have been expanded to include a larger number of explanatory factors, the findings suggest that socially heterogeneous school classes would be the best way of avoiding skewed social selection into further and higher education.[171]

In seventh grade, the students could choose a second foreign language, usually French or German, which was required in order to apply for enrolment in upper-secondary school.[173] In the School Survey, eight out of ten of the students stated that they planned to choose to study a second language. Among the children from upper-middle class families, this proportion was just over 90 percent, while the corresponding proportion among the children from working class families was just over 70 percent. In the ninth grade, it would turn out that half of the total number of students had studied the upper-secondary preparatory program. However, of those who had said they planned to do so in the sixth grade, it was only just over 60 percent who had actually done so. Here too there were substantial social class differences. Of those who had planned to study the upper-secondary preparatory program in grade six, twice as many of the children from upper-middle class families realised this intention than was the case among working class children.

When the children born in 1953 graduated from ninth grade, the labour market for young people was much better than it is today. Four out of ten started work immediately after completing ninth grade, and the same proportion started three- or four-year upper-secondary

"Mum was an office worker and worked at MHF,[172] but she also had an extra job for a few years to make ends meet. At that time she got on a bus that drove round the southern suburbs around five in the morning, picking up women who would do the cleaning at Bromma Airport or somewhere. Then she went to her other job. She really worked a lot. I remember when my little sister started in first grade. On the first day of school, all the children were accompanied by their parents. But my little sister came with me. Mum was at work."

(Jan Andersson)

school programs.[174] Approximately 20 percent started two-year vocational college programs, which did not provide the qualifications required for subsequent university studies. The social class differences remained substantial, however. Among those who started upper-secondary school, seven of ten were upper-middle class children, whereas only one in five came from working class families.

Just over 80 percent of the children who started at upper-secondary school also completed their upper-secondary programs. This meant that of all the children born in 1953, one-third had an upper-secondary school certificate at the end of the 1970s. The corresponding proportion for their parents' generation had been just over ten percent.

Approximately 20 years later, many of these young people had continued their studies, and just under one in five had completed a two-year program of post-upper-secondary education. A similar proportion had completed a university education and the same proportion had not completed any form of post-compulsory-school education. Among the children from working class families, 27 percent had not completed any form of further or higher education, while the corresponding proportion among the two highest social classes was thirteen percent. The corresponding proportions for those who had completed a university education were eight percent for the working class children and 28 percent for the children from the two highest social classes. The children born in 1953 were a product of the class society, but compared to the young people of today, it was much easier for them to find work, despite having little education. In spite of this, poor school performance seemed to have an inpact on health status as children with low marks in the sixth grade shoed a greater risk of experiencing ill-health as adults.[175]

The significance of social capital

In one study based on the project data, the mothers' answers from the 1968 Family Survey were used to analyse the significance of the parents' level of education and the family's social capital for the children's level of success in school, as measured by their grade scores in year nine.[176] The definition of social capital employed in the study was that the parents had spoken with the children about their schoolwork, that they read the children's school books, and that they participated in parent-teacher meetings. The study also examined the significance of the parents' own educational background for their children's school results, and also the significance of a good relationship between parents and children.

The study showed that parental activity had a positive effect on the children's grades, irrespective of the type of activity involved. However, parental attendance at parent-teacher meetings only had a positive effect on the grades of children from families in which the parents had low levels of educational achievement, whereas the other forms of parental activity produced similar increases in the grade scores of all children. The study also found that parents with a high level of education were often more engaged in the various activities examined than parents with a lower level of education.[177] The differences were not substantial, but they were nonetheless clear. For example, just over half of the mothers in families with a high level of education stated that one of the parents read the children's school books, compared to just over 40 percent of the mothers in families with a lower level of education.

Although the parents' active participation had a positive effect on the children's grades, it was first and foremost the parents' level of education that made a fundamental difference. Children in families where the level of parental education was high had grade scores that were 0.3 grade-score units higher than children from families where the level of parental education was low.[178]

In the Family Survey, the mothers also answered questions about the quality of the relationship between parents and children. This same study found that children from families characterised by good parent-child relationships also had slightly better grades than children

"Mum had a business education and went back to work when my twin sister and I were fifteen and our little sister was nine. It was a big step for her, of course, but it wasn't as if we thought it was a good thing for Mum. The big difference was that it was no fun that there was nobody home when we came back from school. You'd come into the building, and smell baking, and you'd feel really happy, until you suddenly realised that it couldn't be coming from our place."
(Ulla Abelin)

from families where the parent-child relationship was not quite as good. Furthermore, a good parent-child relationship was found to reinforce the positive effect of social capital.

A later study produced similar results, but the observation period was extended to include the level of education achieved at a little over 50 years of age.[179] In addition, statistical methods were used to order the effects of different factors chronologically. In the same way as in the previous study, families with higher levels of resources were more engaged in their children's schooling, but the only factor that was directly related to the level of education achieved by middle age was the parents' aspirations. The other forms of family engagement only had an impact on the children's grades, which of course in turn affected the likelihood of continuing into further and higher education. Thus what was most important was that parents had a positive attitude towards school. Since it was more common for families characterised by a high level of education and a good social position to encourage their children's school work, the study's author concluded that what is most important today is to influence people's attitudes towards education.

Siblings and sibling position

We sometimes explain our successes and failures in adult life by reference to our position in the family in which we grew up – whether we were an only child or had siblings, and if so how many siblings we had, and our birth position among these siblings. But do children who grow up with several siblings do better or worse than children with fewer or no siblings? Does the child's position in the sibling group matter? Is the youngest child given more freedom during childhood? Are parents over-ambitious in relation to their first child? Does an only child become more self-centred and egotistical than a child with siblings because he or she receives all the parental attention, and does not have to compete for space with brothers and sisters? Are middle children more likely to feel squeezed by the interests of their siblings, and to be more willing to compromise?

The issue of siblings has been a focus for the research community for a long time now. Research has shown, for example, that of the 37 American presidents from George Washington to Gerald Ford, 20 were first-born sons.[180] As early as 1874, Francis Galton, one of the founders of modern statistics, noted that first-born children and only children were more likely to become prominent scientists.[181]

The greatest interest has been directed towards the number of children in the family, and their respective positions in the sibling group. There is now a great deal of research that has shown the existence of a relationship between family size and the intellectual development of children. The smaller the family, the greater the child's intellectual ability. Research focused on sibling position has also found that the intellectual ability of the first child is greater than that of younger siblings, although the results here are not as clear. There are several possible explanations for these correlations. In larger families, parents do not have as much time or economic resources per child as parents in smaller families. First-born children and only children are exposed to more adult communication, which improves their verbal abilities. Or is there perhaps something in the way siblings interact that benefits children in smaller families? There are of course many other factors that also make a difference. The age difference between siblings, as well as the children's gender and the family's social class should, for example, also be included in analyses.

A number of studies have been conducted in the Metropolitan project with a focus on siblings and the family.[182] Stated briefly, these studies show that older siblings and children with few siblings performed better in the verbal test in the School Survey, and that children with no siblings performed best of all. It was surprising to find that these results held, even though the researcher included controls for a wide range of factors, including the social position of the parents, which showed itself to be the most important variable. Since the children of

single mothers performed no worse than other children, the findings also contradicted theories that emphasised the importance of children having access to both their parents. It was also found that the children, and particularly the sons, of older mothers performed better on the tests included in the School Survey. This may have been due to the life experience of the older mothers making them less self-centred and more focused on the needs of their children.[183]

Finally one study directed its focus on educational achievement. This study found that sibling position and family size had an impact on both the grades and the level of education achieved by the children. Among only children and first-born children in small families, for example, 40 percent graduated from upper-secondary school. Among younger siblings in larger families, the corresponding proportion was only 20 percent. Thus being an only child or the first child in a small family was particularly advantageous.

The significance of childhood conditions for future prospects as adult

Similarities and differences in the conditions experienced by siblings during childhood, such as having grown up in the same family, and gone to the same school but in different classes, may be utilised to analyse the significance of childhood conditions for children's future economic prospects. Social mobility, both upward and downward, is about whether and to what extent the social position of parents affects that of their children. It is often studied with the help of data on the incomes, education and social class of parents and their children, but it can also be examined in other ways. Economists, for example, have

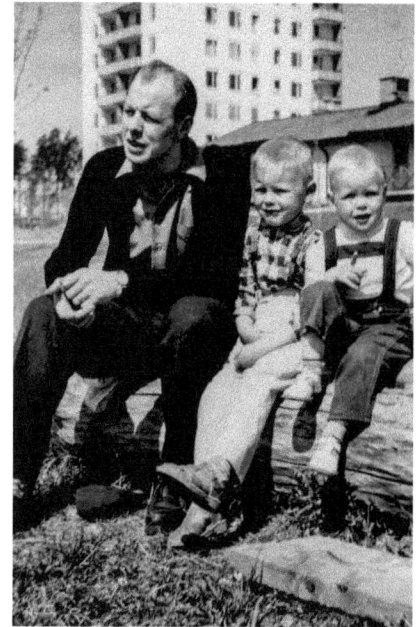

Image 20. Photographer: Ingrid Flyghed. Copyright: Ingrid Flyghed, License: CC-BY-NC-ND.

Image 19. Single child, middle child, big brother or little sister? What impact does birth order have on incomes as adult? Photographer: Arne Sohlström. Copyright: Arne Sohlström, License: CC-BY-NC-ND.

used the correlations among siblings' incomes to assess the extent of the parents' and the childhood environment's impact on children.

Similarities between siblings' incomes are of course not necessarily entirely the result of parents' socio-economic resources, but may also be dependent on attitudes and the immediate environment. The correlation among siblings thus constitutes a broad measure that captures a wider range of important factors than the parents' income, for example. Various studies have also shown that more than half of the family conditions and childhood environment factors that siblings have in common do not covary with the parents' income. It is therefore of interest to look to factors other than parental income in order to explain the covariation in sibling incomes, and a number of economists have made use of the Project Metropolitan data to this end.[184]

Almost one-quarter of the covariation in sibling incomes was explained by factors that they had in common. Of this one-quarter, the parents' socio-economic status (income, education and occupation) explained only 13 percent of the covariation among sisters and 23 percent of the covariation among brothers. The Metropolitan data made it possible to look for other factors that could explain the covariation. To begin with, the researchers examined a large number of indicators of family structure and social problems, which were found to have little effect. However, the amount of explained variance increased substantially when the researchers took into consideration whether the parents helped their children with schoolwork, whether they employed an authoritarian form of parenting, the mothers' attitude towards planning and their propensity to delay gratification, and also the number of books in the home. For sisters, for example, the proportion of the correlation explained by siblinghood increased to 58 percent, while for brothers it increased to 71 percent. The parents' helping their children with schoolwork and the mothers' propensity for planning were particularly important. The researchers had thus uncovered family factors that affected children's future incomes, and that could not exclusively be explained by the family's level of socio-economic resources. This was possible thanks to the large amount of data that Project Metropolitan had brought together. The results of the study do not say anything about income size, but they capture factors that influence the transmission of resources, norms and attitudes across the generations – the factors that play a role in the way children's futures are formed.

Choice of friends, friendship and life after school

In the School Survey, the children were asked to choose three students in their class as their best friends, their best class workmates and those whom they would most like to see as organisers of a class party. The methods used to analyse data of this kind are known as sociometry. Few other data sets include information of this kind. There are small data sets, but hardly any like Project Metropolitan that include over 15,000 students from 619 classes in 587 schools. The length of the follow-up period also makes the Metropolitan dataset unique, and since the data were updated in 2004, the project has produced a number of studies that have attracted a great deal of attention both in Sweden and abroad.

The friendship choices were analysed for the first time in a doctoral dissertation published in 1985.[185] The questions examined focused on the extent to which sociometric status among classmates could be predicted on the basis of individual and/or social variables. The reasons underlying these types of choices, and why certain people are chosen over others, are complex, and a great deal of theoretical work has been conducted in this area. At the time of the School Survey in 1966, the children were at an age when girls and boys tend to spend their time mostly with friends of the same sex. This was also found to be the case in the School Survey data, where few of the children chose friends and workmates of the opposite sex. The choices made with regard to party organisers were not as gender specific however.

The higher the children's grades, the more often they were chosen by their classmates. This was the case for all the types of choices examined, with the exception that girls who were socially active during their leisure time received the most friendship choices. It might be viewed as surprising that grades should play such an important role in the children's popularity. The researcher argued that school grades in part serve to summarise, or covary with, more general characteristics such as cognitive ability, orderliness, ambition, purposefulness and maturity. He also argued that grades are linked to, or serve to summarise, characteristics that more directly influence an individual's interactions with others. These may include flexibility, loyalty, helpfulness, openness, aggressiveness and more or less disruptive behaviour in the classroom. It may also be the case, however, that different individuals reflect popular interests, attitudes or values to a varying extent. The individual making such choices can also obtain status by spending time with those who are successful.

More recently, a further study has been conducted in which network theories have been examined with the help of the friendship choices recorded by Project Metropolitan.[186] It is most common for children to choose best friends of the same sex as themselves, and also to choose people who are like themselves in other respects (a phenomenon known as homophily). This tendency towards similarity has been explained by reference to individual preferences and structural opportunities – how many people one has to choose from. Using the question of whom the children wished to have as a best friend, the researcher wanted to apply a dynamic perspective to the explanation of the tendency towards similarity. The conclusion was that when social ties are formed in a sequence, the current state of a network affects the chances of additional homophilous associations emerging, and that the absolute size of a network is of importance for the degree of homophily that will emerge. Since the absolute size of a network in a school class is fixed and stable over time, the network homophily decreases when the proportion of ties initiated by actors increases, and network homophily increases if the size of the group decreases.

The significance of friendship choices for adult life

Following the updating of the Metropolitan data, a number of studies have been conducted on the significance of the children's friendship choices for their health as adults. The first of these studies was published in 2009.[187] It is rare for social science research to attract as much attention as this particular study. In addition to being featured in Swedish newspapers and on television, articles on the study were also written in Scotland and the USA. The BBC broadcast a program on the research, and a long article was published on the website of the American television presenter Oprah Winfrey. Why did the study cause such a stir?

It is well established that there is a link between social position and health. The higher one's social position, the better one's health, and the longer one's life. However, the majority of studies have only focused on short phases of life, and on people's social status as adults. The updated data from Project Metropolitan provided an opportunity to examine whether this relationship also held over longer periods of time, and whether social status among one's peers as early as the first teenage years could have long-term effects into adulthood.

Sociometric status was measured using the question regarding which children the respondents would most like to have as workmates in school. The children were divided into five status groups on the basis of the number of choices they received: marginalised (no choices), peripheral (one choice), accepted (two to three choices), popular (four to six choices) and favourites (seven or more choices). Since the social class of the parents was included in the analyses, the results show the effect of sociometric status in the classroom in 1966, irrespective of which social class the children's parents came from.

By comparison with the children who were classified as favourites, the risk of being admitted to hospital at some point during the period 1973–2003 increased in line with the declining number of choices that the children had received. Among the marginalised children, the risk of developing heart disease as an adult was five to nine times as high as it was among the most popular children, while the risk for type 2 diabetes was three to four times as high. These are diseases that are often related to lifestyle. Furthermore, the risk of experiencing psychological problems such as anxiety or depression was twice as high among the marginalised children. The marginalised boys were four times as likely to have committed suicide as the most popular children in the class. These children were also three times as likely as the favourites to have received treatment for drug or alcohol problems.

The children's sociometric status, or lack of status, may have led to these poorer health outcomes as a result of behavioural changes and various psychological mechanisms. The results were quite astounding. Was it really possible that the sociometric choices made in a survey, on a single occasion during middle school, could capture effects that manifested themselves over the subsequent four decades? Firstly, it is important to remember that the number of cases involved was often small. The number who had experienced heart problems during the period 1973–2003 was only 124, for example, while 167 had committed suicide. Of the children who had participated in the survey in 1966, 1,420 had been categorised as marginalised. In other words, it was by no means all of the unpopular children who experienced subsequent problems, but compared with the other children, the proportion who did so was greater.

There is also the recurrent dilemma of the chicken and the egg. Might the children who received few sociometric choices in the School Survey already have had mental health issues prior to their participation in the survey? If this was the case, the number of choices received would be the effect of these psychological problems, rather than their cause. The researcher was aware of this problem, but argued that there were other studies that pointed to sociometric status having direct effects on health, and that the relationship was probably the result of a process in which the different factors reinforced one another.

In a subsequent study, the same researcher developed the analysis further, by dividing social isolation into relationships and positions.[188]

The children who did not receive any choices as best friend were defined as lacking relationships, while the children who received no choices as class workmates were categorised as having a marginal position. The analyses included controls for among other things social class, education and psychological problems among the parents, and among the children themselves for cognitive ability, grades, truancy, whether the child had been sent out of class for behavioural reasons, and the child's level of interest in school work.

Children who occupied a marginal position (having not been chosen by anyone as a workmate) were at greater risk than other children of subsequently being admitted to hospital, whereas children who lacked relationships (having not been chosen by anyone as a best friend) were not characterised by a corresponding excess risk for hospitalisation. Among those who were hospitalised, however, the number of days of hospital care was higher among those who lacked relationships. The study's author discussed a number of possible interpretations of the results. It was conceivable that the children who lacked friends in the classroom had important friends outside school instead. Another possibility was that best friends need not necessarily function only as a support, but might also have a negative influence. Why they should have spent more days in hospital could only be a matter for speculation. Here it was possible that having friends might nonetheless have played a positive role in relation to the opportunities for leaving hospital.

In a third study, researchers focused on psychological problems such as anxiety and depression.[189] The same categorisation of sociometric choices was used as in the first article, i.e. with the different groups labelled marginalised, peripheral, accepted and so forth. In this study, the popularity of the boys was not found to have any effect on the risk of subsequent hospitalisation for anxiety or depression. Among the girls who had received few choices, however, there was a substantial excess risk by comparison with those who had received an average or greater than average number of choices. This analysis also included controls for several background factors, such as a range of school-related variables and the social situation of the family.

Why was there an excess risk for girls and not for boys? The researchers assumed that girls and boys valued status and acceptance on the basis of different criteria. On the basis of previous research findings, the researchers discussed the possibility that girls ascribed more importance than boys to appearance, socio-economic status, school success and social competence. This was thought to reflect their greater interest in the home, and in understanding, intimacy and feelings. By contrast, boys ascribed more importance to toughness, physical ability and social characteristics oriented towards independence. This meant that girls became more engaged in, and victimised by, aggression in the context of relationships in which the relationship itself was used as a weapon. As a result, girls who found themselves lower down the "pecking order" were more emotionally vulnerable than boys.

The importance of peer status has been studied further in several recent publications. In one of the studies researchers found that lower peer status in adolescence was associated with smoking in adulthood.[190] Furthermore, two studies developed the analyses of long-term effects of peer status in the school class by clustering outcomes during adulthood (level of education, employment status health etc.) – showing clear negative effects of low peer status.[191]

Mods, Drugs and the Shift to the Left

When the Metropolitan Project children were eleven years old, the first Mods appeared in Stockholm. The phenomenon spread across the country, and adult society was horrified at their clothing, hairstyles and behaviour. A couple of years later, as teenagers, a significant number of the Metropolitan children themselves became Mods. At around the same time, or a little later, many of them also became involved in the left-wing activism of the late 1960s. But an even greater number became neither Mods nor left-wing activists.

Different periods of history are often associated with specific youth cultures, even though many young people never become part of such a culture. At the beginning of the 20th century the Wandervogel movement emerged among German youth as a reaction against the artificiality of the middle class lifestyle. Instead, these young people sought romanticism and a return to nature through country rambles and song. In the 1930s and 1940s, Sweden had "Swingpjattar"[192] and "Nalensnajdare" who identified themselves with jazz music and dance. The arrival of rock and pop music also produced identifiable new youth groups. The 1950s saw the emergence of the "teenager" concept. For many of the children born in 1953, the music of the sixties, produced by bands such as the Beatles and the Rolling Stones, became an important part of their lives. The same period also saw a succession of popular Swedish bands, such as the Tages and the Shanes. At the same time, the teenage years of the children of 1953 coincided with a radicalisation of society, and with the Swedish so-called prog music movement[193].

Image 21. Anti-war demonstration in Stockholm 1970s. Photographer. Sten-Åke Stenberg. Copyright: Sten-Åke Stenberg, License: CC-BY-NC-ND.

How to cite this book chapter:
Stenberg, Sten-Åke. 2018. Mods, Drugs and the Shift to the Left. In: Stenberg, Sten-Åke. *Born in 1953: The story about a post-war Swedish cohort, and a longitudinal research project.* Pp. 153–160. Stockholm: Stockholm University Press. DOI: https://doi.org/10.16993/bav.k. License: CC-BY

Did the Mods go on to lead respectable lives?

The early teenage years of the children born in 1953 coincided with a period when many young people labelled themselves Mods. The Mods are sometimes described as one of the first rebel youth movements in Sweden, and they were most prominent during the mid- to late 1960s. When Project Metropolitan conducted the Family Survey in 1968, the Mods were on the way out, but they remained in the public eye thanks to a film entitled "They Call Us Misfits"[194] by the Swedish filmmaker Stefan Jarl, which premiered that same year. The researchers therefore asked the mothers who participated in the survey whether their 15-year-old children were Mods.

Stefan Jarl's Mods films linked the Mods with the emergence of the drug problem in Sweden. It is unclear, however, how widespread drug use actually was among the youths who called themselves Mods. And until recently there was no research that could describe how things had turned out for these youths later on in life. However, the update of the Metropolitan data provided a unique opportunity to attempt to answer this question, and in 2008, forty years after the Family Survey, two researchers carried out a social analysis of the children whose mothers had described them as Mods. How had their adult lives turned out? Did Stefan Jarl's films paint a representative picture? Did the Mods become social outcasts? Or was their rebellion a manifestation of creativity, which would later lead them to enter artistic occupations? Or had they simply left their rebellious teenage years behind and integrated themselves into mainstream adult society?[195]

A total of 167 mothers had answered that their children were Mods, of which a small majority were boys. There were no particularly conspicuous social differences between the Mods and other youths. One in four of the Mods had grown up in non-skilled manual workers' homes, as compared with fifteen percent of the other children, while ten percent of the Mods, half as many as of the other children, were from upper class or upper-middle class homes. The Mods lived with

"I defined myself as a Mod for a time during my youth. It mostly involved me having written The Beatles and The Rolling Stones (misspelled) on my green army jacket, and having bought a pair of boots from the "Impo shop" on Gamla Brogatan (Old Bridge Street)."
(Sten-Åke Stenberg)

single mothers somewhat more often than other children, and one in four of the Mods, as compared with sixteen percent of the other children, had grown up in a family that had received social welfare benefits.

Although there were no major social differences between the Mods and other children, one might expect their rebellious tendencies to have manifested themselves in their attitudes towards school, their grade scores and their adult lives. In the School Survey of 1966, almost 25 percent of the children whom the mothers would label Mods two years later, and 15 percent of the other children, answered that they were bored by all or almost all school subjects. Just over 40 percent of the future Mods, and 30 percent of the other children, had played truant. In answer to the question on what they thought would be most important for them to be happy as adults, almost half of the children, irrespective of whether or not they would become Mods, answered that being happily married was the most important factor. However, the Mods were more pessimistic about their future prospects. Compared to their classmates, almost twice as many said that their future would be worse than that of others. Three years later, when they left the ninth grade, the Mods had a slightly lower grade score average than other children – 2.9 as compared to 3.2.

How did things turn out for the Mods in later life? Did a disproportionate number of them become drug abusers?[196] Even though many of the Mods had no registered drug abuse, there were fairly substantial differences in relation to the other youths in the Metropolitan data. Among the Mods, fourteen percent had been registered for drug abuse, as compared with only four percent among the other Metropolitan youths. The differences were smaller with regard to involvement in crime. By the age of 25, 29 percent of the Mods and 20 percent of the other youths had been convicted for at least one offence. When the researchers examined the life situation of the former Mods as they approached the age of 50, they found no substantial differences here either. Sixteen percent of the Mods had completed some form of post

"I was "left wing" of course, and participated in the Vietnam demonstrations, and went to meetings and supported a load of organisations. I was involved in the "No to the EEC" movement too. Although today I think the opposite! But my activism went no further than demonstrations, selling pamphlets, shaking the collection tin and going to meetings. I never tried to become more involved in these organisations, to become part of any inner circle."

(Bo Östlund)

upper-secondary education, as compared with 21 percent among the other youths in the data set. The proportion who had a stable position in the labour market was roughly the same as that among the youths who had not been Mods, and there were no indications that the Mods had artistic occupations to a greater extent than others. However, a slightly larger proportion of the former Mods were receiving social welfare benefits. Finally, the family situation of the former Mods was largely the same as that found among the other youths. The majority were either married or cohabiting, just as they had previously wished for. The differences that could be noted between the former Mods and the others in the data set were linked to the fact that the Mods were more often drug abusers. The researchers' analyses showed, however, that the Metropolitan children had been influenced more by their childhood conditions in general than by their membership of a youth subculture. The origins of the drug abuse could thus be traced to the period prior to their becoming Mods. The researchers concluded that parents should not be concerned about youths responding to what is in fact a very normal need to identify with something. Generally speaking, it is substance abuse and other factors that occur earlier on in childhood that may lead to problems later on in life.

The shift to the left

In May of 1968, a period of violent civil unrest was triggered by students in Paris. This was then followed by a time of escalating political radicalisation across large parts of the western world. In Stockholm, students occupied their Students' Union offices, and in the autumn of the same year the Swedish Social Democrats achieved an overall majority in the election to the second chamber of the Swedish parliament. The ongoing escalation of the Vietnam War added further fuel to the denunciations of both capitalism and colonialism, and the atmosphere of social criticism was further exacerbated in Sweden by a major strike at the mines of the iron ore producer LKAB during the winter months of 1969–70. A string of new left-wing organisations came and went. To begin with, the youths who became actively involved were somewhat older than the Metropolitan children born in 1953. However, younger youths were also drawn to the protest movements when they saw pictures of the USA's carpet bombing of Vietnamese villages, and of children burned by napalm; many lost faith in the USA as the "world's biggest democracy".

To begin with this radicalisation was not regarded as being particularly positive. In a 1969 survey of the Swedish population's views of different groups in society, political demonstrators were viewed only slightly more positively than alcoholics and "raggare",[197] and they were viewed in much more negative terms than bureaucrats, capitalists, Russians, foreigners and gypsies.[198] But how big was the left-wing movement in reality?

In 1971, a survey was conducted in Stockholm's schools of the students' political opinions and political participation. Since almost 2,000 of the survey participants were also included in the Metropolitan data set, it was possible to link the two surveys together. The results were presented in two reports.[199] Unfortunately, the original data were destroyed in connection with the anonymisation of the Metropolitan data set in 1986, and it is therefore not possible to study the long-term effects of young people's political activities today. At the time in question, there was no Green Party in Sweden. The Christian Democrats, who were then known as the Christian Democratic Assembly, were not represented in the Swedish parliament. The Left Party was known as the Left Party Communists, and further to the left of this party there were a number of other small communist political groupings. In the survey, these were collectively labelled Marxist-Leninists (M-L).[200]

The study focused on the significance of personality and psychosocial factors for youths' political attitudes. The adoption of this approach was a sensitive issue. Attempting to explain political attitudes on the basis of personality rather than interests and instrumental beliefs involves a risk for the psychologisation of politics. At the same time, we cannot ignore

"I am one of those who has not distanced themselves from their political past. I have been very politically active. My joining the FNL-groups at upper-secondary school has had a major effect on me. It was really good, enlightening and stimulating. I acquired a new circle of friends. I got practice in debating, and learned to stand up for my views. It was also good because I was basically a shy person."

(Weje Sandén)

"Demonstrations have never been my thing. I'm maybe just too comfortable and conventional."

(Manni Thofte)

the possibility that personal factors may have played a role in how receptive young people were to radicalisation at this time. Although it is easy to assume that all young people were politically active during this period, the survey showed that around 40 percent of the survey participants had no particular preference for any of the political parties. Just over one in ten had Communist sympathies, and the same proportion reported Conservative (Moderate Party) sympathies. Support for the Social Democrats was only slightly higher, while the level of support for the Centre Party and the Liberal Party (Folkpartiet) was somewhat lower. The Christian Democrats had the support of under one percent.

The youths with left-wing sympathies participated in demonstrations and often found themselves in open conflict with the established order. Just over 80 percent of them stated that they would participate in a demonstration even if there was a serious risk of conflict with the police. Among the youths with Social Democratic and Liberal sympathies, one-quarter said that they would do so, and perhaps somewhat surprisingly, one in ten of the youths who reported Conservative sympathies stated that they would have participated in a demonstration under these conditions.

The left-wing sympathisers devoted a lot of time to studying Marxism and history, and to writing pamphlets and articles in various journals. As early as the School Survey of 1966, the children who would become left-wing sympathisers showed a somewhat greater interest in verbal expression than other children; they wanted to write stories, read books and learn foreign languages. For example, eight of ten of the youths who would develop Marxist-Leninist sympathies reported that they read the news in daily newspapers, whereas the same proportion among those who would later develop Social Democratic sympathies was a little over 60 percent. These early intellectual interests also manifested themselves in the School Survey's verbal cognition test, where the Marxist-Leninist youths clearly had the highest test scores. There were no major differences on the spatial cognition (pattern folding)[201] and numeracy tests.

People who spend their time in their rooms studying Marxism do not have as much time for outdoor activities, and this also manifested itself clearly in the results of the 1971 survey. Almost 40 percent of the Conservative youths reported outdoor activities as their principal leisure time interest, as compared with only ten percent of the Marxist-Leninist youths. The researcher who conducted the study argued that one factor that may have contributed to this low level of interest in the outdoors was that Marxist-Leninist youths often perceived sport as an activity that produced passivity and dulled people's interest in social issues. Other activities that are often associated with youth – such as going to discos and listening to pop music – were less attractive to Marxist-Leninist youths than to others. However, over half of them reported having smoked hash. The corresponding proportion among the youths with Conservative Party sympathies was one quarter.

During the school strike of 1966, the then 17-year-old future Swedish Prime Minister and Foreign Minister, Carl Bildt, made a statement that would subsequently become the subject of repeated debate. He asserted that school students could not play truant in response to the strike because their attendance at school was prescribed by law. Young left-wing activists often found themselves in conflict with school, however. Grade scores were viewed as the sorting tool of middle class society, and the contents of textbooks were often in conflict with their values. It was therefore not surprising that it was the Marxist-Leninist youths who were most dissatisfied with school (80 percent). In 1971, almost all the Marxist-Leninist students stated that students should have more influence in school. Among those with Conservative Party sympathies, the corresponding proportion was only slightly over half. In both 1966 and 1971, the Marxist-Leninist youths also reported a higher level of interest in creative subjects such as art and literature. When these youths were given the opportunity to choose between different occupations in 1966, the only favoured occupation was that of being a writer. In 1971, it was

"I never participated in an anti-Vietnam War demo. I sympathised, and was a bit leftist in general, but I never got involved in the organised movement. I was suspicious of mass ideology and wanted to find out things for myself. I lived in a collective for a while too, but I called it 'sharing a house'."

(Jan Andersson)

the Communists who reported the poorest relationships with their families. At the same time, however, they generally expressed the highest level of confidence that people in general could be trusted.

Overall there were no major differences between the youths, irrespective of their party sympathies. It is possible that the slightly older youths were more politically active, but among those born in 1953, only a minority had left-wing sympathies in 1971, in fact the largest single group had no specific party preferences. Perhaps the communist youths were romantics to a somewhat greater extent than others, with a passion for social justice? They sought out creative activities and were drawn into the left-wing shift that manifested itself in the election results of this period. When the Vietnam War ended, and the realities of the oppression of the Khmer Rouge and other communist dictatorships became more apparent, most came to understand that reality was more complicated than they had thought during their younger years.

Ingrid

Dreams of the Future

The Metropolitan Project children's future aspirations focused on having a happy marriage and a good job, and a majority had a positive view of their chances of having a good life. A number of studies have examined whether the children's assessments of their future were realistic and why optimistic aspirations were not always fulfilled.

In the 1966 School Survey, the children were asked about how they viewed their future. Their responses can be utilised to study why children have certain perceptions and attitudes, but also to analyse the significance of personality for outcomes later on in life. In answer to the question of what would be most important for them to be happy as adults, just over 40 percent of the boys, and almost 60 percent of the girls, stated that they wanted to be happily married, while a little over 20 percent of the girls and over half of the boys answered that they wanted a good job. Only just over one percent stated that material possessions were most important for them to be happy as adults, for example owning a car or boat. The children were then asked how they thought life would turn out for them. They were asked, for example, whether they thought their future prospects were worse than, better than or the same as those of other children of the same age. Three-quarters thought that their prospects were as good as those of others, one in 10 thought they were worse, and just over fifteen percent felt that their future prospects were better than those of their peers.

One researcher has analysed how well the children's views about their future corresponded with how their lives actually turned out.[202]

Image 22. Artist: Ingrid Stenberg. Copyright: Ingrid Stenberg, License: CC-BY-NC-ND

How to cite this book chapter:
Stenberg, Sten-Åke. 2018. Dreams of the Future. In: Stenberg, Sten-Åke. *Born in 1953: The story about a post-war Swedish cohort, and a longitudinal research project*. Pp. 163–177. Stockholm: Stockholm University Press. DOI: https://doi.org/10.16993/bav.l. License: CC-BY

Did things go better for those who thought their future prospects were better than others'? Did the children's predictions about their future have any significance for their risk of an early death, getting a job or experiencing financial difficulties? Did the children's perceptions reflect their parents' circumstances or their own ambitions and abilities?

What influenced the children's predictions?

People's perceptions and predictions about the future are often related to stereotyped conceptions. These are produced both by experience and in communication with others. Research indicates that children are aware of, and receptive to, stereotypes as early as the age of around ten. This should also have been the case for the Project Metropolitan children when they answered the questions in the School Survey. They knew that difficult conditions at home and poor school results could give rise to future problems. Besides the issue of whether the children's assessments of their future prospects turned out to be correct, it is also interesting to examine whether their perceptions had an effect on how their future lives turned out.

Self-esteem may be linked to expectations, which in turn influence one's future. Children who identify with negative, stigmatising stereotypes may develop a negative view of themselves, which can then result in a vicious circle – expectations are dependent on experiences, which in turn create new experiences. A further explanation for children being able to make reasonable predictions about their future as early as the age of twelve, when the school study was performed, may be found in what is known as motivated action theory. Children with low expectations for their future may feel that they have little to lose and may therefore be more interested in short-term rewards. This means that they are more likely to test various challenging behaviours, such as taking drugs for example.

In order to examine these issues, the researcher made use of the following survey question: "If you compare your future prospects with those of the majority of other people your age, do you think your prospects are worse, as good as, or better than others'?" By the year 2002, almost one in ten of the children who in 1966 had answered that their prospects for the future were much worse than others' had died. Among the children who had felt that their prospects were about the same as others', just under four percent had died. At the same time, the analyses produced the somewhat surprising finding that compared to children who assessed their future prospects as being about the same as others', the mortality rate was almost twice as high among children who assessed their prospects to be much better than those of others. Similar results were found for the proportions of youths who had received social welfare benefits at some point during the period 1991–2002, for the risk of being without an income for a long period of time and for the risk having to live on sickness benefits, unemployment benefit etc.

Nor were the children's perceptions about their future prospects merely a reflection of their childhood conditions (social class, family break up, neglect etc.) or their abilities (grade scores, popularity etc.). When these factors were included in the analysis, there was still a certain correlation between the children's future expectations and their incomes as adults. Other factors that were not included in the survey may of course have played a significant role, but the children's perceptions about their future prospects nonetheless played some part in how their lives turned out as adults.

Why did things turn out worse for many of the children who believed that things would go better for them than for others? The answer to this question was concealed in the substantial differences that existed within this group of young people. In order to better understand the causal mechanisms involved, the researcher divided the group into four sub-groups on the basis of their average grade scores. The analysis then showed that positive views about the future were not enough to compensate for poor school grades. For those youths who had poor grades and who believed they would have a much better future than others, adult life turned out much worse than they expected. At the same time, among those with high grade scores who also believed that their future prospects were better than others', adult life turned out much better than it did for their peers. The data also showed that the children who had unrealistically optimistic views about their future also wanted much more than others to be remembered as leaders among their peers or as being good at sports. In answer to a survey question asking whether they would choose to take 100 SEK now or 1,000 SEK in five years, many more answered that they would take the 100 SEK now, and more than half stated that they would like to quit school immediately. This proportion was even higher than it was among the children who felt they had the most unfavourable future prospects. Of these, 38 percent wanted to quit school immediately. Finally, a much larger number stated that they did not talk to their parents about their career plans.

The children who turned out to have unrealistic future expectations placed more value on immediate rewards. This was also the case with the children who had realistic but negative expectations of their future prospects. Thus we cannot be sure why they answered the way they did. In order to make further progress, the researchers would have had to interview the children again, which was of course impossible. We can, however, conclude that these children probably needed more help at school. The same problems are no doubt still to be found today, and if these children could be given help while still at school, things might turn out better for them as adults.

Incentives that can be measured in monetary terms play an important role in economic theory. Therefore, the survey question on whether the children would prefer to have 100 SEK today, or would rather wait five years to be given 1,000 SEK, has attracted considerable interest. In the field of economics, this is referred to as the discount rate; those who are not prepared to wait assess their future to be so uncertain that they don't want to risk waiting for rewards later on in life. There are few, if any, studies that have been able to follow those who have answered a question of this kind over such a long period as is possible using the Metropolitan data. Given such a lengthy chronological perspective, it is reasonable to assume that long-term effects will be mediated via various life events that have occurred along the way. One such finding was also noted in a study which found an association between the children's level of patience and their school results, which in turn affected their life chances.[203] Those who did not want to wait for the larger sum of money earned lower incomes in middle age, spent more days unemployed, and were at higher risk of obesity and of becoming mothers as teenagers. Although the results were striking, the researchers cautioned against drawing conclusions about causality, since there are many aspects of life that cannot be accounted for by the data included in the study.

Another group of economists adopted a similar perspective, but this time examined whether the children's willingness to delay gratification was linked to the risk of involvement in crime.[204] According to economic theory, individuals who consider committing offences make an economic calculation which compares the immediate reward with the price they risk having to pay later – in this case a possible prison sentence. In this study, the survey question on whether the children would prefer 100 SEK now or to wait and receive 1,000 SEK was used as a measure of the individuals' patience. The study's results supported the hypothesis that the children who chose 100 SEK today were also at higher risk of committing crimes later in life. There are two possible policy conclusions that follow from this finding. It can be used as an argument either for introducing harsher sentences, or for improving the education system so that children become more patient. The researchers were themselves inclined towards the latter alternative.

Anxious? Competitive? Indifferent?

In another study, the children were divided into groups labelled anxious, competitive and indifferent. The categorisation was based on how the children had answered the following questions: Some people worry about the future, others are not at all worried. What about you? Do you think what you become when you grow up is important, or doesn't it matter? Do you compare your future prospects with those of others?[205]

The question examined was whether these personality differences affected the risk of experiencing economic difficulties as an adult (receiving social welfare benefits at some point between 1990 and 2000), the risk of dying prior to the year 2000, and the possibilities of completing higher education (at least three years of university-level education by 1990). Since the children's perceptions had largely been formed by their childhood conditions, the researcher did the same as in the study described above, and included controls for gender, family social class in 1963, social welfare recipiency during childhood, mental health and alcohol problems among the parents, interventions by the child welfare committee as a result of parental conduct, and possible involvement in crime by the father.

Approximately one child in ten had been assigned one of the three different personality types. They included almost as many girls as boys, but the indifferent children came from the lower social classes to a greater extent. One possible explanation for this difference may be that children from the lower classes, as a result of their experiences of poor conditions, do not perceive themselves as being in control of their lives. The statistical analyses showed that indifference had an impact on the risk of experiencing economic problems as an adult and of not attaining a higher education, irrespective of the children's family background. The most surprising result was that the risk of an early death was 58 percent higher among the competitive children. It is possible that the competitive children had what are termed Type A personalities, which are among other things characterised by a strong focus on competitiveness. Other studies have found people with this personality type to be at higher risk of heart disease.

Social mobility

Social differences may be assessed in different ways. Such assessments focus either on whether the situation itself is fair and how it affects living conditions, or on people's ability to make the best of opportunities and realise their dreams, irrespective of their social position. If the opportunities for earning money and becoming successful are evenly distributed, it is easier to accept the social differences that exist. People with a conservative political perspective tend to emphasise the issue of equal opportunities, whereas those towards the left of the political spectrum instead focus on the existence of a class-based society per se. Conservatives often advocate a meritocratic view, and argue that individuals should get what they "deserve" according to their abilities. Those on the left argue that the more unequal a society is, the lower the degree of social mobility. The Project Metropolitan data have been used in a number of studies to examine the issue of social mobility from childhood to adulthood. Economists usually measure social differences in society on the basis of the distribution of incomes and wealth. Sociologists, on the other hand, have often used social class as their frame of reference. These methods complement one another, and need not be seen as conflicting. Both economists and sociologists have studied social mobility using the Metropolitan data.[206]

One study took its point of departure in the French sociologist Pierre Bourdieu's theories on economic, cultural and social capital.[207] Social position was determined on the basis of a combination of education and occupation. Upward mobility was defined as both parents in the child's family having completed no more than the six years of obligatory education that were required at the time, and that neither of the parents were in the upper or upper-middle classes in 1968. At the same time, the child was to have started university-level studies, or had a job that required a university degree or similar, by 1985 at the latest.

Social class differences had a clear impact at school. The mean score on the cognitive test conducted in the School Survey in sixth

"Through my university studies I found myself in the type of radical and intellectual circles in which I felt I actually belonged. But it was a double-edged sword.

I was torn between joy at spending time in an environment filled with books, films, politics and intellectual conversations and a feeling of still not really belonging.

It is the dilemma of social mobility. You find yourself among middle-class intellectuals and you don't belong there, despite the fact that you have the right external attributes. You seek out 'the old gang' and you don't fit in there either. So you keep on searching."

(Bo Östlund)

"We lived in a detached house in Södra Ängby in Bromma. Then there was Blackeberg with the rental flats on the other side of the metro line, and the school was right in between. So half the class came from Södra Ängby and the other half from the rental flats. As a result you became aware of class differences quite early. And you could see very early on which of the boys from Blackeberg that things wouldn't go well for. And they didn't either. But the conscientious girls from Blackeberg kept on being conscientious. And the boys from Södra Ängby became directors and lawyers."

(Lotta Samuelsson Aschberg)

grade was 70 points. The children from higher social classes scored an average of 79 points, and those from the lower classes an average of 64 points. The same difference could be seen in the mean grade scores from the children's final year in compulsory education, with children from the higher social classes having an average grade score of 3.7 and those from the lower classes scoring 3.0. Differences of this kind are well-established, and show that cognitive ability is not merely a question of biology. What opportunities did the children from lower social classes have for upward mobility? The results showed that despite coming from the lower social classes, those children who succeeded in being upwardly mobile had results that were similar to those of the children from the higher classes. In the cognitive test, they had scored an average of 80 points, and their mean grade score in the ninth grade was 3.8, and had been as high as 3.7 as early as the sixth grade. The children's school performance was thus a crucial factor.

A family's cultural capital was defined using five questions from the Family Survey on the parents' attitudes towards education. These included, for example, whether education provided a more secure future and whether schools placed too much weight on theoretical subjects. Social capital was defined with the help of the Family Survey's questions on the parents' help with their children's schoolwork. As has been shown by other studies, the children from the higher social classes had access to the highest levels of both cultural and social capital.

If the children's parents had a positive attitude towards education, and if they devoted a considerable amount of time to helping their children with their schoolwork, this provided the children from the lower social classes with a level of cultural and social capital that increased their opportunities for upward social mobility. However, if their parents had a negative attitude towards education, then children who were given a lot of help with their schoolwork were no more upwardly mobile than children who were not given help. In fact, the children who were given help appeared to do worse. It is possible that this may be an indicator of authoritative parenting, with the parents' apparent interest being more focused on exercising control than on helping their children.

It was also found that the composition of the family was not important. The children of single parents had as much chance of being upwardly mobile as children who grew up with two parents.

The culture of conscientiousness

In the mid-1990s, a man called Ronny Ambjörnsson published an autobiography entitled *My first name is Ronny* (*Mitt förnamn är Ronny*).[208] Ambjörnsson is a professor emeritus of the history of science and idéas, and the book was about his own journey across the class divide. In Sweden, Ronny is one of a number of names ending in the letter "y" that were commonly given to their children by working class parents. Ambjörnsson was a child of the working class, and sought explanations for his own upward mobility in the culture of conscientiousness that had characterised his parents during the rapid structural and institutional changes that Sweden had experienced, with dramatically improved living standards and the expansion of the education system. Ambjörnsson argued that the culture of conscientiousness was characteristic of parts of the working class at the turn of the 20th century.[209] It was a culture characterised by among other things self-control, planning, purposefulness, hard work and a suspicion of the expression of emotion. It also involved a strong belief that knowledge and education could reform not only the individual but also society as a whole. The roots of this culture were to be found in the temperance and labour movements.

The same researcher who conducted the above mentioned study on social mobility broadened Ambjörnsson's personal perspective and made use of the Metropolitan data to test whether his arguments also held up in relation to others.[210] The children's childhood conditions were categorised on the basis of different levels of privilege. Among

"You should work. Not be self-satisfied. Pay your way. It was important for Mum and Dad that we should get an education. You should be well-behaved, do your homework."

(Weje Sandén)

those with a higher level of privilege, the study counted children with a parent who had graduated from upper-secondary school and/or a parent with a higher-level salaried occupation. Among the less privileged were counted those whose parents had at most completed the six years of obligatory schooling, and children with both parents from the working class or lower middle class. Social mobility was defined in the same way as in the previous study, on the basis of occupation and education. Children from a less privileged background were then divided into three groups: those who had been upwardly socially mobile with regard to both education and occupation; those who had not been upwardly mobile in relation to either education or occupation; and those who had been upwardly mobile in relation to one but not the other. It is possible, for example, to obtain a high-status occupation without a university education. The children from privileged backgrounds were divided into those who retained their social position, those who did not do so, and those who did so in relation to either occupation or education.

A measure of the culture of conscientiousness was then constructed on the basis of six questions from the Family Survey: Do you like to plan for the long term? Do you think it pays to plan for the future? Do you think you get more out of life if you always think before you act? Do you like saving up to buy something big? Do you like doing things that you haven't planned in advance? Do you think that you might as well take the opportunity to have good things now as think about having good things in the future? Attitudes towards higher education were measured using the questions: Does school place too much weight on theoretical knowledge and too little on practical skills? Do you think that completing a more advanced level of education gives people a more secure future?

Questions on attitudes towards continuing into upper secondary education, and on which occupation the children should aim for, were posed both to the children themselves in the School Survey of 1966, and to the mothers in the Family Survey of 1968. Both surveys also included questions on how the children and parents respectively wanted the children to be remembered by their classmates.

The results largely confirmed Ambjörnsson's arguments. A well-developed culture of conscientiousness within the family improved the likelihood of upward social mobility. Similarly, there was a correlation between the children's social mobility and the parents' attitudes towards higher education. The children who would turn out to be upwardly socially mobile also perceived higher levels of parental expectations than other children. However, children from more privileged families who experienced strong pressure to maintain their parents' social position tended less often to continue into higher education or to obtain a higher status occupational position. Perhaps this was an expression of rebellion against the demands placed on them by their parents.

Downward social mobility

At the beginning of the 1990s, Sweden experienced a serious economic crisis. During the period 1990–1994, the number of people in employment declined by 550,000 and unemployment rose from just over two to a little over eight percent. The educational requirements for getting a job increased, and the opportunities for today's young people to become established in the labour market are worse than for those who were born in 1953. Despite this, the factors that explain downward social mobility may be the same today as they were 40–50 years ago, and one study has used the Metropolitan data to examine this issue.[211]

Earlier studies have found that the risk for downward social mobility increases if the parental generation has been upwardly socially mobile without the help of education. This research found that in such cases, the attitudes and habits that parents carry with them from their childhood social position had not changed, which they had in cases where upward social mobility had been based on education.

The children's downward social mobility took the form of a readjustment to what was viewed as normal, or to the social position of their grandparents. Downward social mobility thus became a form of consolidation rather than something that involved a loss. If the social mobility of parents had been based on education, however, this was assumed to have produced a change in norms and relationships, and to have been more stable for this reason. [212]

The French sociologist Bourdieu's theory on cultural capital has also been linked to these arguments. Bourdieu argued that social classes differ from one another as a result of their levels of economic, social and cultural capital. Each class has what is termed a habitus, i.e. a system of values and motives that form people's perceptions of the world around them. Habitus is only affected gradually by social mobility between classes. Bourdieu refers to situations in which a person's habitus is not suited to a new social position, and where the person does not seem to fit into a social situation, as the Don Quixote effect. These ideas were in part confirmed when they were tested using data from Project Metropolitan. There was no general correlation between parents' upward social mobility and the social mobility of their children. However, children of parents with a low level of education in combination with a high social position were at markedly higher risk of becoming downwardly socially mobile than the children of parents with a high social position and a high level of education. This might be an indicator of a Don Quixote effect, but attitudes also had an independent effect, irrespective of social class. Positive attitudes towards education among parents improve the social position of their children.

Occupational aspirations and gender segregation in the labour market

Although the Swedish labour market has changed a great deal since the 1950s, it is still segregated in the sense that certain occupations are dominated by women and others by men. The foundations of these sex differences are probably laid in childhood, and if we want to even out these differences in occupational choices, we should start with children. Both devaluation theory and socialisation theory have been important for developing an understanding of differences in occupational choices. The former argues that traditionally female occupations have been devalued by society and that fewer boys have chosen such occupations as a result. The latter theory emphasises the importance of socialisation processes, i.e. that children do the same as their friends, who during childhood are often of the same sex. The long follow-up period of Project Metropolitan provides unique opportunities to study changes in children's occupational aspirations, from their childhood perceptions to the reality of their labour market situation as adults.

There are two recent studies that have focused on the Metropolitan children's occupational aspirations. One of these studies examined how their choices were linked to their classmates' future occupational aspirations, while the other looked at the relationship between these aspirations and their actual occupational situation when they were almost 30 years of age.

In the School Survey, there were 54 occupations that the children were asked whether wanted to become, did not want to become, or didn't know whether they wanted to become. The questions examined in these studies were whether it was possible to explain these choices on the basis of knowledge about their classmates' choices and the gender composition in the classroom, and whether they later came to have the jobs that they had aspired to as children.

In the study that attempted to understand how the children's choices were affected by other children in the class, the occupations were divided into seven categories based on the proportion of women in these occupations at the time of the School Survey.[213] Each child was then given a score based on how many gender-atypical choices he or she made, and these were summed for each class. Social interaction patterns were analysed using a question about who the children usu-ally spent their leisure time with (mostly boys, mostly girls, mostly both boys and girls, mostly adults, or that they were most often by themselves). The composition of the class itself was measured using the proportion of girls, and the girl or boy who received most 'best friend' choices was defined as having central status. The individual children's scores for gender-atypical choices were then also used as an explanation in the analysis. Finally, the analysis also included the socio-economic status of the children's families and the children's grade scores.

The results showed that the central girl's level of openness to male-dominated occupations influenced the other girls in the class such that they also had a more positive attitude towards such occu-pations. The proportion of girls in the class was found to be unim-portant, but the girls who spent most of their leisure time with other girls made more gender-typical choices than girls who did not do so. It is difficult, however, to know whether the children were attracted to others who thought like them, or whether they were influenced by the views of those they spent their time with. Among the boys, neither the gender composition of the class nor the central boy in the class had an effect on their occupational preferences, but those who spent a large part of their leisure time with girls had a somewhat more positive attitude towards occupations dominated by women. Boys with low grade scores, unlike girls, had a more positive attitude towards gen-der-atypical occupations. One explanation for the gender difference noted in this regard might be the fact that the occupations dominated by women were also low status occupations.

The researchers concluded that the results provided some support for devaluation theory. If the central girl in the class made gender-atyp-ical choices, this had a powerful effect on the other girls, whereas the central boy in the class had no such effect. Thus at the general level, the status of female occupations should be raised, for example by means of pay increases.

A subsequent study showed that there was a greater degree of gender-segregation in the actual occupational choices that the children had made by the time they were almost 30 years of age, than there had been in their occupational aspirations at age thirteen.[214] It was particularly clear that girls had not entered the male-dominated occupations that they had aspired to. In 2008, only 14 percent of people worked in gender-neutral occupations (in which women accounted for between 40 and 60 percent of the workforce). When the occupations of the children born in 1953 were examined in 1980, the corresponding proportion was five percent. In other words, we still have a long way to go before achieving gender equality on the labour market.

Crime and Punishment

The issue of crime has been a high-priority field of research in Project Metropolitan. Researchers have among other things studied who becomes involved in crime, the significance of childhood conditions and school, whether criminal behaviour is inherited, how many young offenders continued their criminal careers, drug abuse, drink driving offences and the effects of prison sentences.

Right from the start of Project Metropolitan, crime was one of the most important areas of research, and the first report on the topic was published in 1977. Up to now, just over 50 studies have used the data to focus on crime in one way or another. By comparison with other data sets on crime, the Metropolitan data provide many advantages. One is that the crime data cover a comparatively long period of time – from 1966 to 1984 – and another that the data set includes information on both boys and girls (men and women). Furthermore, the data include information on the fathers' involvement in crime. The studies have employed a range of different perspectives, and in addition to describing the extent of the study participants' offending, researchers have sought to identify explanations for involvement in crime and have also analysed its consequences.

Different theories on the causes of crime both compete with and complement one another. This is also true of the Project Metropolitan studies, in which researchers have analysed the data set on the basis of different perspectives. Some of these perspectives direct their focus at individuals' conditions. Researchers employing such perspectives look for explanations in subcultures or in the frustration that individuals

Image 23. Arrest: Photographer: Ronald Kieve. Copyright: Ronald Kieve, License: CC-BY-NC-ND.

How to cite this book chapter:
Stenberg, Sten-Åke. 2018. Crime and Punishment. In: Stenberg, Sten-Åke. *Born in 1953: The story about a post-war Swedish cohort, and a longitudinal research project.* Pp. 179–192. Stockholm: Stockholm University Press. DOI: https://doi.org/10.16993/bav.m. License: CC-BY

may feel when the distance becomes too great between their own opportunities and general, societal goals regarding the attainment of goods and status.

Similar explanatory models have been based on psychosocial explanations, with links to a book by *Richard G Wilkinson and Kate Pickett*.[215] Other researchers instead make use of control theories, and explain crime by reference to individuals having weak bonds to parents and school. Labelling theories explain offending as an effect of the environment's reactions to individual behaviour. These theories argue that when individuals repeatedly experience negative reactions to their behaviour, they eventually incorporate these negative expectations into their own personality, so that they end up becoming what their environment expects them to be. There are also theories that seek explanations outside the individual, and that instead emphasise factors such as the so-called opportunity structure – "opportunity makes the thief".

Many people have broken the law at some point in their lives. Although not everyone who does so has to face the legal consequences of their actions, the proportion of the population with a criminal conviction is quite substantial. In a study of offending among people born in 1960, the Swedish National Council for Crime Prevention showed that almost 40 percent of the men, and ten percent of the women, had at some time been convicted of a criminal offence. Viewed in terms of the cohort as a whole, this means that one in four of those born in 1960 had a criminal conviction.[216]

Crime data were collected from a number of different sources. These included the police's National Crime Register, from which information was collected for the period between 1966 and the first six months of 1984. This register includes information on both offences and sanctions. Project Metropolitan also collected data on interventions by the child welfare committees during the period 1960–1972. In addition, data were collected from the same source for the period 1953–1959, but these related only to problems concerning the parents. The police register included information on theft, violent offences, vandalism, fraud, serious traffic offences, drug offences and other crimes. Less serious offences, such as speeding, were not registered. The data collected from the child welfare committees included information on theft, violence/vandalism, drug and alcohol abuse, drunkenness and solvent abuse, and adjustment problems. Unlike the police register, the information from the child welfare committees only covered the Greater Stockholm area.

Who committed offences?

During the period 1966–1984, one-fifth of the Project Metropolitan children were registered for crime. Not unexpectedly, more boys committed offences than girls – one-third of the boys and seven percent of the girls. The group as a whole committed a total of 28,000 offences, of which the boys accounted for 25,000.[217] By comparison with the whole Swedish population, however, the proportion of Metropolitan children was smaller. This is no doubt due to the fact that the Metropolitan study included offences registered during a limited period of time – just under 20 years.

Many people only commit offences during their youth, and then never again. However, those who continue to commit offences risk ending up with serious problems. Men who had committed offences prior to the age of nineteen and who then continued their involvement in crime accounted for just over 75 percent of the offending among the men. Among the women, the corresponding proportion was approximately 50 percent. During the Metropolitan children's teenage years, theft was the most common offence. In adulthood, motoring offences and fraud also became common, and these three offence types together accounted for two-thirds of the total number of offences. The largest proportion of violent offences, one-third, were committed by men who continued their involvement in crime after their teenage years. Drug offences were somewhat more common among women, but the biggest difference between the sexes was that the young men more often committed traffic offences whereas the women were more commonly involved in fraud.

Those who committed offences generally came from worse childhood conditions than those who were never registered for crime. By comparison with the children who did not commit offences, a larger number of the offenders had grown up in the families of unskilled workers; they had more often experienced a family break-up, and many had parents with alcohol abuse and mental health issues. For example, one-quarter of those who committed offences both in their youth and as adults had parents who had been alcohol abusers or had mental health problems, or fathers who had been registered for crime. However, although a larger proportion of the offenders had experienced problems in childhood, the majority of them had not.

The Metropolitan Project includes four sources of information on drug abuse: Being registered in the Social Services Register (child welfare committees), the Hospital Discharge Register (patient data), the needle-mark survey, and for the boys there are data that were recorded at the time of their entry into national service. The needle-mark survey was conducted at the Kronoberg remand centre in Stockholm by the remand doctor, Nils Bejerot. The survey registered all those placed on remand who had needle marks resulting from intravenous drug use. The information on drug abuse at entry into national service is rarely used since it only relates to boys, and there is reason to suspect that the information provided may have been exaggerated by boys who did not want to do national service, or who hoped to be given a less demanding form of national service. The project includes information on drug abuse from the ages of thirteen to thirty. The first three data sources together include information on 564 individuals with drug problems, of which 369 were boys.

Drugs

Many of those who grew up in Greater Stockholm during the 1960s and 1970s often encountered drugs. The drug problems experienced by those born in 1953 were the focus of a doctoral dissertation published in 1986.[218] Among other things, this dissertation showed that just under five percent of the men in the Metropolitan project, and almost three percent of the women, had been registered for drug abuse.

The dissertation also showed that the children who used drugs had experienced more adverse childhood conditions than others across a broad range of areas. They had therefore grown up in circumstances that were in many ways similar to those found among the children who had been registered for crime. The girls who used drugs had experienced particularly difficult childhood conditions.

Drug abuse is also intimately associated with involvement in crime, not only because it is an offence in itself, but also because crime may be used as a means of obtaining money to finance drug abuse. The quickest way of obtaining the large sums of money required is through theft and robbery offences.

Premature death is a rather blunt but simple measure of experiences of difficult life conditions. Up to 1983, eight percent of the boys and almost four percent of the girls who had been registered for drug abuse had died. The corresponding proportions for the other children in the study were two and just under one percent respectively. The majority of the deaths among the registered drug abusers, 60 percent, appear to have been the result of overdoses or violence.

As early as the sixth grade, the children who would later abuse drugs had worse school results than other children, and a larger proportion had been required to repeat a school year. In the School Survey, three times as many answered that they were bored by all or almost all school subjects. A little over four times as many of the boys, and three times as many of the girls, had played truant at some point, and twice as many had been sent from the class by a teacher. Finally, school behaviour and performance also manifested itself in the desire to continue studying. In sixth grade, almost half of the children who did not become drug abusers stated that they intended to continue into upper-secondary school. Among those who would later use drugs, the proportion was considerably lower – just under one-third of the boys, and one-fifth of the girls. When they subsequently actually chose whether or not to go to upper-secondary school, less than one-fifth of those who would become drug abusers chose to apply. Of those who did, half of the boys and one-third of the girls were accepted. Among the other children, a good deal more than half applied to upper-secondary school, and virtually all of these were accepted.

The children who were to become drug abusers did not spend much of their leisure time at home with their families. Although few of them had drug problems as early as the sixth grade, the children who later developed such problems spent their Saturdays at home considerably less often than other children. Among the boys who would later become drug abusers, less than one-third preferred to spend their Saturday evenings indoors watching television or listening to the radio, as compared with almost half of the boys who did not develop drug problems. They also spent much more time than other children socialising with the opposite sex. It is possible that their drug abuse was in part linked to their having matured early, and by extension to a different lifestyle. Over the longer term, their drug abuse also resulted in other problems such as unemployment and dependency on social welfare benefits.[219]

Three studies have made use of the updated Metropolitan data to follow the children who became drug abusers into late middle age. The results are disheartening and may be viewed as unsurprising, but it is important to be able to document what actually happened to them. This is particularly true since there are few studies that have been able to follow the same individuals over such a long period of their lives.

"At secondary and upper-secondary school I smoked a lot of hash. But I was never a drinker. After upper-secondary school I hitch-hiked around and worked for a few years. Still kept doing the hash, in bad company, and it finished with prison for just over six months. At the remand centre I pulled myself together and started to study, and wanted to go to university. All credit to the prison service, they had very good teachers.

Otherwise my time at the remand centre was not what I would call a beneficial experience in any way. It was just bad. A terrible waste of time that I put myself through. But it was a blow that became a turning point. Afterwards, I've never tried to hide it, but it's not something that I've boasted about either."

(Jan Andersson, Future Director General of the Swedish National Council for Crime Prevention)

When the Metropolitan children had reached the age of 37, just over three-quarters of those who had not abused drugs were employed or engaged in studies, as compared with just over one-third of the drug abusers. At the same point, 16 percent of those who had abused drugs had already died, as compared with two percent of those with no history of drug abuse.[220]

Drug abuse played an important role for the risk of continued criminal behaviour and also for the risk of premature mortality. By age 56, almost 40 percent of the men and 30 percent of the women who had been involved in both crime and drug abuse during their youth had died. The corresponding proportions among those who had committed offences but not been registered for drug abuse were nine percent and seven percent respectively. Research has shown that women who engage in offending often experience greater difficulties in later life than male offenders. However, if drug abuse is taken into account, the difference becomes less marked. What is more, the differences between those who had only engaged in offending and those who had also abused drugs also increased over time.[221]

The significance of school

The Swedish Independent Schools Reform has led to a concentration of children from different social backgrounds in different schools, and to a debate concerning what effects this might produce over the longer term. This issue has also been the subject of a study based on the Project Metropolitan data. This study concerned how the social composition of schools at the sixth grade level affected the risk that children would later commit offences.[222] A total of 123 schools were included in the study, and there were only eight schools in which no children had been registered for crime during their school years. At the same time, there were a similar number of schools from which as many as one-fifth of the children, or more, had been registered for crime by the police. Furthermore,

"The youngest of my sisters died. She went off the rails early and became a drug abuser. Then I decided never to end up there myself. I probably smoked a bit of weed at some point, and I smoked cigarettes until my first child was born, and then for a few years after I turned 40. But never these days. And I've been teetotal my whole life."

(Bo Östlund)

students from ten percent of the schools accounted for over half of the offences committed by boys.

The size of the school or class did not however have any effect on the risk that the children would commit offences either during their school years or later on in life. The factors that mattered most at the individual level were cognitive ability, whether or not the family was intact, the child's interest for schoolwork, and how much time was devoted to doing homework. In schools where the children performed well on the cognitive abilities tests, the level of criminal activity during their school years was lower. In schools where the children had on average performed less well in these tests, the risk for involvement in crime was higher. This was the case irrespective of how well the individual child had performed on the tests, and children who performed poorly were at particularly high risk of committing offences if they attended a school where the average result was poor.

There is an interaction between the school environment and individual characteristics, and children who have problems of their own find things even more difficult in schools with high levels of problems, such as crime for example. The study's author concluded that educational policy should attempt to ensure that schools are socially heterogeneous, and that schools with problems should be provided with increased social, educational and economic resources. If this research result is generalizable, the conclusion would be that the segregation produced by the Independent Schools Reform has made it more difficult to help children with problems.

Mental illness and crime

We often hear in the media about serious offences committed by people suffering from mental illness. A number of researchers have used the Project Metropolitan data to examine the relationship between mental illness and crime.[223] How common was it that those who engaged in offending also had mental health problems?[224] As expected, it was found that people suffering from mental illness committed offences to a greater extent than those who were healthy. During the years between sixteen and thirty years of age, one-third of the men who were not suffering from mental illness, and six percent of the women, were registered for crime. Among those suffering from mental illness, the corresponding figures were one-half and one-fifth respectively. Although the excess risk for crime was substantial among those with mental health problems, the number of individuals involved was small, since the number of healthy individuals was so much larger than the number who were mentally ill. A total of 2,500 healthy men had committed offences during this period of their lives, as against 41 who were suffering from serious mental illness. Among the women, of course, the numbers were much smaller (389 and 15 respectively). Among those who had received medical care for mental health diagnoses related to alcohol and drugs, almost all the men and seven of ten of the women had committed offences.

One reason that those with mental illness are registered for crime more often than others may be that they are at greater risk of getting caught. Sometimes they return to or stay at the scene of the crime and behave in a suspicious manner.

How did life turn out?

One of the first studies that was conducted after the Project Metropolitan data had been updated focused on how the study participants' involvement in crime affected their lives as adults. How had they fared as they approached their fiftieth birthdays? How had their lives turned out after perhaps being students, having families and getting jobs? Had they achieved the goal that many had expressed in the School Survey of becoming "happily married"?

The study showed that among the men who had not committed offences, two-thirds were married or cohabiting with children in 2001, as compared with 56 percent of those who had committed offences during their youth. Among those who had committed offences both as youths and later (to age 31), the corresponding figure was only 37 percent. Almost five times as many of those who had committed offences were on disability pensions, and a little over four times as many were social welfare recipients. The risk of premature death prior to the age of 50 was generally low. Of the men who had not committed offences, 2.1 percent had died by 2001, whereas among those men who had committed offences, the figure was much higher, 13 percent. The situation among the women was similar to that found among the men. However, a considerably larger proportion of the women who had committed offences were on disability pensions. Of the women with no criminal history, 1.7 percent had died, while the corresponding figure among the women who had committed offences was almost 14 percent.

In another study, the researchers constructed a summary measure of social exclusion that included the degree of labour market attachment, being on a disability pension and social welfare recipiency.[225] A statistical analysis showed that once a large number of background factors had been controlled for, those who had only committed offences during their youth were at no greater risk of social exclusion in middle age than those who had not committed offences. However, those who committed offences both in their youth and as adults continued to exhibit a greatly increased risk of social exclusion. Poverty and social problems during childhood were of no significance for the risk of becoming socially excluded. By contrast, this risk was increased substantially by poor grades and drug abuse, although these factors did not explain everything. This means that there must be factors other than the social problems included in the study that contributed to the offenders being unable to break the behavioural patterns from their youth and early adulthood. Is it possible, for example, that others' attitudes towards them, and the attitudes of public sector agencies, may have played an important role? The Metropolitan data do not include measures that would allow us to examine such a hypothesis however.

Effects across the generations

Social heritability is not only about the transfer of resources from one generation to another, but also involves the way people identify with their parents in ways that affect career choices, interests and behaviours. In one of the most recent studies based on the Metropolitan data, two economists analysed the risk that the children of fathers who had been registered for crime would also commit offences themselves.[226] When fathers had been registered for at least one offence, the risk of their children committing offences was more than twice as high as it was for children whose fathers had not been registered for crime.[227] For each additional offence committed by the fathers, the number of offences the sons were expected to commit increased by 0.3, while the corresponding increase for daughters was over 0.5 offences. The types of offences committed by the fathers were of no significance for these risk levels. The likelihood that conditions and risks associated with the childhood family will be transferred across the generations is of course not limited to criminality. The level of education that children achieve is powerfully influenced by their parents' level of education, and by comparison with the level of social heritability related to education, the heritability of criminality was found to be weaker. However, criminality was found to be subject to a greater level of heritability than poverty. When the analyses included controls for various aspects of human capital among the parents, such as education, a large proportion of the risk of inheriting criminal behaviour disappeared, although 20–43 percent of the total effect of the fathers' involvement in crime remained.

The authors of the article that presented the findings of this study did not limit themselves to noting that they had identified a heritability effect, but also sought explanations for this. The fathers' registered crime was divided into three periods: those who had only been convicted prior to 1953, when the children were born; those who had only been convicted subsequent to the birth of the children; and those who had convictions during both periods. Since the effects were strongest if the fathers had committed offences subsequent to 1953, it seemed reasonable to interpret this in terms of the children having viewed the fathers as a form of role model. This explanation was given more weight when it was noted that sons who had an unusually good relationship with their fathers in 1968 behaved more like their fathers than sons whose relationship with their fathers had not been as good. If a father and son have a good relationship, the child behaves like the father, for better or worse.

Explanations for the Metropolitan boys' criminal behaviour were also sought in a study conducted in the field of social medicine using similar data.[228] Here too it was found that the fathers' involvement in crime increased the risk that the boys would commit offences, and boys whose fathers abused alcohol were almost twice as likely to commit offences as boys whose fathers did not do so. In contrast to many other studies, the researchers in this case also assessed the effect of this risk factor, i.e. the fathers' alcohol abuse, on the total crime level within the cohort.[229] Not all boys who commit offences have fathers who have been registered for crime, of course, and for those who do not, this risk factor cannot have an effect. And the disappearance of a powerful risk factor need not necessarily result in any major reduction in the extent of the social problem being examined. It was found that the total crime level would only have declined by three percent if the fathers had not abused alcohol. The only factor that would have reduced crime substantially would have been if the boys themselves had not abused alcohol and drugs. This would have reduced the cohort's total crime level by almost 18 percent.

Between 25 and 40 percent of all deaths in traffic are alcohol-related.[230] Two economists analysed the risk that children would become drink drivers if their fathers had been.[231] Although the problem of drink driving has attracted a great deal of attention, few studies have examined how the drink driving of fathers affects their children.

Of all the boys in the study, a little over eight percent, or just over 600 boys, had been convicted of drink driving, and these boys had been registered for an average of 1.59 offences. Only half of one percent of the girls had been convicted of drink driving, and these girls had been registered for an average of 1.61 offences. When the relationship between the drink driving of the fathers and that of their children was examined, the study only used information relating to the fathers for the period 1953–1972, and the children had to have been living with the family when the fathers committed these offences.

Of the boys whose fathers had driven while under the influence, 18 percent were themselves registered for drink driving at some time between the ages of 16 and 31. Among the other boys, the corresponding proportion was eight percent. When the age-range for the boys was reduced to 16–19 years, the proportions were nine and three percent respectively. Thus the risk for drink driving was two to three times as high among boys whose fathers had been registered for drink driving offences.

In this study too, the researchers assessed how the total level of drink driving among the boys would change if their fathers had never been convicted of this offence. The powerful effect noted at the individual level would not have led to any major reduction in the size of the problem as a whole. As has been noted, a total of just over 600 of the boys born in 1953 were convicted of drink driving, but of these, only 121 had a father who had also been convicted of this offence. Of these, eight of ten had not become drink drivers. Thus it is important to distinguish between the level of risk and the extent of a problem.

As might be expected, the proportions were much lower among the girls, but the same difference was found on the basis of whether or not the father had been convicted of drink driving. Half of one percent of the girls with fathers who had not been convicted of drink driving were convicted of the offence themselves, as compared with three percent of the girls whose fathers had been convicted.

335 years in prison

The effects of imprisonment have been a matter of considerable debate, and a great deal of criticism has been directed at the use of long prison sentences. On the basis of labelling theory, critics have often argued that this form of punishment in fact serves to reinforce a criminal identity and that prisons constitute a training ground for future involvement in crime. During the 1980s, the crime policy focus shifted from the offender to the crime victim. The positive effects of prison sentences were no longer viewed solely in terms of the offender, but also in terms of providing law-abiding citizens with protection from criminals. Imprisonment was argued to produce an incapacitation effect by preventing the inmate from committing new offences.

In 1991, a doctoral dissertation was published that examined the effects of prison sentences.[232] During the period 1966–1984, 2,686 of the Metropolitan children had been registered for a total of 7,716 convictions, of which 5,030 involved cases of reoffending. Those who were sent to prison spent a total of 335 years behind bars. The actual incapacitation effect was calculated in terms of the mean conviction frequency during the period in which the individuals would have been at risk of being convicted if they had not been in prison. The results showed that if the conviction risk for those sentenced to prison had been the same as that of the other Metropolitan children, the incapacitation effect would have reduced the total number of offences by approximately three percent, and the number of more serious crimes by between five and six percent.

If all of those who relapsed into serious crime had been given a two-year prison sentence for their first serious offence, 28 percent of the total number of convictions for serious offences would have been prevented. But this would have produced a 500 percent increase in the number of prison inmates. If only those who relapsed into violent and drug offences were given a two-year sentence, the number of convictions for serious crime would have been reduced by just under seven percent, but the number of prison inmates would have more than doubled.

The dissertation concluded that even though the majority would agree both that crime should be made more difficult and that prison sentences should be avoided, "differences in the relative strength of these values lead people to adopt different positions". The issue of how many offenders should be locked up, and for how long, is a question of resources and values.

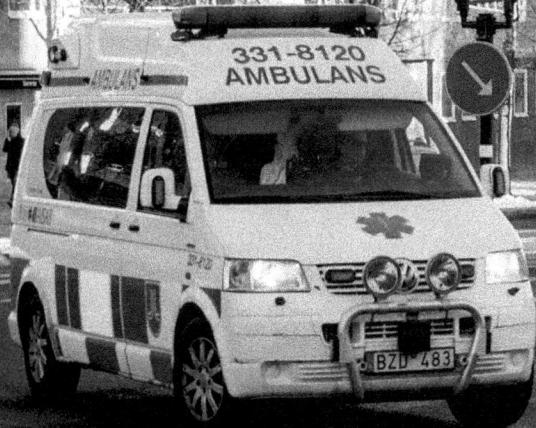

Social Disadvantage, Violence and Ill-health

How and why do the social and economic conditions of children affect their later lives? Why do some succeed in life, despite experiencing poor conditions in childhood? These questions have been examined from a number of different perspectives by several Project Metropolitan studies.

Different concepts are used to describe the most disadvantaged groups in society. The traditional term "poverty" is still used in the research, and is usually measured on the basis of income and social welfare recipiency.[233] Social marginalisation and exclusion are commonly used to highlight the fact that economic resources are not the only important factor. The contemporary Swedish debate also includes frequent references to the concept of "outsidership". Several of the Project Metropolitan studies have adopted a broader focus on the issue of poverty by looking at more than low incomes, and the researchers have primarily employed the concept of social exclusion.

Economic hardship and social problems during childhood can produce effects all the way into middle age. Why does childhood play such an important role? Shouldn't schooling and social policy be able to level out the playing field? Life is long, and a great deal can happen between childhood and middle age. In order to understand how childhood conditions influence the lives of adults, a number of studies have sought to identify incidents and changes during the life course that have an effect on adult life in the form of events that transmit the effects of childhood conditions into later life. Researchers have also made use of the economic crisis that Sweden experienced at the beginning of the 1990s, and which saw the level of unemployment rise

Image 24. Stockholm South General Hospital. Photographer: Sten-Åke Stenberg. Copyright: Sten-Åke Stenberg, License: CC-BY-NC-ND.

How to cite this book chapter:
Stenberg, Sten-Åke. 2018. Social Disadvantage, Violence and Ill-health. In: Stenberg, Sten-Åke. *Born in 1953: The story about a post-war Swedish cohort, and a longitudinal research project.* Pp. 195–211. Stockholm: Stockholm University Press. DOI: https://doi.org/10.16993/bav.n. License: CC-BY

dramatically. Could childhood factors contribute to explaining why some people became long-term unemployed during the economic crisis? Were they affected by something from their childhood that made them particularly vulnerable to the rising level of unemployment?

There are several different theories that attempt to explain how and why poverty and social problems in childhood affect the risk of experiencing similar problems during adult life. Some of these theories focus on socialisation processes and culture. Poor people are assumed to behave differently from others. They are assumed to have less ambition and their values are assumed to be characterised by passivity, short-termism and resignation. There is then a risk that this "culture of poverty" will be passed on across the generations. One well-known example of this perspective is found in the work of the American anthropologist Oscar Lewis, who studied the residents of a Mexican village during the 1960s.[234]

Other theories highlight the importance of resources. Those who grow up in families characterised by problems and a lack of resources are less well-equipped for adult life. Poor children do not have the same educational and leisure time opportunities as rich children. The American sociologist Glen H. Elder, working within the framework of so-called life course theory, has employed a research perspective that emphasises the way that resources both limit and create opportunities for individual choices.[235]

A similar perspective focuses on what is termed cumulative disadvantage. This perspective argues that a lack of resources in childhood increases the risk for additional negative effects, which leads to the situation becoming worse over time.[236] At the same time, this perspective also underlines the importance of turning points, which can change individuals' lives for better or for worse.[237] In summary, these explanations and theories range between the extremes of arguing that "the mould of a man's fortune is in his own hands" or that everything is dependent on circumstances outside the individual's control. As usual, the truth probably lies somewhere in between.

In one study, researchers attempted to identify factors in the period between childhood and adult life which mediated the risk that childhood economic hardship would lead to labour market problems in adulthood.[238] The study found that children who had grown up in families that experienced lasting poverty, which continued into adolescence, were at particularly high risk of experiencing problems in middle age. This was interpreted as providing support for theories of cumulative disadvantage. The most important intermediary factors were involvement in crime, drug abuse and having achieved a low level of education by the age of 25. At the same time, the study also noted that the group with weak ties to the labour market as adults was for the most part comprised of people who had not experienced problems during childhood. Similarly, a majority of those who had experienced difficult childhood conditions did not have any major problems as adults. Although it had been possible to identify heightened levels of risk, these excess risks contributed little to the prediction of labour market problems in middle age.

Finally, the study analysed those who, despite being only weakly attached to the labour market in their early adult lives, nonetheless became more successful when they were older. What could explain their having achieved this success in spite of having started at a disadvantage? Would it be possible to identify positive turning points? The study found that it was first and foremost those who had been able to acquire resources by means of education, or by having a family, whose chances improved substantially. But were there additional explanations?

In a later study, the researchers went further and refined their analyses.[239] This study focused on two overarching research questions. One of these was whether, and how, poverty and social problems during childhood were related to one another. The other was how these two factors together served to increase the risk for social exclusion in adulthood. Do risk factors experienced in adulthood have more negative effects for those who experienced social problems and a lack of resources during childhood?

When different explanatory factors were analysed in a way that allowed the researchers to control for the order in which they had emerged over the life course, no effects were found that went directly from childhood to middle age. Instead the links were mediated by problems experienced in the period between these life stages, of which the most important were involvement in deviant behaviour and educational failure during the teenage years and in early adulthood. Ill-health and poverty in the early adult years also played a mediating role, albeit a less important one. The study also showed that social problems in the childhood family were primarily transmitted into middle age via deviant behaviour and poverty, as a result of failing to achieve educational success. There was also, of course, a strong relationship between poverty and social problems during childhood.

Although these patterns were clear, the processes involved were complex. For example, part of the effect of educational failure was mediated via involvement in crime and drug abuse during the individuals' teenage years. Since the effect that was transmitted via norm-breaking behaviour and social exclusion was much more powerful in middle age than the effect transmitted via education, the researchers concluded that involvement in drugs and crime was much more dangerous than educational failure.

In part the results were as expected, but it was important that the researchers had been able to show how the effect of childhood conditions on adult life was transmitted via different intermediate events, and the finding that childhood resource deficiencies have an indirect effect on adult life sends an important message, among other things for the school system. It means that it is possible to compensate children from disadvantaged conditions in a way that will enable them to succeed as adults.

Finally, the researchers examined how the children born in 1953 were affected by the economic crisis of the early 1990s. Were there early-life factors that significantly increased their risk of experiencing long-term unemployment followed by social exclusion? Among those who were part of the so-called core labour force[240] in 1991, just over seven percent experienced a period of long-term unemployment at least once during the economic crisis of 1992–1995. This proportion was twice as large for those from the core labour force group who had experienced poverty or social problems during their childhood years. The same applied to those who had low grades in their final year of compulsory school or who had been registered for deviant behaviour. Further, those who had experienced both a lack of resources during childhood and long-term unemployment during the early 1990s were at the highest risk of experiencing social exclusion later on in life (being positioned outside the labour market or receiving social welfare benefits in 2000–2001). Did this mean that they were more vulnerable to the effects of long-term unemployment? This is a difficult question to answer, but the statistical analyses did not suggest that this was the case. In fact, the analyses showed the reverse. It was those who came from most favourable childhood conditions who experienced the most adverse effects of long-term unemployment. This finding was interpreted as being due to a "saturation effect", i.e. that additional resource deficiencies no longer have any major effect once your resources have fallen below a certain level.

In a follow-up article, the researchers directed a special focus at the significance of involvement in crime for cumulative social problems, and how this was affected by the economic crisis of the early 1990s.[241] The differences in income and labour market attachment between those with and without a history of involvement in crime increased, which was viewed as a confirmation of the theory of cumulative disadvantage. This trend was further amplified by the unemployment crisis of the 1990s. Although there was no difference in the relative trends between men and women, the difference in absolute terms was substantial, to the women's disadvantage. This may be due to involvement in crime producing a greater stigmatisation effect among women, since offending represents a clearer breach of social norms for women than for men.

Three subsequent studies have enhanced the analysis of the significance of childhood for social, economic, and health-related disadvantaged in adulthood by applying a so-called person-oriented approach.[242] Instead of studying specific events, such as unemployment, statistical methods were employed to create groups in which unemployment, social welfare recipiency, mental health problems and low educational achievement appeared in different combinations, summarised for the period from the beginning of the 1990s until 2007. Four different groups were identified in one of the studies.[243] The first, which included 72 percent of the individuals in the study, had average scores on the variables examined, and therefore served as a comparison group. The individuals in the second group had relatively low levels of educational achievement and higher levels of social welfare recipiency and mental health problems. The third group only had higher levels of unemployment, and in the fourth group, the individuals had low levels of educational achievement as well as high levels of unemployment, social welfare recipiency, and mental health problems. The analyses included the explanatory childhood factors social class, parents' education, family income, social recipiency, family type, number of siblings, parents' alcohol problems and mental health. The results showed that all adverse family-related factors in childhood were independently linked to an increased risk of ending up in a different cluster than "average". When the researcher included all explanatory in the analysis family type and parental mental health did not show any statistically significant association with the outcome profiles.

The second study was also based on a person-oriented approach, but here the researchers further developed their approach by focusing on eight different life-course trajectories of unemployment, social welfare recipiency and mental health problems, which were divided up by gender, and in which problems could vary over time during the period 1992–2008.[244] Just over 60 percent of the individuals in the study, among men and women alike, had no problems and were therefore used as comparison groups. The statistical analyses then identified seven problem profiles for the men and women respectively, in which unemployment, social welfare recipiency and mental health problems appeared in different combinations between 1992 and 2008. The childhood family conditions that were assumed to affect which profile the individuals would belong to were alcohol problems, mental illness, social welfare recipiency and involvement in crime. Finally, the researchers utilised the individuals' level of educational achievement at age 37 as a factor that could mediate the effects of negative childhood conditions with regard to which profile group they found themselves in as adults.

For men, difficult childhood conditions were most strongly associated with profiles in which unemployment was combined with social welfare recipiency, with or without mental health problems, and this pattern was not specific to any particular period of adult life. Among women, difficult childhood conditions were primarily associated with combinations that included unemployment, social welfare recipiency and mental health problems, either throughout the entire period 1992–2008, or with a peak during the 1990s. At the same time, few correlations were found between childhood conditions and individual problem-types as adults for either men or women. The researchers therefore concluded that it was important to study adult life on the basis of combinations of conditions, such as unemployment and social welfare recipiency. Of the individual problems experienced during childhood, parental alcohol problems and parental involvement in crime were found to have the strongest correlations with negative conditions in adulthood. Finally, educational achievement was found to have a clear mediating effect. This might be due to a combination of personality, behaviour and factors associated with the individuals' social networks.

The third study was also based on life trajectories, and focused on covariance over time among the same problems as were examined in the second study.[245] In this new study, however, the focus was directed at mortality, and the different problem profiles were used to explain the risk of death.

The results showed that unemployment alone did not affect the mortality risk, but that the combination of unemployment, social welfare recipiency and mental health problems produced a significant increase in this risk. It was also found that those who had more permanent problems were at greater risk than those who experienced problems over a shorter period. One important conclusion was therefore that the mortality rate was not higher for those who were only temporarily affected by the high levels of unemployment during the early 1990s. The researchers noted that although the profiles constituted the study's principal focus, mortality was also clearly affected by individual factors from childhood, such as a low level of educational achievement and economic hardship within the family. No major differences were found between the sexes.

Welfare dependency

Means-tested benefits, such as income support and housing benefit, are a subject of constant debate. Are those who really need it getting help? Are benefit levels too high or too low? What types of demand can be made of those who receive benefits? Do these forms of assistance lead to passivity and dependency, which may in the worst case lead to the children of families who receive benefits eventually also themselves living on benefits? These questions have not only been raised in Sweden. In the USA, they were a matter of considerable debate in the mid-1990s, and in 1996 the Clinton administration tightened the rules for means-tested assistance. Among other things, a maximum time limit was introduced for how long a household could receive benefits.

The changes in the benefit system in the USA also influenced the debate about, and the view of, means-tested assistance in Sweden. Inspired by this debate, one researcher conducted an analysis of

Information on social welfare recipiency during childhood was collected by the project for three different periods: 1953–59, 1960–65 and 1966–72. For each of these periods, the project has collected information on the number of years during which the household received social welfare payments, but not which specific years.

the possible inter-generational effects of social welfare recipiency in Sweden.[246] The issue examined was whether it was possible to trace an effect between generations, such that children from families who had received social welfare benefits were at greater risk of becoming social welfare recipients themselves.

The factors that might explain a possible inter-generational effect were in part the same as those identified in studies of social exclusion. Firstly, it was possible that welfare recipiency might produce a "culture of poverty" in which the income from means-tested assistance became part of the child's socialisation. Secondly, children who grew up in families that received social welfare benefits might have access to fewer resources than other children, which could in turn result in an increased risk of needing social welfare benefits themselves as adults. A third explanation, which is similar to that focused on the culture of poverty, is based on the American political scientist Charles Murray's critique of social policy.[247] Since poverty and unemployment are a precondition for the receipt of welfare benefits, Murray argued that means-tested benefits produced an incentive to fail. Welfare recipients become caught in a poverty trap. Although he is not cited, Murray's views are present in the Swedish debate on, for example, how much persons receiving welfare benefits should be able to work before they lose their right to such benefits.

By analysing how social welfare recipiency during childhood (1953–72) was linked to social welfare recipiency during adult life (1982–83), this Swedish study was able to examine the possible negative effects of social welfare benefits. Firstly, it was found that the children's risk of requiring social welfare benefits as adults increased with the number of years during which their families had received social welfare during childhood. Among the children whose families had not received social welfare assistance during childhood, six percent received social welfare as adults. For children whose families had received social welfare payments for one to two years, this proportion increased to thirteen percent. The risk of requiring social benefits increased gradually thereafter in line with the number of years of social welfare recipiency during childhood. Of those children whose families had been social welfare recipients throughout their childhood years, half had themselves received social welfare payments as adults during the years examined by the study (1982–83).

The next stage of the analysis compared the inter-generational effects between Sweden and the USA. This comparison showed that the effect was much stronger in Sweden. Of those who had received social welfare benefits in Sweden during the years 1982–1983, 43 percent had grown up in families which had also received social welfare payments. The corresponding figure in the USA was 25 percent.[248] The comparison was not entirely unproblematic, since the Swedish research was based on register data, and the American study on interviews, and the periods examined in the two countries differed from one another. Still, the disparity noted between Sweden and the USA is so large that we can reasonably conclude that it reflects a real difference.

Finally, the study also analysed the reasons that social welfare dependency appeared to be transmitted across the generations in Sweden. Was there anything to indicate that the welfare benefits in themselves produced negative effects? The answer was sought by dividing up the children whose childhood families had received social welfare benefits so that those whose fathers were registered for crime, and children who had themselves manifested signs of deviant behaviour, were removed. The children who remained were thus those who had received welfare benefits, but who had no indications of problems other than a lack of economic resources. Among these children there was no increase in the risk for of becoming social welfare recipients as adults. This excess risk did exist, however, if the children's fathers had been registered for crime and/or the children themselves had shown signs of deviant behaviour.

In summary, the results were interpreted such that the stronger inter-generational effect found in Sweden, compared to the USA, was viewed as being due to Sweden's better developed social policy. A larger number of the American social welfare recipients would not have had to apply for means-tested welfare assistance if they had lived in Sweden, since they would have been able to live on the income from various forms of social insurance. What was most important, however, was that the analysis had not been able to identify any negative effect of social welfare benefits per se. The study found no support for the idea of a benefit dependency culture.

Suicidal behaviour – attepted and completed suicide

In one the studies conducted in the Metropolitan project, researchers sought to explain why a number of men had attempted to commit suicide during the period between 1970 and 1984.[249] Potential causal factors were identified theoretically, primarily with the help of Emile Durkheim's classic work on suicide from 1897 and the American sociologist Robert Merton's 1938 theory on deviant behaviour. Briefly stated, the crucial factors were social solidarity and the sense of being part of society. Durkheim also argued that poverty functioned as a school for self-control and thereby served to prevent suicide. Merton's theory claimed that the frustration an individual may feel as a result of an inability to achieve goals that are generally viewed as attainable, such as being able to acquire a car by legal means, could lead to a shift in the threshold for engaging in theft or turning to violence among the poorest members of society. Merton never specifically referred to suicide, but the researchers who conducted this study argued that this too could be seen as a reaction to the tensions that arise when those experiencing poverty lack the opportunities to achieve generally accepted social goals. If this were the case, in contrast to the view espoused by Durkheim, poverty would increase the risk for suicide.

The Metropolitan Project contains data that made it possible to examine the causes of suicide. The study found that the risk for suicide was higher among boys who in the School Survey had stated that they were mostly alone, or who had played truant. Over the longer term, a boy's perception that he was lonely, either in reality or only in his perceptions, and truancy that led him to withdraw from the fellowship provided by school, could lead to suicidal behaviour. Poverty, measured in terms of social welfare recipiency in the childhood family, was also found to increase the risk for suicide. However, it was primarily shorter periods of poverty that were important. This finding was cautiously interpreted as indicating that a relatively brief period of poverty can be more harmful, at least in relation to the suicide risk, than experiencing poverty as the "normal" condition during childhood. In these cases, a short period of poverty represents a clearer break with what is perceived as being normal.

The study's results should be interpreted with caution. Needless to say, not all the children who felt lonely or who were poor later attempted to take their own lives. During the period examined, the study included 33 cases of suicide.[250] However, the identified risks support the view that it is important for schools to focus attention on children who are lonely, and not only on those who engage in externalising and disruptive behaviours.

Virginia Woolf, who herself committed suicide in 1941, was quick to focus on how women become locked into their social roles. In the essay *A Room of One's Own* (1929/1998), Woolf imagines what would have happened if Shakespeare had a sister with the same gifts and talent as himself, and concludes that "any woman born with a great gift in the sixteenth century would have certainly gone crazed, shot herself, or ended her days in some lonely cottage outside the village, half witch, half wizard, feared and mocked at". This observation was used by one researcher to introduce an article on gender differences in suicidal behaviour.[251] Although girls have better results early on in their educational careers, they have lagged behind boys in the field of higher education, particularly during the 1950s and 1960s. This has been explained as being the result of a conscious choice not to invest in education and a career, since women who became more successful than men in male-dominated areas would jeopardise their chances of living up to gender-role expectations, such as having a family. The study therefore hypothesised that girls with high grades in year six would be at higher risk of attempting to commit suicide, and of actually doing so than boys (during the period 1969–1984), and that families with high levels of educational ambition might be able to reduce a hypothetical risk of this kind.

The results of the study show that girls with above average grades were at increased risk of attempting or committing suicide, but that this was not the case for boys. In contrast to the study's second hypothesis, however, the excess risk was only found for girls who had grown up in families supportive to education. At the same time, the results also showed that both girls and boys who underperformed were at increased risk of suicidal behaviour. Among these, however, it was only the girls who thought that their families would prefer them to be remembered as performing well in school over being well-liked by their classmates who were at increased risk. This was not the case among the boys.

The rather depressing conclusion was therefore that parents who supported their daughters in performing well at school also increased their daughters' risk of engaging in self-harming behaviour. By contrast, parents who were content with their daughters being liked by their classmates, and thereby following the gender roles of the time, served to protect their daughters against self-harming behaviours, irrespective of their school performance.

A more recent study found that children who reported that they spent most of their time alone in the 6th grade were approximately twice as likely to commit suicide in early and middle adulthood compared to peers who spent most of their time with other people. It should be noted that the analyses also included indicators of well-established suicidogenic risk factors measured both prior to (e.g., pre-natal stress, social welfare recipiency and family rupture) and (e.g., unemployment, mental disorder and parasuicide) of the survey in the 6th grade. The researcher concludes that a lack of social recognition in early life, which is the essence of loneliness, might in itself be sufficiently detrimental to have long-lasting suicidogenic effects. Recognition and feeling significant to others is important for self-esteem, which ultimately protects the individual against questioning her/his own existence.[252]

Violence against oneself and others

Violence directed against other people is a criminal offence, but not violence directed against oneself. A recent study has analysed the causes of, and the differences between, these two types of violence.[253] The study was based on theories of inequality and health developed by Richard G. Wilkinson, who is one of the authors of the aforementioned book on equality entitled *The Spirit Level. Why More Equal Societies Almost Always Do Better*.[254] Wilkinson and his colleagues argued that social status, friendship and stress during childhood and youth are the psychosocial factors that have the strongest effect on health in later life. The researcher who conducted this particular study of violence argued that the same should be true of this form of behaviour, and that the risk for violence should therefore increase in cases where there is a lack of self-esteem, trust and a sense of belonging.

It is by comparing ourselves with others that we become conscious of our status, or our position in the social hierarchy. A lowly position may result in destructive psychological effects such as poor self-confidence, insecurity, feelings of exclusion and alienation. At the same time, we compare ourselves with others to a varying extent. People who do not tend to compare themselves with others are more stable and experience fewer problems.

As has already been noted, the Metropolitan data include information on social welfare recipiency. However, since the receipt of welfare benefits has been associated with stigma and shame, welfare recipiency works well as a measure of an individual's social status.

Social science data rarely include information on the extent to which people compare themselves with others, and it is therefore difficult to test Wilkinson's arguments empirically. However, the school survey included questions of this kind, both in terms of how the children assessed their future prospects in relation to the prospects of others, and how often they compared their own future prospects with others'.

The school survey also provided researchers with a unique opportunity to examine the elements of reciprocity, intimacy and investment in social relationships, which Wilkinson had combined in the generic concept of friendship. The survey questionnaire asked the children to name three classmates whom they viewed as best friends. If any of these choices was reciprocal – if the child who chose the friend was also chosen by this friend – this was counted as the child being part of a reciprocal relationship. The children were also asked whom they usually spent their leisure time with. The children who answered that they were mostly by themselves were defined as having insufficient close social relationships. Another question in the survey asked whether the children were part of any club, association or similar, and these answers were interpreted as a measure of the children's social embeddedness. Exposure to stress early in life was measured using data on whether the mothers had been single during pregnancy, and whether they had experienced family changes, such as divorce, during the first years of the child's life. Violence was measured in two ways: suicide/attempted suicide, and whether the individual had registered convictions for murder, manslaughter, involuntary manslaughter, assault, reckless endangerment, rape, child abuse, procuring for prostitution and robbery. The results showed that low status – social welfare recipiency – increased the risk for both forms of violence, whereas having poor future prospects only increased the risk for externalising violence. However, those who often compared their future prospects with those of others were at increased risk for both types of violence.

Sociological theories have described human identity as a reflection of the perceptions of others, which may be true reflections or merely the interpretations of the individual concerned. In this way, people make themselves the object of others' opinions. On the basis of these theories and the results of the study, the researcher speculated about whether children who had not yet developed a strong sense of their own identity might be particularly sensitive to frequent social comparisons. Perceiving oneself too much through the eyes of others leads to such children losing touch with their internal subjective ability to feel harmonious and satisfied with themselves, which it was argued might ultimately lead to the self-rebelling through violence.

The experience of various stress factors during childhood was not correlated with violence later in life. The relationship between social embeddedness (social relations) and violence proved to be complex. An increased risk for violence against others was only found among those who did not have any friends at school. Children who perceived themselves as lonely or who did not participate in clubs or associations were at increased risk of engaging in violence against themselves. What caused this difference? The self-perceived measure of loneliness was broader in the sense that it was not linked to any specific environment such as school or a club. Since the analysis included controls for other social contacts, the result was interpreted as indicating that a deep subjective sense of loneliness produces dangerous conditions for self-harming behaviour – violence directed against oneself. On the other hand, not having a friendship choice reciprocated in the classroom was interpreted as an explicit rejection of a social relationship with one or more clearly identified others, which ultimately leads to the individual directing the resulting aggression against other people.

Anorexia

Anorexia nervosa is a specific form of self-harming behaviour that has attracted an increasing amount of attention over recent decades. Of the Project Metropolitan children, nineteen girls and three boys were diagnosed with this disorder during the period 1969–2002.

Since only serious cases are admitted to hospital, this probably represents a rather limited estimate of the actual extent of this problem among the Metropolitan children. Despite the relatively small number of cases, the Metropolitan data nonetheless made it possible to look for social causes of Anorexia.[255]

The risk of being diagnosed with the disorder was higher among girls whose mothers were highly educated and for girls who often compared their future prospects with those of others. The risk was highest when the mothers were also housewives. Other studies have also found that girls of highly educated mothers are at greater risk of developing anorexia. There are a number of possible reasons for this. Highly educated mothers may have identified the problem in their daughters to a greater extent as a result of their higher levels of knowledge. It is also possible that housewives with a high level of education place particularly high demands on their daughters. If these mothers themselves had the disorder, they also had greater opportunities to pass this problem on to their daughters. Why were girls who more often compared their future prospects with those of others at a higher risk of developing anorexia? Perhaps this comparison included their highly educated mothers. Other studies have shown comparisons of this kind to be linked to an increased risk for anorexia. Daughters with highly educated mothers may feel more pressure to perform than others.

PROJECT METROPOLITAN

A longitudinal study of a Stockholm cohort

RESEARCH REPORT No 35

KRIMINELLA KARRIÄRER OCH PÅFÖLJDSVAL

Criminality
Violence
the Mental
Disordered

THE STOCKHOLM
METROPOLITAN PROJECT

Sheilagh Hodgins and
Carl-Gunnar Janson

PROJECT
METROPOLITAN

A LONGITUDINAL STUDY
OF A STOCKHOLM COHORT

Director: Professor Carl-Gunnar Janson

Criminality and Violence among the

PROJECT METROPOLITAN 37

METROPOLITAN 23
Stockholm cohort

PROJECT
A longitudinal

RESEARCH REPORT

TVILLINGAR — EN

SIV FISCHBEIN
BRITTA ALIN ÅKERMAN

RUBRICERAD JOBB

What are the Results of the Research?

Have the results produced to date by Project Metropolitan increased our understanding of social conditions in Sweden during the post-war period? Have they produced even more general knowledge about social conditions, irrespective of time and place? In my view, they have.

The Metropolitan data cover a broad spectrum of social conditions, and during the first decades of the project most of the effort was devoted to collecting information. During the crisis of 1986, when doubts were raised about the entire project, energy was focused on directions other than research. Although a large number of reports were published prior to the year 2000, it is in fact only since the millennium that the research has manifested significant progress. And in the coming decades we can hopefully look forward to, among other things, interesting studies of the ageing process viewed from a life course perspective.

Many studies have shown that childhood factors, such as family conditions and school results, have an impact on life far into middle age. But when the Project Metropolitan children were given the chance to answer questions about their lives and their futures as early as age twelve, many of them were already aware of the nature of their life chances. Ideally, we would like all children to view their futures with curiosity and excitement, and to be able to imagine that almost anything is possible. In reality, however, the Metropolitan children, including those for whom things did not turn out particularly well, were disconcertingly aware of their future opportunities, or lack of

Image 25. Photographer: Sten-Åke Stenberg. Copyright: Sten-Åke Stenberg, License: CC-BY-NC-ND.

How to cite this book chapter:
Stenberg, Sten-Åke. 2018. What are the Results of the Research?. In: Stenberg, Sten-Åke. *Born in 1953: The story about a post-war Swedish cohort, and a longitudinal research project.* Pp. 213–215. Stockholm: Stockholm University Press. DOI: https://doi.org/10.16993/bav.o. License: CC-BY

opportunities, as early as the sixth grade. This knowledge ought to be used to influence adult society to attempt to prevent adult life from becoming a self-fulfilling prophecy for children.

Other studies show, however, that childhood conditions do not impact on adult life directly, but rather that different life circumstances serve to transmit or curb the effects of childhood. It is possible to change negative conditions so that life becomes better over the longer term, which is important knowledge for adult society to take on board. For example, one study shows that our perceptions of the Swedish Mods, which have been powerfully influenced by Stefan Jarl's trilogy of Mods films, are not correct. Living a provocative lifestyle during puberty need not lead to long-term problems – the crucial factor was whether or not these youths became drug abusers.

Much of the Project Metropolitan research has focused on crime and social marginalisation. These studies have provided descriptions of the extent and character of youth crime. This has provided a basis for understanding the links between crime and drug abuse. The Metropolitan children were one of the first generations to be confronted with the widespread availability of drugs. Sadly, the research findings also suggest a relatively powerful inter-generational effect, with the fathers' criminality emerging as an important risk factor for their children. This may provide important lessons for today's school system and social services. During the 1980s, the view that crime could be reduced by incapacitating offenders by means of long periods of incarceration became very popular. One of the doctoral dissertations written using the Project Metropolitan data effectively sounded the death knell for this view. The costs would be far too high in relation to the effects produced.

School and the parents' attitudes toward education played an important role for the children's futures. If the school system of the 1960s can be compared with that of today, and if the goal of schooling is to ensure that all children are given the same educational opportunities, the findings produced by Project Metropolitan also show that current school policy may be on the wrong track. Children with poor educational prospects appear to benefit from attending classes in which many of the children come from more promising conditions. At the same time, children from more promising environments do not do any worse as a result of attending classes with large numbers of children from homes that lack educational experience. It is better to mix poorer students with better students than to separate them into different teaching groups.

Project Metropolitan has shown that externalising and disruptive children are not the only ones who need extra help in school. The children who were quiet and lonely were at increased risk of engaging in self-harming behaviours later in life, which might have been avoided if adults had helped to break their social isolation. Here too, the unique data collected in the School Survey have played a central role. The information on friendship choices has improved our understanding of the effects of popularity and isolation respectively. When researchers were able to show that popular children experience fewer health problems in adult life than less popular children, the results had a global impact.

The Swedish social class system is also a central factor in many of the Metropolitan studies. The Metropolitan children were born into a city in which people from different social classes could live next door to one another. Today the lower social classes have more or less completely disappeared from the central areas of Stockholm, with the exception of beggars and the homeless. The same pattern can be seen in the residential movements of the Metropolitan children.

I believe that the Project Metropolitan data still contain a great deal of untapped knowledge. Most of the Metropolitan children are still alive, and we are now approaching our autumn years. Our experiences during this phase of our lives will probably be very different, depending on our place in the class system, and the varying experiences that have influenced us from childhood.

PART III
ON THE FREEDOM, UTILITY AND RESPONSIBILITIES OF RESEARCH

Project Metropolitan and the Future of Social Research

At the time of writing, more than half a century has passed since the start of Project Metropolitan. The history of the project has at times been dramatic. Those of us who work as researchers hope that the future will be less turbulent, and perhaps this book will contribute to an improved understanding of our work. At the same time, of course, the boundary between research and the personal integrity of the individual is never drawn definitively, once and for all. The debate on the risks and benefits of research will continue. This is of benefit to research, and it is fundamental to democracy.

When Project Metropolitan began, the idea of using computers as a daily work tool had hardly even been considered. The researchers of the time collected data on thousands of individuals and conducted statistical analyses with the help of punch cards, mechanical calculating machines and typewriters. The researchers' enthusiasm for the task at hand, having the opportunity to follow a whole generation of young people, weighed more heavily than the problems they could envisage. With the benefit of hindsight, many of these researchers have wondered whether they would have had the courage to take on a similar project if the opportunity had presented itself again. Their academic lives would undoubtedly have been considerably more comfortable if they had devoted themselves to simpler and less controversial tasks than Project Metropolitan.

It is not only the overwhelming nature of the work that makes today's researchers apprehensive about starting such large projects as the Metropolitan study. University efficiency is increasingly being measured and quantified in terms of the number of publications

How to cite this book chapter:
Stenberg, Sten-Åke. 2018. Project Metropolitan and the Future of Social Research. In: Stenberg, Sten-Åke. *Born in 1953: The story about a post-war Swedish cohort, and a longitudinal research project.* Pp. 219–228. Stockholm: Stockholm University Press. DOI: https://doi.org/10.16993/bav.p. License: CC-BY

produced. Projects that require years of extensive data collection do not lead to speedy publication, since it may be decades before the data are ready to study and interesting findings may be produced. Researchers who do not publish articles quickly cannot count on either research funding or continued employment, which may in turn lead to short-termism and over-simplification; taking pride in the development of a data set that will bear fruit over the longer term carries no weight on an academic CV. It will not help the researcher to obtain academic posts, and does little to increase the chances of receiving funding from the research councils.

As we have seen in the introductory section of this book, at the time when Project Metropolitan was initiated, social research was not subject to extensive legal regulation. Research was autonomous, and it was entirely up to those who administered data registers, or who were asked to participate in an interview, to determine whether the researchers would be given access to the information they sought. The work was for the most part governed only by fundamental ethical rules and the confidentiality legislation. The computerisation of society later served to increase concerns about what this new technology might mean for the individual's personal integrity, and for the opportunities for central authorities to exercise control over people. As early as 1974, Sweden introduced a regulatory Data Act. There then followed a period in which the regulation of research increased, which in some ways reached a crescendo in the Project Metropolitan debate. When it became clear in the early 1990s that it was not reasonable to regulate the media and the arts on the basis of the data legislation, control of these areas was abandoned, while the authorities continued to regulate social research.

The legislation that regulates research is rather impenetrable. For register-based research projects, this legislation means among other things that information from different administrative registers may only be combined with the objective of examining a clearly specified research question: databases are viewed as being illegal. Statistics

Sweden has therefore discontinued the project register that made it possible to update the Metropolitan (Stockholm Birth Cohort) data with new, up-to-date information from various registers. All of the work carried out at the beginning of the 2000s to resurrect Project Metropolitan was based on this link. This decision awakens associations with the so-called Luddites, who at the beginning of the 19th century destroyed machinery that they viewed as threatening during the industrial revolution. The only difference today is that it is the prestigious public sector agency Statistics Sweden that is destroying the results of technological progress. The legislation is not entirely clear, and it would have been possible to arrive at a different decision. But with expanding regulation and legislation, there follows an expanding corps of lawyers. These often have a different perspective to that of the researchers, and today it is the lawyers who make the decisions.

In 2016, however, on the basis of Project Metropolitan, the Swedish research council Forte awarded Stockholm University substantial funding for a new research program (11.5 million SEK over three years, with a good chance that both the grant amount and its term would be doubled). The program, entitled Reproduction of inequality through linked lives (RELINK), includes updating and extending the Project Metropolitan data. In addition to updating existing register data, the material will become multigenerational, by adding linked register data on the cohort members' parents, siblings, children, nieces and nephews. This will enable RELINK to provide answers to questions about how the cohort members' life trajectories have been moulded by those of previous generations, and also about the extent to which the life trajectories of siblings and childhood friends are similar across the life course, and the effects this has on the lives of subsequent generations. In January 2018, following a long period of indecision, Statistics Sweden finally determined to allow the probability matching process to be repeated, and Project Metropolitan and the Stockholm Birth Cohort will soon be reborn as "Stockholm

Folke Fridell's 1955 novel, *Bjälken i ditt öga (The Beam in Your Eye)*, is about the Katrineholm Study, one of the first large-scale Swedish sociological surveys. In the first chapter, two sociologists named Mia and Sven are sitting on the train to Katrineholm. They have the card index – the "victim list" – of those to be interviewed on their laps. Fridell describes these people as naïve and sociology as being superficial, while at the same time describing sociologists as wanting to intrude into the sanctity of individuals' private lives in an unpleasant way: "With this train that is soon to leave, we are going to be travelling into these people in order to learn. To ask, to listen and to know. And then finally to put it all together." Fridell misunderstood sociologists, who are not interested in people's "innermost secrets" but rather in social patterns.

Birth Cohort Multigenerational Study (SBC Multigen)", with great potential.

It would be going too far in the current context to provide a detailed description of the relevant legislation and how it is interpreted by different public sector authorities in Sweden. In May 2018, the EU's new data directive came into force, and at the time of writing it is difficult to predict what this will mean for social research.

The freedom of research and the media

The history of Project Metropolitan may also be viewed in the light of issues relating to the quality and freedom of research. What constitutes good research and bad research respectively? Good research may lead to important and interesting findings, but need not necessarily do so. Bad research rarely leads to anything good. Project Metropolitan, often viewed as representing the field of sociology, has been criticised as an example of bad research. The critics have argued that the project has been superficial and that standardised questionnaires cannot capture the complexity of human social existence. Sociological researchers have also been compared with social engineers, who are attempting to put people's lives in order with the help of schematic presentations of research results. In their zeal they have been accused of crossing the boundaries of personal privacy, and of threatening the personal integrity of the individual.

Which methods and materials should researchers be able to use? In the mid-1980s, many of the most ardent critics of Project Metropolitan were journalists. Not long after the Metropolitan debate, the same criticisms were turned on the media themselves; newspapers also maintained registers containing personal information, which was forbidden by the contemporary data legislation. At the beginning of the 1990s, however, the government made it clear that the Swedish constitution took priority over the Data Act, and since then journalists and artists have been able to conduct their work free from interference.

Like journalists, the goal of researchers is to produce new knowledge that contributes to a better understanding of people and society – with a focus on everything from how Prime Ministers think to whether levels of poverty have increased. Their methods are also similar in many ways. Both groups employ interviews and study documents and registers. The principal differences between the two perhaps lie in the way that journalists rarely work with large data sets that require statistical expertise, and that research should have a basis in theory. Another difference is that journalists have a more short-term perspective, since news, by definition, is expected to be topical. Researchers do not need to be in such a hurry, but should rather be given the opportunity to reflect and conduct more detailed analyses. Further, journalists are usually employed by firms operating in the private sector, sometimes with public sector funding. Most researchers, however, are public sector employees, although some do work in the private sector, for example at various market research companies.

Both the media and the research community have been accused of violating people's privacy. The media, for example, may publish intimate details on individuals' private lives and the names of crime suspects who are later found to have been wrongfully indicted. By contrast, there are few if any examples of researchers publishing information that has violated the personal integrity of specific individuals. Individual identities are almost never of interest to researchers, with the exception of research on well-known figures such as politicians, leaders of industry and authors. In the context of the research process, however, individuals without names and personal identity numbers may provide information that facilitates the production of generalisable knowledge. Interviews may constitute the basis for the formulation of hypotheses and for problematising theories. Studies of this kind may not be published if there is any way in which the individuals involved may be identified. Instead, researchers employ pseudonyms and invent names for geographical locations. Nor have the results of this type of research ever been criticised for violating individuals'

"At present it is difficult for researchers to collect and assemble sensitive personal data for future research purposes. This may for example affect longitudinal studies where a variety of information is typically collected for a large number of individuals and intended for future research projects whose specific objectives are not yet known."

(Ministry of Education, Remit of the committee "Preconditions for register based research", Kommittedirektiv: Förutsättningar för registerbaserad Dir. 2013:8.)

integrity. Instead, the focus of the integrity debate has been directed at the compilation of databases that contain information on large numbers of individuals over a long period of time. Project Metropolitan was one example of this. The very fact that researchers' databases have included sensitive information about people has been perceived as threatening. The fact that the statistical analyses have been conducted using anonymised data has been viewed as being less important.

People frequently feel they have been violated by media reports, and every now and then proposals are made for the regulation of journalism. But every time privacy protections are proposed at the journalist's expense, these are rejected as an assault on the freedom of speech and the foundations of democracy. At the same time, calls for greater freedom from the research community are often viewed as a threat, not only to the integrity of citizens, but also to freedom and democracy. In such cases, social research is defined as part of the state's control apparatus. The researcher's view is quite the opposite of course – researchers work in the hope that their findings will serve to strengthen democracy by dispelling prejudices and providing a more secure foundation for societal debate.

Although the methods employed by social researchers, and their goal of revealing new knowledge, are often similar to those of journalists, they do not enjoy the same protections. Since the debate on Project Metropolitan, the regulation of research has been intensified. A journalist can access registers and interview people about their health, criminal offending, political opinions and ethnic background without applying for permission to do so. A researcher would be committing a criminal offence if he or she did so without first obtaining the permission of a research ethics review board.[256] There are arguments for viewing this as a good thing. Ethical review forces the researcher to consider ethical issues, and it creates legitimacy and confidence in society at large. It may, however, also be a bad thing. The ethical review process may become overly regulated and formalised. The focus will come to be directed at the application itself, and once it has been approved, the researcher's interest in the ethical issues may decline. Ethical problems arise continuously, and they cannot be exhaustively formulated in legal texts. They should constitute an integral part of the research process, and not something that has been settled following the meeting of an ethics review board – a meeting in which the researchers do not themselves participate, but whose outcome they are informed of in terms of either an approved application or a requirement to supplement the application with missing information. The public suspicion of research might also increase – it must be dangerous if such extensive controls are necessary. There is also a risk that the otherwise so highly esteemed principle of the freedom of research will ultimately be negatively affected.

We all have boundaries that we do not want others to cross, but where does the line go between personal integrity and what the media usually refer to as the public interest? A journalist's work is protected by the Press Freedom Act, whereas the work of the researcher is controlled by legislation and public sector authorities. The freedom of research does not enjoy the same protections as the media. This does not mean that I am arguing for any restriction of the freedoms that are currently enjoyed by journalists and artists, and there are of course certain limits to journalistic freedom. But newspapers are rarely found guilty of libel.

Politics, views of society and Project Metropolitan

By comparison with the situation in dictatorships, Swedish social research is of course free. The question is why a democracy should need such powerful protections against social research? The views expressed about Project Metropolitan and sociological research have been linked to political convictions. Centre-right commentators, who have a more individualistic perspective, have ascribed more importance to the individual, the family and the market. Individual integrity has been assigned greater weight than knowledge about society. Social democrats and social liberals have more often been the allies of research. Their goal has been to use politics to change society, and to improve people's life chances and the distribution of income and wealth. Achieving these aims requires knowledge on which to base decisions. Research can provide this knowledge.

Sten Johansson, a Swedish sociologist and former Director General of Statistics Sweden, argued that statistics should be maintained on people's living conditions in areas such as health, housing and personal security in the same way as statistics on national accounts and the balance of payments.[257] Since health and housing standards cannot be measured in monetary terms in the same way, something else is needed, and here the sociologists' questionnaires and register studies have an important role to play. These describe the nature of living conditions; and then citizens, via public debate and through their elected representatives, formulate how things should be and what should be done to achieve these goals. This is now well-established practice, inter alia within international organisations such as the EU, where statistics also serve the function of providing a basis for decisions on reform. Forty years ago, this was still a new idea.

Many of those whose political sympathies lie to the left of the social democratic position have expressed criticism of this type of research, viewing it as an instrument of control wielded by the bourgeois state. The Danish Metropolitan project was greatly harmed by the student revolt at the University of Copenhagen. The project was accused of being reactionary and of providing those in power with information that could be exploited to manipulate and oppress the people. A salient example of this phenomenon in Sweden can be seen in the author Jan Myrdal's refusal to participate in the Population and Housing Census of 1990.[258]

Scientific methods

The methods employed by social science are a matter of debate. A line is sometimes drawn between quantitative and qualitative methods. Stated simply, quantitative research is based on data that include large numbers of individuals and that are analysed using statistical methods. Qualitative research, on the other hand, studies fewer observations and attempts to understand events and individuals' lives at a more detailed level. Tensions have often arisen between these two methodological perspectives. Qualitative researchers have criticised their quantitative colleagues for being superficial, for using underdeveloped theories and for being politically conservative. Quantitative researchers have criticised qualitative research for being too subjective and because it is impossible to draw generalisable conclusions on the basis of its findings. As we have seen, when the debate on Project Metropolitan was at its most intense, the criticism of the project from the academic world often came from researchers with a qualitative focus.

This conflict has not been resolved and the same undertone of criticism regarding conservative and radical research remains today. This discussion is a hopeless one, since different problems require different methods. Nor is it likely that social science will ever become as homogeneous as the natural sciences. Social science will never be able to predict events such as the fall of the Berlin wall with any great precision, nor provide detailed advice on how to combat gang crime. Research can provide various pieces of the puzzle, but will never be able to do it with the same precision as that with which we can predict the movements of heavenly bodies or build bridges. This does not mean that everything is relative, however, or that there are "alternative facts". Today what we need is serious research based on facts, which shows that society cannot be manipulated by opinions and ideologies.

Social researchers are often good at describing and explaining what has happened, but find it much more difficult to predict what will happen in the future. Both predictions and history may be disputed. Political and economic interests have a stake in describing social trends from different points of view. Scientific transparency and the use of

"There was a centre-right criticism of this trend whose undertones focused on a risk of it becoming totalitarian – the implication was 'imagine if Stalin had possessed a computer; imagine how much worse he would have been.' And from the left there was loud criticism from the Marxist perspective, which argued that the state apparatus is primarily a tool used by the elite or high finance to discipline the masses, to keep the people in order. From this perspective, of course, a computerised, omniscient state was also something dangerous. The criticism came from two directions, and the Social Democrats found themselves in the middle, and probably tried to argue that [the criticisms] merely represented insidious attacks on our welfare society." (Anders R. Olsson in Klein 2008, p. 13.)

methods that can be scrutinized and verified enable researchers to contribute to improving our knowledge of social processes. Diversity, clarity and transparency about its sources are what give research its legitimacy. Since researchers also arrive at different conclusions, they are also part of the public debate. Social science can serve to bolster democracy by providing a basis for debate and decision making that is as free as possible from the biases produced by preconceived ideas. In this way, social science can contribute to the questioning of prejudices and may strengthen the foundations of a free and open society.

Endnotes

1. Sometimes referred to as "the Swedish Middle Way", the Folkhem was viewed as lying midway between capitalism and socialism. The basis of the Folkhem vision is that an entire society ought to function like a small family in which everybody contributes. https://en.wikipedia.org/wiki/Folkhemmet https://www.britannica.com/topic/peoples-home

2. The area did not correspond exactly to what is now referred to as Greater Stockholm.

3. The name Metropolitan was taken from the aeroplane Convair Metropolitan which at the time linked the Scandinavian capital cities together.

4. Svalastoga 1947

5. One of the most prominent was the study by Douglas, a paediatrician, of all children born in the UK during a certain week in March 1946. The study is known by the name "The 1946 National Birth Cohort" (NBC) and the Metropolitan studies in Sweden and Denmark were structured in a fairly similar way. Unlike the Swedish Metropolitan study, the NBC has not been anonymised, but is instead still being updated today. Svalastoga was also familiar with the Scandinavian studies conducted by the sociologist Gunnar Boalt, however, and those of the educationalists Thorsten Husén and Kjell Härnqvist. Other later studies also influenced his interest, such as the psychologist John C. Flanagan's American project "Talents", Girod's Geneva project, Illsley's Aberdeen study and the British cohort study from 1958. For a presentation of the background to the project, see also Janson 2000.

6. Today the concept "longitudinal" is most commonly used.

7. Svalastoga 1964.

8. Svalastoga 1964; statement in *Aftenposten*, evening edition, November 27, 1964.

9. The Kinsey reports were the result of a major study of sexual behaviour, Kinsey et al. 1948, 1953.

10. *Aftenposten*, Thursday morning, September 24, 1964, p. 16

11. *Aftenposten*, Friday morning, September 25, 1964, p. 2

12. *Aftenposten*, Monday morning, November 16, 1964, p. 2

13. *Aftenposten*, Wednesday morning, November 18, 1964, p. 2. Sverre Holm was the incumbent of Norway's first Chair in Sociology, established in 1949.

14. *Aftenposten*, Thursday morning, November 19, 1964, p. 2. Andenæs, like Svalastoga, had been interned at Grini during the war.

15. *Aftenposten*, Thursday morning, November 19, 1964, p. 2.

16. *Aftenposten*, Thursday morning, December 17, 1964, p. 19.

17. Svalastoga 1964, p. 4.

18. The description of the situation at the Department of Sociology is largely based on Gundelach 2001.

19. Gundelach 2001.

20. *Kurasje*, No. 1, 1970, p. 2.

21. Minutes of the Metropolitan meeting, Thursday January 30, 1975. Secretary: Tom Rishøj, Project Metropolitan archive.

22. Letter of May 5, 1994 from Erik Høgh to Carl-Gunnar Janson, Project Metropolitan archive.

23. Osler et al. 2004. Osler et al. 2006.

24. The Stockholm area was defined as the City of Stockholm and municipalities around Stockholm that met three criteria in 1960: more than 50 per cent of the population should be living in urban areas; less than one-third of the population should be working in agriculture and more than fifteen percent of the economically active population should be commuting to central Stockholm. This corresponded to the definition of "counties" employed in the American census.

25. Letter sent in March 1966 to school directors, head teachers and certain teachers in Greater Stockholm, signed by Ingvar Ohlsson, Director General of the Kungliga Statistiska Centralbyrån (subsequently Statistics Sweden), and Torgny Segerstedt, Professor and Chairman of the Swedish Council for Social Science Research.

26. News from the National Board of Education, 8/3/1966, Reference number 1816/66 P. Project Metropolitan archive.

27. Letter sent in March 1966 to school directors, head teachers and certain teachers, signed by Börje Svensson (Association of Teachers in Colleges and Departments of Education), Olle Anderberg (National Union of Teachers), Sören Carlson (National Association of Legal Guardians), Tore Ahlström (Association of School Principals and Directors of Education), Einar Kahls (Association of Specialist and Technical Teachers), Helmer Norman (Swedish Association for Remedial Teaching) and Martin Widén (Swedish Teachers' Union). Project Metropolitan archive.

28. These surveys had been conducted within the framework of the IS-project (Individual-statistics project) at the University of Gothenburg and the ETF project (Evaluation through Follow-up of Students) at the Stockholm Institute of Education, which were combined into a single research project at the University of Gothenburg entitled "Evaluation through Follow-up" (ETF) in 1990. The first data collection took place during the spring term of 1961 and included pupils born on the 5th, 15th and 25th of any month in 1948. At the time of this data collection, the majority of the approximately 12,000 participating pupils were in the sixth grade of elementary education. The school administrative data that were collected were then supplemented annually with additional data until 1969. In the spring term of 1966, a new wave of data collection was initiated in the same way, this time for pupils born on the 5th, 15th or 25th of any month in 1953. Project Metropolitan then coordinated its data collection with this survey. Information for approximately one-tenth of the cohort, or approximately 10,000 pupils, was then supplemented annually until 1974.

29. It is not possible to describe the entire questionnaire here, but the code books are available on the project's website: www.stockholmbirth-cohort.su.se.

30. The test focused on three areas, one verbal (opposites), one spatial (sheet folding) and one numerical (number series). These tests are still employed today in the project Evaluation through Follow-up (ETF) at the University of Gothenburg. Kjell Härnqvist (1921–2006) was a professor of education and educational psychology at the University of Gothenburg. He was Vice-Chancellor of the university for a while, and from 1981 was also a member of the Royal Swedish Academy of Sciences.

31. Instructions to Statistics Sweden's interviewers: Project Metropolitan 1968 P 0763 Instruction of LOKO, Project Metropolitan archive.

32. Carl-Gunnar Janson, handwritten document, 1986, Project Metropolitan archive.

33. Work report for Project Metropolitan 1967–69, p. 4, Project Metropolitan archive.

34. Janson 1970.

35. Swedish Police Authority.

36. Work report for Project Metropolitan, July 1, 1972–March 1, 1974, p. 4, Project Metropolitan archive.

37. Work report for Project Metropolitan, July 1, 1972–March 1, 1974, p. 5, Project Metropolitan archive.

38. Data Protection Authority, reference no. 785–74, decision dated June 21, 1976.

39. Data Protection Authority, reference no. 2035–75, decision dated November 19, 1975.

40. Data Protection Authority, reference no. 785–74, decision dated June 21, 1976.

41. The Living Conditions Survey (ULF) has been conducted by Statistics Sweden on the instruction of the Swedish Parliament since 1975. Since 2008, the survey has been integrated with EU-SILC (EU Statistics on Income and Living Conditions).

42. Kerstin Anér (1920–1991) was among other things a Doctor of Philosophy, a producer at Radio Sweden, a Member of Parliament for the Swedish Liberals and an Undersecretary of State at the Ministry of Education. In 1977, she co-authored the book *Du och datorn* (You and the Computer) with Jan Freese and Charles Gavatin.

43. *Svenska Dagbladet*, May 10, 1975. Once Anér had made this explicit reference to the Metropolitan Project, the project leadership created a system to further "prevent or obstruct the use of the project's data tapes by outsiders".

44. Freese 1976.

45. Freese 1976, p. 36.

46. SOU 2012:20.

47. It could however be argued that the combination of data from different existing registers does result in the production of new data. This new data does not however become more than the sum of its constituent parts.

48. Project Report 1976/1977, Project Metropolitan archive.

49. Stockholm University, Faculty of Social Sciences, 20–04-1977, reference no. 1603/77.

50. Data Protection Authority, Director General C. G. Källner 05-05-1977, reference no. 728–77

51. A decision whose implementation would subsequently be postponed.

52. Data Protection Authority, Director General C. G. Källner 05-05-1977, reference no. 728–77

53. Opening address at the conference of the Swedish Medical Research Council, Stockholm, November 11, 1976.

54. Data Protection Authority decision 02-03-1979, reference no. 1886–78.

55. Application to the Data Protection Authority 17-09-1981, Data Protection Authority's reference no. 1842–81.

56. Letter from the Data Protection Authority 16-10-1981, reference no. 1842–81

57. Including personal identity numbers.

58. Letter from the Department of Sociology 02-11-1981, Project Metropolitan archive.

59. Data Protection Authority, Decision 03-12-1981, reference no. 1842–81

60. Letter to the Data Protection Authority 07-12-1984; Data Protection Authority's reference no. 2782–84.

61. Application from the Department of Sociology 16-01-1985.

62. Data Protection Authority, Decision 04-03-1985, reference no. 2782–84.

63. Work report July 1, 1984-June 30, 1986, written by Pär Sparén, Project Metropolitan archive.

64. The Swedish National Archive 20-01-1986, reference no. 44-86-63.

65. The following authority members participated at the meeting: Jan Freese (Director General), Gunnar Hökmark (Conservative), Erna Möller (senior physician), Olle Nilsson (Editor-in-Chief), Åke Polstam (Centre Party), Per-Gunnar Vinge (Federation of Swedish Industries, former head of the Swedish Security Service), Lennart Nordström (substitute) (Swedish Agency for Public Management), Director Nils Rydén, Acting Director Gustaf Adolf Westman and Departmental Director Mats Björklund. Four authority members, the Social Democrats (SAP) Birgitta Frejhagen, Lars Hedfors and Kurt-Ove Johansson, and Kerstin Gustafsson (Legal Officer at the Swedish Confederation of Professional Employees - TCO) abstained from voting.

66. Qwerin 1987.

67. Qwerin 1987. An historical review of the issue of personal integrity protection in the public debate may be found in SOU 2007:22.

68. SOU 1987:31.

69. As early as April 29, 1966, *Dagens Nyheter* had reported, that the project had been awarded funding by the "Parliamentary Tercentenary Foundation", and in an editorial comment a few days later (May 2, 1966) the project was presented as an example of good research. The *Göteborgs-Posten* newspaper published a critical article on the project on September 29, 1975, under the headline: "Secret data on private lives collected on computers by students".

70. According to a new proposal for a *Biobank Act*, the individual has in certain instances, e.g. in cases relating to biological samples, the right to be "forgotten", i.e. to have samples retained in the biobank destroyed. But this right does not extend to data that have already been extracted from the biobank and saved in a data register established for research purposes. A new proposal for European legislation expresses a desire to extend individuals' "rights to be forgotten", but exempts research from these rules, and states that if data are essential for research, then they may be retained without consent. The "right to be forgotten" is thus on the way to gaining ground, both in Sweden and elsewhere.

71. In practice, the Centre for Epidemiology at the National Board of Health and Welfare complied with individuals' requests to be removed

from their registers in the 1990s, which led to a small number of data entries being removed, perhaps ten of several hundred thousand. These requests were granted in order to avoid provoking protests and a subsequent debate.

72. If anything, *Aftonbladet* had an even worse memory than *Dagens Nyheter*, since on December 26, 1984, the paper had published an article stating that "'It's true', Swedish researchers find the same results among children in Stockholm," in which Peter L. Martens presented his research on the children of divorced parents. The results showed, in line with findings from American research, that it was a "myth that the children of divorced parents have a tougher time in school than children whose parents are living together."

73. *Expressen* had also previously published positive coverage of the project. On September 20, 1979, the paper had published an article under the headline "He is following 15,000 youths for 20 years – The project that is the work of a lifetime." The reporter Margareta Rost had met Carl-Gunnar Janson: "Almost 20 years ago, he started working with Project Metropolitan. The project is about youths in Stockholm and what happens to them from birth to the age of thirty."

74. *Dagens Nyheter* March 6, 1986. The signatories comprised Sune Bergström, Professor Emeritus and Nobel prize winner in medicine, Torgny T:son Segerstedt, Professor Emeritus and former university vice-chancellor, Martin Holmdahl, Vice-Chancellor of Uppsala University, Kjell Härnquist, Vice-Chancellor of Gothenburg University, Lars Beckman, Vice-Chancellor of Umeå University, Sven Erlander, Vice-Chancellor of Linköping University, Staffan Helmfrid, Vice-Chancellor of Stockholm University, Håkan Westling, Vice-Chancellor of Lund University, Bengt Samuelsson, Vice-Chancellor of the Karolinska Institute and Nobel prize winner in medicine and Sten Johansson, Director General of Statistics Sweden.

75. Waldenström 2010, internet.

76. The minutes of the meeting, which took place on February 26, 1986, were taken by Marja Walldén. Those present were Nils Rydén, G.A. Westman and Mats Björklund from the Data Protection Authority, and Ann-Marie Janson and Marja Walldén from the project. The minutes

were sent to the Data Protection Authority, with a request for confirmation that they constituted a correct reflection of what was said. I have found no such confirmation in the Project Metropolitan Archive.

77. Data Protection Authority 24-04-1986, reference no. 977–86.

78. Message appended to Data Protection Authority minutes 21-05-1986, no. 3.

79. Supreme Commander, operational command, 21-05-1986, Säk 903:61977.

80. Ordinance (1953:716).

81. Decision of the Chancellor of Justice 27-10-1986, reference no. 1729-86-20.

82. At the beginning of the 2000s, Professor Christopher Gillberg of Gothenburg University refused to make his data available to two other researchers. Instead he destroyed the data set, and for doing so was sentenced to a fine. He succeeded in bringing his case before the European Court of Human Rights, but to no effect. Gillberg allowed his medical ethics to take precedence over the law. One important difference, however, was that Gillberg had not been required to anonymise his data set. https://en.wikipedia.org/wiki/Christopher_Gillberg

83. *Dagens Nyheter* March 13, 1986. Anna Christensen was Professor of Civil Law at Lund University. https://en.wikipedia.org/wiki/Anna_Christensen

84. https://en.wikipedia.org/wiki/Folkhemmet https://www.britannica.com/topic/peoples-home

85. *Aftonbladet* March 14, 1987.

86. *Aftonbladet* December 4, 1987.

87. Olsson 2004.

88. Government decision 21-05-1987, reference no. Ju 3533-86, in Olsson 2004, p. 38.

89. Olsson 1991; Olsson 2004, p. 38.

90. Olsson 1991, p. 39, reference to reference no. 306/91.

91. Olsson 1991, p. 39, reference to Ministry of Justice, reference no. 93–3260.

92. In September 2008, for example, Billy Rimgård published the blog "Beneath a steel sky", with the headline "The file on my father – perspectives on surveillance", on his father's excerpt from the Project Metropolitan register, http://www.monotoni.se/bass/2008/09/akten-om-min-pappa/.

93. The Centre for Health Equity Studies (CHESS) is a collaboration between the Karolinska Institute and Stockholm University. In 2018 Centre for Health Equity Studies (CHESS) merged with Centre for Social Research on Alcohol and Drugs (SoRAD) creating the Department of Public Health Sciences at Stockholm University. https://www.su.se/publichealth/english/about-us/history

94. The Karolinska Institute Regional Research Ethics Review Board. Decision 2003-12-01, case 739, reference no. 03–629. At the time, the project had the working title BAST, but was then renamed The Stockholm Birth Cohort. Following two additional applications, the Regional Research Ethics Review Board in Stockholm gave its approval for the project's data and follow-up period to be extended (reference nos. 04–628T and 2008/1991–32).

95. The Swedish term "avidentifierad" ("de-identified") was previously used, but is today only applied to data that cannot be linked to an individual either in theory or practice. The term anonymised refers to data that can be linked to individuals with the help of a key or by means of reverse identification. The essential factor is that such a linking process is theoretically possible, irrespective of the fact that it is in reality also prohibited.

96. The procedure has been described in more detail in two articles: Stenberg & Vågerö 2006; Stenberg et al. 2007.

97. The HSIA datatbase was discontinued by Statistics of Sweden in 2018 thereby making it impossible to update Stockolm Birth Cohort. The matching procedure is now repeated in the project RELINK. See chapter Project Metropolitan and Future of Social Research. https://www.su.se/publichealth/english/research/research-areas/reproduction-of-inequality-through-linked-lives-relink .

98. The number of individuals in the study had declined, since over 1,000 had died.

99. On June 13, 2008 *Dagens Nyheter* published a long article on the updating of Project Metropolitan under the headline "Controversial register given new life".

100. One might object that people's right to self-determination must be respected in relation to information they have provided. People may feel aggrieved about having their information used in research that they themselves do not wish to participate in, irrespective of whether this research involves any risks. Once the data had been anonymised, however, they had the same status as other forms of register data. Much of today's medical and social research is based on data of this kind, with the benefits being viewed as outweighing any risks involved.

101. Personal Data Act (Personuppgiftslagen 1998:204); Directive 95/46/EC of the European Parliament and of the Council of the European Union of October 24, 1995 on the protection of individuals with regard to the processing of personal data and on the free movement of such data.

102. Assessment of applications for grants for large databases (2007) and the Data Infrastructure Committee's (DISC) proposals for funding KFI/DISC 23-01-2008, Memorandum, Swedish Research Council (Vetenskapsrådet); reference no. 825-2007-7487.

103. Swedish Data Protection Authority, reference no. 1776–2010.

104. Regional Research Ethics Review Board in Stockholm, reference no. 2011/1907-31/5.

105. See, for example, the Data Protection Authority's decision of April 18, 2012, reference no. 811–2011, p. 3: "data sets which include so many variables relating to registered individuals mean that it is possible to identify those registered by means of so-called reverse identification."

106. The Official Statistics Act states that: "Data from the official statistics may not be combined with other information in order to ascertain an individual's identity." Official Statistics Act, SFS 2001:99, 6 §.

107. Sverige nu 2012, questionnaire from SIFO, May-August 2012.

108. LIF policy 2010:1, Rules for non-intervention studies and financial support for quality registers, October 2010.

109. The research ethics review process is conducted by six Regional Ethical Review Boards, which in turn have different boards for different research areas, with social science research being included in the "other research" category. The regional boards are governed by a Central Research Ethics Review Board, which formulates guidelines and to which decisions made by the regional boards may be appealed.

110. Every now and then, governmental inquiries and public sector agencies attempt to define what constitutes research. A recent example can be found in the work of the governmental inquiry published in SOU 2012:20, which states that "Research seeks new knowledge, whereas development work employs knowledge to develop new or improved products, systems, processes or methods. The difference between the two may be described such that research is focused on discovery, whereas development work is focused on invention."

111. Application to the Data Protection Authority 17-09-1981, Data Protection Authority reference no. 1842–81.

112. According to the government bill 2007/08:44 *Certain issues regarding research ethics review etc.*, the points of departure for the research ethics review process have largely been drawn from the European Council's Convention on Human Rights and Biomedicine (DIR/JUR [96] 14).

113. Government bill 2002/03:50, p. 105.

114. Dahlquist 2011.

115. The Finnish alcohol researcher Klaus Mäkelä makes the same observation in a critical study of the Swedish Ethical Review Act: Mäkelä 2008.

116. Conditions of use for the MedMera store card, Point 5.

117. All publications that include Metropolitan/Stockholm Birth Cohort Data can be found on the homepage of the project: https://www.stockholmbirthcohort.su.se/research/publications.

118. The Million Programme (Swedish: Miljonprogrammet) is the common name for an ambitious public housing programme implemented in Sweden between 1965 and 1974 by the governing Swedish Social Democratic Party to make sure everyone could have a home at a reasonable price. The aim was to construct a million new dwellings during the programme's ten-year period. At the time, the Million Programme was

the most ambitious building programme in the world to build one million new homes in a nation with a population of eight million. At the same time, a large proportion of the older unmodernised housing stock was demolished. https://en.wikipedia.org/wiki/Million_Programme.

119. A new partner's children in changing family constellations/relationships.

120. Mums who spend time in cafés drinking café lattes in the company of their small children.

121. Payed days home from work due to child care.

122. It is of course impossible to mention every publication based on the Project Metropolitan in a book such as this one. My primary focus has been on the areas in those fields where most studies have been performed. The data set is also so rich that new areas will develop and expand in the future. Examples of recent publications which have not been included in this overview is a study by Carl Bonander and Carolina Jernbro (2017) about injury risks among children with cognitive impairment as well as Kassman's (2017) investigation of the association between scouting in childhood and income later in life.

123. The presentation of research results is not as exact as in the original scientific texts. Interested readers may themselves look up the original sources.

124. My calculation.

125. *Jordemodern*, March 1955, p. 138.

126. This also includes some who were born in private hospitals and in an ambulance. The mean term of pregnancy for these children was much shorter than normal, and we may therefore assume that these were in large part unplanned births.

127. In 1930, 76 percent of children were born at home. Socialstyrelsen SOSF 1990:22.

128. Since to be included in the Metropolitan data, the children had to have been alive in 1963, it is likely that a larger number of children were born in the lower social classes, where the child mortality rate was higher.

129. Medical Board (Medicinalstyrelsen): Rapport överinspektion av förlossningsanstalterna i Stockholms län, *Jordemodern*, January 1955, pp. 31–36.

130. Difficulty producing milk.

131. Jordemodern. October 1954, p. 408.

132. Waldegren (ed.) 1956, p. 2544.

133. In an article entitled "Breastfeeding regimes during the new-born period" published in *Jordemodern* in February 1955, p. 52, the doctor Gert von Sydow describes how dreary the process of delivering babies to their mothers for breastfeeding could be at the beginning of the 1950s: "It is perhaps sufficient, as an illustration, to conjure up the dreary image of the trolley of packages, lined up like sardines in a crate, that is still wheeled around the corridors of many Swedish hospitals, and which stops at door after door at predetermined times, using numbered tags to distribute children to each mother, for feeding."

134. Embring 1955, p. 43.

135. Embring 1955, p. 43.

136. Hyrenius & Zackrisson 1955.

137. The original was published in 1946, and has since been translated into 39 languages and has sold 50 million copies around the world.

138. Spock 1946, p. 3.

139. Children's Village for troubled children.

140. Czerny & Keller 1906.

141. Bratt 1946, p. 58. The author was the founder of the Erica Foundation, https://www.studyinstockholm.se/university/erica-foundation/.

142. Herlitz 1945a, p. 132.

143. Smedberg1945, p. 81.

144. Hamrin-Thorell 1945, p. 150.

145. Herlitz 1945b, p. 253.

146. Martens 1976; 1981.

147. Martens 1981.

148. Unless otherwise stated, this section is based on Nordlöf 2001.

149. Board of Directors, Allmänna barnhuset (General Children's Home) 1969.

150. Today women can have children with the help of anonymous sperm donors and surrogate mothers. At the same time, there is substantial interest in genealogical research, and television shows follow celebrities as they seek to uncover their roots. Here there is a contradiction between a need among adults to become parents, and children's interest in knowing their backgrounds, which has yet to be seriously discussed.

151. Board of Directors, Allmänna barnhuset 1955, p. 39, pp. 61–62.

152. Board of Directors, Allmänna barnhuset 1955, p. 62.

153. Board of Directors, Allmänna barnhuset 1955, p. 39.

154. Board of Directors, Allmänna barnhuset 1955, p. 64.

155. Board of Directors, Allmänna barnhuset 1955, p. 65.

156. Vinnerljung 1996.

157. Vinnerljung et al. 2006; Vinnerljung & Sallnäs 2008.

158. SOU 2011:9; SOU 2011:61.

159. Arvidsson 2016.

160. Lindquist & Santavirta 2012; 2014.

161. When they were between 19 and 31 years old.

162. Brännström et al. 2017a.

163. Brännström et al. 2017b.

164. Gao et al. 2017.

165. Allmost all areas mentioned in this sections have English descriptions in Wikipedia.

166. One million new homes were built between 1965 and 1974: https://en.wikipedia.org/wiki/Million_Programme

167. Wikström 1989.

168. Timms 1989.

169. Brännström 2004; Lindahl 2011.

170. The most theoretical study program was called the "upper-secondary preparatory" program; then there were programs with a narrower focus: humanist, technical, socio-economic and aesthetic. Finally, there were programs that could not lead to upper-secondary studies: general practical, technical-practical, commercial, and household technology. https://en.wikipedia.org/wiki/Education_in_Sweden

171. Koskinen & Stenberg 2012.

172. The Swedish Abstaining Motorists´ Association.

173. Bergryd et al. 1988. Much of the information presented on education is drawn from this report.

174. Axelsson1994.

175. Almquist 2013.

176. von Otter & Stenberg 2012.

177. It was unusual for the parental generation to have graduated from upper-secondary school. Families in which one of the parents had completed upper-secondary school were counted as having a high level of education, and families in which neither parent had graduated from upper-secondary school were categorised as having a low level of education.

178. Grades varied from 1 to 5. The explicit intent of policy-makers was to have normally distributed grades at the national level, with a mean value of 3.

179. Von Otter 2014.

180. Renshon 1975.

181. Galton 1874.

182. Walldén 1982, 1988, 1990, 1992, 1994.

183. Professor Marja Walldén, who had conducted the research, stated that she believed this might be the explanation in an interview published by the Swedish newspaper *Svenska Dagbladet* on October 13, 2004.

184. Björklund et al. 2010.

185. Stütz 1985.

186. Grund 2014.

187. Almquist 2009.

188. Almquist 2011.

189. Modin et al. 2011.

190. Almquist & Östlund 2012.

191. Almquist & Brännström 2013; Almquist & Brännström 2014.

192. They were inspired by Zoot Suits, https://en.wikipedia.org/wiki/Zoot_suit

193. https://en.wikipedia.org/wiki/Progg

194. "De kallar oss mods", https://en.wikipedia.org/wiki/They_Call_Us_Misfits

195. This section is based on Alm & Nilsson 2008; Alm & Nilsson 2011.

196. The Project Metropolitan data on drug abuse come from three different sources: the Social Services Register, the Hospital Discharge Register and the so-called needle-mark study conducted at the Kronoberg remand centre in Stockholm. These data cover the period until 1983.

197. https://en.wikipedia.org/wiki/Raggare

198. Cerha 1973, p. 63.

199. Frändén 1977, 1979.

200. Examples of these organisations include the Communist League Marxist-Leninists (KFML), the Marxist-Leninist League for the Formation of the Communist Party of Sweden (MLK), the League of Revolutionary Marxists (RMF) and the Communist League (FK).

201. The spatial cognition test involved pictures of figures that were to be folded. The response alternatives were images of the results of different folding options.

202. Halleröd 2011.

203. Golsteyn et al. 2013.

204. Åkerlund et al. 2014, 2016.

205. Alm 2011a.

206. Carroll & Eriksson 2005; Alm 2005; Alm 2006; Björklund et al. 2010.

207. Alm 2005.

208. Ambjörnsson 1996.

209. Ambjörnsson 2001.

210. Alm 2006.

211. Alm 2011b.

212. Richardson 1977.

213. Alm & Bäckman 2014.

214. Alm 2015b.

215. Wilkinson & Picket 2009.

216. Svensson 2000.

217. Unless otherwise stated, the following description is primarily based on Nilsson & Estrada 2009.

218. Torstensson 1987. The majority of this section is based on this study.

219. Nilsson & Estrada 2009.

220. Alm 2015a.

221. Nilsson et al. 2014, Bäckman et al. 2017.

222. Lindström 1995.

223. Hodgins & Janson 2002.

224. Since offenders who had been sentenced to forensic psychiatric care were not included, these figures represent an underestimate of the actual number of men diagnosed with serious psychiatric disorders. If these are included, the number of individuals suffering from mental illness increases by six percent. Nor is there any data available on those with mental health problems who had not been admitted to hospital.

225. Nilsson & Estrada 2011.

226. Hjalmarsson & Lindquist 2012.

227. These risks were actually expressed in terms of odds and odds ratios. For the boys, the odds were 2.06 times as high as for those whose fathers had not committed offences. For the girls, the odds were 2.66 times as high.

228. af Klinteberg et al. 2011.

229. The measure is known as the Population Attributional Fraction (PAF).

230. Vägverket 2008.

231. Hjalmarsson & Lindquist 2010.

232. Andersson 1991.

233. The labels applied to the assistance provided to those living in the worst economic conditions have also shifted over time. For a long period in the 20th century, it was referred to as poverty assistance, then social assistance, social welfare benefit, financial assistance, and today: income support. https://en.wikipedia.org/wiki/Welfare_in_Sweden

234. Lewis 1968.

235. Elder 1998.

236. Dannefer 2003; DiPrete & Eirich 2006.

237. Laub & Sampson 2003.

238. Bäckman & Nilsson 2007.

239. Bäckman & Nilsson 2011.

240. Those who had incomes from employment amounting to more than 3.5 so-called Price-Base Amounts, for at least two of three consecutive years.

241. Nilsson et al. 2013.

242. Bergman & Trost 2006.

243. Almquist 2016.

244. Almquist & Brännström 2018.

245. Torssander & Almquist 2017.

246. Stenberg 2000.

247. Murray 1984.

248. Rank & Cheng 1995.

249. Rojas & Stenberg 2010.

250. The study data included a larger number than this, but a number of cases had to be excluded as a result of missing data on other variables.

251. Rojas 2013.

252. Rojas 2018.

253. Rojas 2012.

254. Wilkinson & Pickett 2009.

255. Ahrén et al. 2011.

256. One example of this can be seen in a study published in the broadsheet *Dagens Nyheter* on September 18, 2012. The journalists had examined in detail every refugee child who had arrived in Sweden unaccompanied by an adult since 2006, a total of 316 children. How had their situation developed in the fields of education, debt, income, crime and marriage? In addition, four of the individuals were interviewed, and their pictures published. The same study could very well have been conducted by a social scientist, but not without the approval of a research ethics review board. It is also likely that a social scientist would not have been given permission to publish pictures and the names of those interviewed.

257. Johansson 1979.

258. The journalist Anders R. Olsson summarised this debate as follows: "There was a centre-right criticism of this trend whose undertones focused on a risk of it becoming totalitarian – the implication was 'imagine if Stalin had possessed a computer; imagine how much worse he would have been.' And from the left there was loud criticism from the Marxist perspective, which argued that the state apparatus is primarily a tool used by the elite or high finance to discipline the masses, to keep the people in order. From this perspective, of course, a computerised, omniscient state was also something dangerous. The criticism came from two directions, and the Social Democrats found themselves in the middle, and probably tried to argue that [the criticisms] merely represented insidious attacks on our welfare society." Klein 2008, p. 13.

References

Ahrén, Jennie C., Flaminia F. Chiesa, Britt af Klinteberg, & Ilona Koupil (2011) "Psychosocial determinants and family background in anorexia nervosa. Results from the Stockholm Birth Cohort Study", *International Journal of Eating Disorders* 45 (3): 362–369.

Åkerlund, David, Bart H. H. Golsteyn, Hans Grönqvist & Lena Lindahl (2014) Time Preferences and Criminal Behavior. Bonn: IZA DP No. 8168.

Åkerlund, David, Bart H. H. Golsteyn, Hans Grönqvist & Lena Lindahl (2016) "Time discounting and criminal behavior", Proceedings of the National Academy of Sciences of the United States of America PNAS 113(22): 6160–6165.

Alm, Susanne (2005) "Born to run? The importance of cultural and social capital for upward mobility". In: Carroll, Eero & Lena Eriksson (eds.) *Welfare politics cross-examined. Eclecticist analytical perspectives on Sweden and the developed world, from 1880s to the 2000s.* Amsterdam: Aksant.

Alm, Susanne (2006) *Drivkrafter bakom klassresan – kvantitativa data i fallstudiebelysning [Driving forces behind class mobility – Quantitative data in case studies].* Stockholm: Institute for Futures Studies, Working Report 2006:1.

Alm, Susanne (2011a) "The worried, the competitive and the indifferent – Approaches to the future in youth, their roots and outcomes in adult life", *Futures* 43: 552–562.

Alm, Susanne (2011b) "Downward social mobility across generations: The role of parental mobility and education", *Sociological Research Online* 13 (3) 2.

Alm, Susanne (2015a) "Hur gick det för 1960- och 1970-talets svenska narkotikamissbrukare?" [What happened to the Swedish drug abusers of the 1960's and 1970's?], *Nordic Studies on Alcohol and Drugs* 32: 109–132.

Alm, Susanne (2015b) "Dreams meeting reality? A gendered perspective on the relationship between occupational preferences in early adolescence and actual occupation in adulthood", *Journal of Youth Studies* 18 (8): 1077–1095.

Alm, Susanne & Anders Nilsson (2008) "Samhällets olycksbarn, kreatörer eller Svensson? Modsens framtid i backspegeln" [Social outcasts, free creators or mainstream citizens? The future of the Swedish mods in retrospect], *Socialvetenskaplig tidskrift* 1: 20–36.

Alm, Susanne & Anders Nilsson (2011) "Cause for concern or moral panic? The prospects of the Swedish mods in retrospect", *Journal of Youth Studies* 14 (7): 777–793.

Alm, Susanne & Olof Bäckman (2014) "Openness to Gender Atypical Occupations in Youth: Do Peer Groups and School Classes Matter?", *Journal of Early Adolescence* 35 (79): 97–119.

Almquist, Ylva (2009) "Peer status in school and adult disease risk: a 30-year follow-up study of disease-specific morbidity in a Stockholm cohort", *Journal of Epidemiology and Community Health* 63 (12): 1028–1034.

Almquist, Ylva (2011) "Social isolation in the classroom and adult health: A longitudinal study of a 1953 cohort", *Advances in Life Course Research* 16: 1–12.

Almquist, Ylva (2013) "School performance as a precursor of adult health: Exploring associations to disease-specific hospital care and their possible explanations", *Scandinavian Journal of Public Health* 41(1): 81–91.

Almquist, Ylva B. (2016) "Childhood origins and adult destinations: The impact of childhood living conditions on coexisting disadvantages in adulthood", *International Journal of Social Welfare* 25: 176–186.

Almquist, Ylva B. & Viveca Östberg (2012) "Social relationships and subsequent health-related behaviours: linkages between adolescent peer status and levels of adult smoking in a Stockholm cohort", *Addiction* 108: 629–637.

Almquist, Ylva B. & Lars Brännström (2013) "Childhood friendship and the clustering of adverse circumstances in adulthood – a longitudinal study of a Stockholm cohort", *Longitudinal and Life Course Studies* 4(3): 180–195.

Almquist, Ylva B. & Lars Brännström (2014) "Childhood peer status and the clustering of social, economic, and health-related circumstances in adulthood", *Social Science & Medicine* 105: 67–75.

Almquist, Ylva B. & Lars Brännström (2018) "Childhood adversity and trajectories of disadvantage through adulthood: Findings from the Stockholm Birth Cohort Study", *Social Indicators Research* 136 (1): 225–245.

Almquist, Ylva B., Josephine Jackisch, Hilma Forsman, Karl Gauffin, Bo Vinnerljung, Anders Hjern, & Lars Brännström (2018) "A decade lost: Does educational success mitigate the increased risks of premature death among children with experience of out-of-home care?", *Journal of Epidemiology and Community Health*, DOI: https://doi.org/10.1136/jech-2018-210487.

Ambjörnsson, Ronny (1996) Mitt förnamn är Ronny [My name is Ronny]. Stockholm: Bonniers Alba Essä.

Ambjörnsson, Ronny (2001) Den skötsamme arbetaren [The conscientious worker]. Stockholm: Carlssons.

Andersson, Jan (1991) *Kriminella karriärer och påföljdsval* [Criminal careers and choice between forms of penalty]. Stockholm University: Department of Sociology, Project Metropolitan Research Report No 35.

Arvidsson, Malin (2016) *Att ersätta det oersättliga: statlig gottgörelse för ofrivillig sterilisering och vanvård av omhändertagna barn [Compensation of irretrievable matters: State redress for involuntary sterilization and abuse in out-of-home care for children]*. Örebro: Örebro University.

Axelsson, Christina (1994) *Educational selection by gender and class origin*. In: Gusrafsson, Lars (ed.) *Studies of a Stockholm Cohort*. Stockholm University: Department of Sociology, Project Metropolitan Research Report No 39.

Bergman, Lars R. & Kari Trost (2006) "The person-oriented versus the variable-oriented approach: Are they complementary, opposite, or exploring different worlds?", *Merrill-Palmer Quaterly*, 52(3): 601–632.

Bergryd, Ulla, Gunnar Boalt & Carl-Gunnar Janson (1988) *Selection to higher education, a comparison between two Stockholm cohorts* in *Research Notes*. Stockholm University: Department of Sociology, Project Metropolitan Research Report No 25.

Billy Rimgårds blogg "Beneath a steel sky" under rubriken "Akten om min pappa – perspektiv på övervakning": http://www.monotoni.se/bass/2008/09/akten-om-min-pappa/ July 2018.

Björklund, Anders, Lena Lindahl & Matthew J Lindquist (2010) "What more than parental income, education and occupation? An exploration of what Swedish siblings get from their parents", *The B.E. Journal of Economic Analysis & Policy* 10 (1): 1–38.

Bonander, Carl & Carolina Jernbro (2017) "Does gender moderate the association between intellectual ability and accidential injuries? Evidence from the 1953 Stockholm Birth Cohort study", *Accident Analysis and Prevention* 106: 109–114.

Bratt, Hanna (1946) *Där vetenskap och kärleksbud mötas i uppfostringsfrågor [Where science and love meet in child rearing]*. Stockholm: Kooperativa Förbundet.

Brännström, Lars (2004) "Poor places, poor prospects? Counterfactual models of neighborhood effects in social exclusion in Stockholm, Sweden", *Urban Studies* 41 (13): 2515–2537.

Brännström, Lars, Hilma Forsman, Bo Vinnerljung och Ylva B. Almquist (2017a) "The truly disadvantaged? Midlife outcome dynamics of individuals with experiences of out-of-home care", *Child Abuse & Neglect* 67: 408–418.

Brännström, Lars, Bo Vinnerljung, Hilma Forsman & Ylva B. Almquist (2017b) "Children placed in out-of-home care as midlife adults: Are they still disadvantaged or have they caught up with their peers?". *Child Maltreatment* 22 (3): 205–214.

Bäckman, Olof & Anders Nilsson (2007) *Childhood poverty and labour market exclusion. Findings from a Swedish birth cohort*. Stockholm: Institute for Futures Studies, Working Report no13.

Bäckman, Olof & Anders Nilsson (2011) "Social exkludering i ett livsförloppsperspektiv" [Social exclusion in a life course perspective]. In: Alm, Susanne, Olof Bäckman, Anna Gavanas & Anders Nilsson (eds.)

Utanförskap [Exclusion]. Stockholm: Dialogos förlag, Institute for Futures Studies.

Bäckman, Olof, Felipe Estrada and Anders Nilsson (2017) "Substance abuse, crime and the life course". In: A.A.J. Blokland and V.R. van der Geest (eds.), *Routledge international handbook of life-course criminology*. Abingdon Oxon: Routledge. (Release: March 2017)

Carroll, Eero & Lena Eriksson (eds.) (2005) *Welfare politics cross-examined. Eclecticist analytical perspectives on Sweden and the developed world, from 1880s to the 2000s*. Amsterdam: Aksant.

Cerha, Jarko (1973) *Masskommunikation med de jämlika [Mass communication with the equal]*. Stockholm: Almqvist & Wiksell.

Czerny, Adalbert & Arthur Keller (1906) *Des Kindes, Ernährung, Ernährungsstörungen und Ernährungsterapi: ein Handbuch für Ärzte [Children, nutrition, nutrition disturbance, and nutrition therapy]*. Leipzig und Wien: Franz Deuticke.

Dahlquist, Gisela (2011) "Hippokrates i vår tid" [Hippokrates in our time], *Läkartidningen* 47 (108): 2438–2440.

Dannefer, Dale (2003) "Cumulative advantage/disadvantage and the life course: Cross-fertilizing age and social science theory", *Journal of Gerontology: Social Sciences* 58b: S327–337.

DiPrete, Thomas A. & Gregory M. Eirich (2006) "Cumulative advantage as a mechanism for inequality: A review of theoretical and empirical developments", *Annual Review of Sociology* 32: 271–297.

Direktionen över Allmänna barnhuset [Board of Directors, General Children's Home] (1955) *Adoption: en vägledning för myndigheter, tjänstemän och förtroendemän, vilka ha att syssla med frågor angående adoption [Adoption: A guide for authorities, civil servants and trustees]*. Stockholm: Allmänna barnhuset i samråd med Medicinalstyrelsen och Socialstyrelsen.

Direktionen över Allmänna barnhuset [Board of Directors, General Children's Home] (1969) *Adoption: en vägledning för myndigheter, tjänstemän och förtroendemän, vilka har att syssla med frågor rörande adoption [Adoption: A guide for authorities, civil servants and trustees responsible for adoptions]*. Stockholm: Allmänna barnhuset.

Giele, Janet Z. & Glen H. Elder (eds.) (1998) *Methods of life course research: qualitative and quantitative approaches.* Thousand Oaks, California; London UK: SAGE.

Elofsson, Åke (1945) "Om arv och hemmiljö" [About heredity and home environment]. In: Siwe, Sture & Folke Borg (eds.) *Allt om barn [All about children].* Malmö: Richters förlag.

Embring, Margareta (1955) *Mamma-Pappa-Barn [Mom-Dad-Child].* Stockholm: Wahlström & Widstrand.

Freese, Jan (1976) *Data och livskvalitet – Om dataregister och deras användning [Data and quality of life – About data bases and their use].* Stockholm: Liber Förlag.

Freese, Jan, together with Kerstin Anér & Charles Gavatin (1977) *Du och datorn [You and the Computer].* Stockholm: Forum.

Freese, Jan (1987) *Den maktfullkomliga oförmågan [The high-handed inability].* Stockholm: Wahlström & Widstrand.

Fridell, Folke (1955) *Bjälken i ditt öga [The beam in your eye].* Stockholm: LT.

Fränden, Olof (1977) *Who where the young leftists?* Stockholm University: Department of Sociology, Project Metropolitan Research Report No 8.

Fränden, Olof (1979) *Further notes on young leftists.* Stockholm University: Department of Sociology, Project Metropolitan Research Report No 11.

Galton, Francis (1874) *English men of science: Their nature and culture.* London: Macmillan.

Gao, Menghan, Lars Brännström, Ylva B. Almquist (2017) "Exposure to out-of-home care in childhood and adult all-cause mortality: a cohort study", *International Journal of Epidemiology* 46: 1010–1017.

Golsteyn, Bart H. H., Hans Grönqvist & Lena Lindahl (2013) "Adolescent time preferences predict lifetime outcomes", *The Economic Journal* 124: F739-F761.

Grund, Thomas (2014) "Network size and network homophily: Same-sex friendships in 595 Scandinavian schools" in Manzo, Gianluca (eds.) *Analytical Sociology: Actions and Networks*, WileyBlackwell: Hoboken, NJ.

Gundelach, Peter (2001)"1980 og årene efter: Undergang og genopstandelse" [1980 and following years: Destruction and resurrection] postscript in Wolf, Preben *Sociologi, Københavns universitet 1479-1979, bind Vi.2 [Sociology. University of Copenhagen 1479-1979, vol 2]*. Copenhagen: Københavns universitet.

Halleröd, Björn (2011) "What do children know about their futures: Do children's expectations predict outcomes in middle age?", *Social Forces* 90 (1): 65–84.

Hamrin-Thorell, Ruth (1945) "Spädbarnets skötsel" [The baby's care]. In: Hamrin-Thorell, Ruth (eds.) *Föräldrar och barn, en handbok för unga föräldrar [Parents and children, a handbook for young parents]*. Stockholm: Lars Hökerbergs bokförlag.

Herlitz, Gillis (1945a) "Hygien och vård under förskoleåldern" [Hygiene and Care during the Pre-school years]. In: Siwe, Sture & Folke Borg (eds.) *Allt om barn [All about children]*. Malmö: Richters förlag.

Herlitz, Gillis (1945b) "Några vanliga ovanor hos barn" [Some common bad habits in children]. In: Hamrin-Thorell, Ruth (eds.) *Föräldrar och barn, en handbok för unga föräldrar [Parents and children, a handbook for young parents]*. Stockholm: Lars Hökerbergs bokförlag.

Hjalmarsson, Randi & Matthew J. Lindquist (2010) "Driving under the influence of our fathers", *The B.E. Journal of Economic Analysis & Policy* 10 (1): 1–15.

Hjalmarsson, Randi & Matthew J. Lindquist (2012) "Like godfather, like son: Exploring the intergenerational nature of crime", *Journal of Human Resources* 47 (2): 550–582.

Hodgins, Sheilagh & Carl-Gunnar Janson (2002) *Criminality and violence among the mentally disordered. The Stockholm Metropolitan Project*. Cambridge: Cambridge University Press.

Hyrenius, Hannes & Uno Zackrisson (1955) *Undersökningar rörande barn i ofullständiga familjer: 1. utom äktenskap födda barn i Göteborg 1928-1954 [Investigations about Children in Incomplete Families: 1. Illegitimate childen born in Gothenburg 1928-1954]*. Stockholm:

Almqvist & Wicksell, Skriftserie/Statistiska institutionen, Göteborgs universitet, 0072–5110, 2.

Janson, Carl-Gunnar (1970) "Juvenile delinquency in Sweden", *Youth & Society* 2 (2): 207–231.

Janson, Carl-Gunnar (ed.) (2000) *Seven Swedish longitudinal studies in the behavioral sciences*. Stockholm: Forskningsrådsnämnden, 2000:8.

Johansson, Sten (1979) *Mot en teori för social rapportering [Towards a theory on social report]*. Stockholm: Swedish Institute for Social Research.

Kälvesten, Anna-Lisa (1956) "Spädbarnets sociologi" [The sociology of the baby], *Tiden* 6: 357–366.

Kassman, Anders (2017) "One of all the others – a life course study of scouts, social capital, and stratification in the Swedish 'Folkhem'", *Journal of Civil Society* 13 (1): 71–89.

Kinsey, Alfred C., Wardell B. Pomeroy & Clyde E. Martin (1948) *Sexual behavior in the human male*. Philadelphia: Saunders.

Kinsey, Alfred C., Wardell B. Pomeroy, Clyde E. Martin & Paul H. Gerhard (1953) *Sexual behavior in the human female*. Philadelphia: Saunders.

Klein, Kajsa (ed.) (2008) *Integritetsdebatten åren kring 1984 - Transkript av ett vittnesseminarium vid Tekniska museet i Stockholm den 30 november 2007 [The debate about personal integrity during the years around 1984 – Transcript from a witness seminar at the national museum of science and technology in Stockholm November 30, 2007]*. Stockholm: KTH the Royal Institute of Technology.

af Klinteberg, Britt, Ylva Almquist, Ulla Beijer & Per-Anders Rydelius (2011) "Family psychosocial characteristics influencing criminal behaviour and mortality – possible mediating factors: a longitudinal study of male and female subjects in the Stockholm Birth Cohort", *BMC Public Health* 11 (756): 1–14.

Kommittédirektiv [Government Commitee Directive] 2013:8. Förutsättningar för registerbaserad forskning [Preconditions for registry based research].

Koskinen, Johan & Sten-Åke Stenberg (2012) "Bayesian analysis of multilevel probit models for data with friendship dependencies", *Journal of Educational and Behavioral Statistics* 37 (2): 203–230.

Läkemedelsindustriföreningens Service AB (LIF) [The Research-Based Pharmaceutical Industry Inc. (LIF)] LIF policy 2010:1, Regler för icke-interventionsstudier och ekonomiskt stöd till kvalitetsregister, oktober 2010 [Rules for non-intervention studies and economic support to quality registers].

Laub, John H. & Robert J. Sampson (2003) *Shared beginnings, divergent lives. Delinquent boys at age 70.* Cambridge (MA): Harvard University Press.

Lewis, Oscar (1968) *La vida, a Puerto Rican family in the culture of poverty: San Juan and New York.* London: Panter Books.

Lindahl, Lena (2011) "A comparison of family and neighborhood effects on grades, test scores, educational attainment and income – evidence from Sweden", *Journal of Economical Inequality* 9: 207–226.

Lindquist, Matthew J. & Torsten Santavirta (2012) *Does placing children in out-of-home care increase their adult criminality?* Stockholm University: Swedish Institute for Social Research, Working paper 8/12.

Lindquist, Matthew J. and Santavirta, Torsten (2014) "Does placing children in foster care increase their adult criminality?", *Labour Economics* 31: 72–83.

Lindström, Peter (1995) *School context and delinquency – The impact of social class structure and academic balance.* Stockholm University: Department of Sociology, Project Metropolitan Research Report No 41.

Martens, Peter L (1976) *Patterns of child rearing ideology.* Stockholm University: Department of Sociology, Project Metropolitan Research Report No 5.

Martens, Peter L (1981) *Socioeconomic status, family structure and socialization of early adolescent children.* Stockholm University: Department of Sociology, Project Metropolitan Research Report No 16.

Metropolitan Project, Stockholm Birth Cohort – homepage: www.stockholmbirthcohort.su.se July 2018.

Modin, Bitte, Viveka Östberg & Ylva Almquist (2011) "Childhood peer status and adult susceptibility to anxiety and depression. A 30-year follow-up", *Journal of Abnormal Child Psychology* 39: 187–199.

Murray, Charles (1984) *Losing ground. American social policy 1950–1980.* New York: Basic Books.

Mäkelä, Klaus (2008) "Den nya svenska etikprövningslagen" [The new Swedish ethical review act], *Nordisk alkohol- och narkotikatidskrift* 25(3): 223–231.

Nilsson, Anders & Felipe Estrada (2009) *Kriminalitet och livschanser – uppväxtvillkor, brottslighet och levnadsförhållanden som vuxen [Criminality and life chances – upbringing, criminality, and living conditions as adult]* Stockholm: Institute for Futures Studies, Working report 2009:20.

Nilsson, Anders & Estrada, Felipe (2011). "Established or excluded? A longitudinal study of criminality, work and family formation", *European Journal of Criminology* 8 (3): 229–245.

Nilsson, Anders, Olof Bäckman & Felipe Estrada (2013) "Involvement in crime, individual resources and structural constraints", *British Journal of Criminology* 53 (2): 297–318.

Nilsson, Anders, Felipe Estrada & Olof Bäckman (2014) "Offending, drug abuse and life chanses – a longitudinal study of a Stockholm birth cohort", *Journal of Scandinavian Studies in Criminology and Crime Prevention* 15(2): 128–142.

Nordlöf, Barbro (2001) *Svenska adoptioner i Stockholm 1918–1973 [Swedish adoptions in Stockholm 1918–1973].* Stockholms stad [Stockholm municipality]: FoU-rapport 2001:8.

Olsson, Anders R. (1991) *IT och det fria ordet – myten om Storebror [IT and the free word – the myth about Big Brother].* Stockholm: Juridik & Samhälle.

Olsson, Anders R. (2004) *Privatliv & Internet – som olja och vatten?* [Private life & Internet – as oil and water]. Stockholm: TELDOK och KFB – kommunikationsforskningsberedningen, Telematik 2004, KFB-Rapport 2000:16, TELDOK Rapport 134.

Osler, Merete, Anne-Marie Nybo Anderssen, Rikke Lund, David G. Batty, Charlotte Ørsted Hougaard, Mogens Trab Damsgaard, Pernille Due & Bjørn E. Holstein (2004) "Revitalising the Metropolit 1953 Danish male birth cohort: background, aims and design", *Paediatric and Perinatal Epidemiology* 18: 385–394.

Osler, Merete, Rikke Lund, Margit Kriegbaum, Ulla Christensen & Anne-Marie Nybo Andersen (2006) "Cohort profile: The Metropolit 1953 Danish male birth cohort", *International Journal of Epidemiology* 35: 541–545.

von Otter, Cecilia & Sten-Åke Stenberg, (2012) *Social capital, human capital and parent-child relation quality: interacting for children's educational achievement?* British Journal of Sociology of Education 36(7): 996–1016.

von Otter, Cecilia (2014) "Family resources and mid-life level of education: a longitudinal study of the mediating influence of childhood parental involvement", *British Educational Research Journal* 40 (3): 555–574.

Proposition 2002/03:50 Etikprövning av forskning [Ethics and research].

Qwerin, Gunilla (1987), *Metropolit i massmedia: En studie av hur Metropolitprojektet bevakades och beskrevs av TV och Stockholmstidningarna [The Metropolitan Project in mass media: A study of how the Metropolitan Project was covered and described in TV and the Stockholm papers].* Stockholm: Allmänna förlaget, BRÅ forskning, 1987:4.

Rank, Mark R. & Li-Chen Cheng (1995) "Welfare use across generations: How important are the ties that bind?", *Journal of Marriage and the Family* 57: 673–684.

Renshon, Stanley A (1975) "Birth order and political socialization". In: Schwarz, David C & Sandra K Schwarz (eds.) *New Directions in Political Socialization.* New York: The Free Press.

Richardson, C. James (1977) "The problem of downward mobility", *British Journal of Sociology* 28 (3): 303–320.

Rojas, Yerko (2012) " Self-directed and interpersonal male violence in adolescence and young adulthood: a 30-year follow up of a Stockholm cohort", *Sociology of Health & Illness* 34 (1): 16–30.

Rojas, Yerko (2013) "School performance and gender differences in suicidal behaviour - a 30-year follow-up of a Stockholm cohort born in 1953", *Gender and Education* 25(5): 578–594.

Rojas, Yerko (2018). "Long-term suicidogenic effect of being mostly alone as a child in a Stockholm birth cohort – restating the role of social isolation in suicide", *Suicidology Online (accepted)*

Rojas, Yerko & Sten-Åke Stenberg (2010) "Early life circumstances and male suicide – A 30-year follow-up of a Stockholm cohort born in 1953", *Social Science & Medicine* 70: 420–427.

SIFO *Sverige nu 2012, enkät från SIFO, maj-augusti 2012*. [SIFO Sifo Research International *Sweden now 2012, Questionnaire from SIFO, May-August 2012*] https://en.wikipedia.org/wiki/Sifo

Siwe, Sture & Folke Borg (eds.) (1945) *Allt om barn, en handbok för föräldrar och lärare [All about children, a handbook for parents and teachers]*. Malmö: Richters förlag.

Smedberg, Lisa (1945) "Spädbarnets vård" [Caring for the Baby]. In: Siwe, Sture och Folke Borg (eds.) *Allt om barn [All about children]*. Malmö: Richters förlag.

Socialstyrelsen [The National Board of Health and Welfare] SOSFS 1990:22 [The Board's administrative provisions and general advice are published in SOSFS] *Allmänna råd om hemförlossning [General advice about home delivery] https://www.socialstyrelsen.se/english*.

Spock, Benjamin (1946) *The Common Sense Book of Baby and Child Care*. Duell, New York City: Sloan and Pearce.

Stenberg, Sten-Åke (2000) "Inheritance of welfare recipiency: An intergenerational study of social assistance recipiency in postwar Sweden", *Journal of Marriage and the Family* 62: 228–239.

Stenberg, Sten-Åke & Denny Vågerö (2006) "Cohort profile: The Stockholm birth cohort of 1953", *International Journal of Epidemiology* 35 (3): 546–548.

Stenberg, Sten-Åke, Denny Vågerö, Reidar Österman, Emma Arvidsson, Cecilia von Otter & Carl-Gunnar Janson (2007) "Stockholm birth cohort study 1953–2003: A new tool for life-course studies", *Scandinavian Journal of Public Health* 35: 104–110.

Stütz, Göran (1985) *Kamratstatus. En sociologisk studie av faktorer relaterade till kamratstatus bland skolelever i årskurs 6 i ett storstadsområde [Peer status. A sociological study of factors related to peer status among school children in grade 6 in a metropolitan area].* Stockholm: Department of Sociology, Project Metropolitan Research Report No 22.

Svalastoga, Kaare (1947) "Sosial ulikhet i en fangeleir" [Social Inequality in a Prison Camp]. In: Lange, August & Johan Schreiner (eds.) *Griniboken II [The Grini Book II].* Oslo: Gyldendal norsk forlag.

Svalastoga, Kaare (1964) *Projekt Metropolit – En orientering [The Metropolitan Project – an overview].* University of Copenhagen: Department of Sociology, Metropolitarkivet [Metropolitan Archive].

Svensson, Robert (2000) *Strategiska brott. Vilka brott förutsäger en fortsatt brottskarriär?* [Strategic crime. Which crimes predicts a continued crime career?]. Stockholm: The Swedish National Council for Crime Prevention, Brå-rapport 2000:3.

von Sydow, Gert (1955) "Amningsregim under nyföddperioden" [Breastfeeding regimes during the new-born period], *Jordemodern*, February.

Timms, D. W. G. (1989) "Overcrowding in childhood and mental health in early adulthood. A review with evidence from Stockholm". In: *Effects of housing conditions.* Stockholm University: Department of Sociology, Project Metropolitan Research Report No 27.

Torssander, Jenny & Ylva B. Almquist (2017) "Trajectories of economic, work- and health-related disadvantage and subsequent mortality risk: Findings from the 1953 Stockholm Birth Cohort", *Advances in Life Course Research* 31:57–67.

Torstensson, Marie (1987) *Drug-abusers in a metropolitan cohort.* Stockholm University: Department of Sociology, Project Metropolitan Research Report No 24.

Villkor för Coop medlemsprogram och Coop MedMera-kort 2012 [Terms and Conditions for Coop's Membership Program].

Vinnerljung, Bo (1996) *Fosterbarn som vuxna [Foster children as adults].* Lund: Arkiv förlag.

Vinnerljung, Bo & Marie Sallnäs (2008) "Into adulthood: a follow-up study of 718 young people who were placed in out-of-home care during their teens", *Child and Family Social Work*, 13 (2): 144–155.

Vinnerljung, Bo, Knut Sundell & Cecilia Andrée Löfholm (2006) "Former Stockholm child protection cases as young adults: Do outcomes differ between those that received services and those that did not?", *Child and Youth Services Review* 28 (1): 59–77.

Vägverket [Swedish Transport Administration] (2008) *Alkohol, droger och trafik [Alcohol, drugs, and traffic]*. Borlänge: Vägverket [Swedish Transport Administration], Broschyr 6.

Waldegren, Lennart (ed.) (1956) *Stockholmskalendern 1956 [The Stockholm Calendar 1956]*. Stockholm: Förlag Stockholms adresskalender, Esselte AB.

Waldenström Daniel (2010) "Ökande bortfall hotar svensk välfärdsstatistik", EKONOMISTATS Nationalekonomer om samhället, politiken och vetenskapen. http://ekonomistas.se/2010/11/19/okande-bortfall-hotar-svensk-valfardsstatistik/ July 2018.

Walldén, Marja (1982) *Sibling position and mental capacity*. Stockholm University: Department of Sociology, Project Metropolitan Research Report No 20.

Walldén, Marja (1988) "Birth weight and birth order". In: *Research Notes*. Stockholm University: Department of Sociology, Project Metropolitan Research Report No 25.

Walldén, Marja (1990) *Sibling position and mental capacity - reconsidered*. Stockholm University: Department of Sociology, Project Metropolitan Research Report No 31.

Walldén, Marja (1992) *Sibling position and the educational career*. Stockholm University: Department of Sociology, Project Metropolitan Research Report No 37.

Walldén, Marja (1994) "Sibling position and the educational process – the study of a Swedish birth cohort". In *Studies of a Stockholm Cohort*. Stockholm University: Department of Sociology, Project Metropolitan Research Report No 39.

Wikström, P-O. H. (1989) "Housing and offending. The relationship at the individual level in childhood and youth". In: *Effects of Housing Conditions*. Stockholm University: Department of Sociology, Project Metropolitan Research Report No 27.

Wilkinson, Richard G. & Kate Pickett (2009) *The Spirit Level -Why Equality is Better for Everyone*. London: Allen Lane.

Swedish Government Official Reports (Statens Offentliga Utredningar, SOU)

SOU 1987:31 *Integritetsskyddet i informationssamhället 4. Personregistrering och användning av personnummer [Protecting integrity in the information society: 4. Individual registers and use of personal identification numbers].*

SOU 2007:22 *Skyddet för den personliga integriteten – kartläggning och analys [Protection of personal integrity – Overview and analysis].*

SOU 2011:9. *Barnen som samhället svek – åtgärder med anledning av övergrepp och allvarliga försummelser i samhällsvården [The Children who were betrayed by society – Provisions due to abuse and neglect in foster care].*

SOU 2011:61. *Vanvård i social barnavård [Neglect in child protection services].*

SOU 2012: 20 *Kvalitetssäkring av forskning och utveckling vid statliga myndigheter [Assuring quality in research and development at government agencies].*

SOU 2014:45 (2014) Unik kunskap genom registerforskning [Unique knowledge through register-based research].

English – Swedish names of organisations and sources

Active Housekeeping – Aktiv hushållning
Association of School Principals and Directors of
Education – Skolledarförbundet
Association of Specialist and Technical Teachers – Svenska Facklärar-
förbundet
Association of Teachers in Colleges and Departments of Education –
Lärarhögskolornas och Seminariernas Lärarförbund
Board of Education for the City and County of Stockholm – Skol-
nämnden för Stockholms stad och län
Chancellor of Justice – Justitiekanslern
Centre Party – Centerpartiet
ERM, The ethical council for market research surveys – Etiska Rådet
för Marknadsundersökningar
Federation of Swedish Industries – Industriförbundet
General Children's Home – Allmänna barnhuset
Karolinska Institute Regional Research Ethics Review Board –
Karolinska Institutets regional forskningsetikkommitté
Local Education Authority in Stockholm – Skoldirektionen i
Stockholm
Medical Board – Medicinalstyrelsen
National Association of Legal Guardians – Målsmännens
riksförbund
National Board of Education – Skolöverstyrelsen
National Board of Health and Welfare – Socialstyrelsen
National Security Vetting Directive – Personalkungörelsen
National Union of Teachers – Lärarnas Riksförbund
Neglect and Abuse Inquiry – Vanvårdsutredningen
News from the National Board of Education – Aktuellt från Skol-
överstyrelsen
Ordinance - Förordning
Press Ombudsman (PO) – Allmänhetens Pressombudsman

Professional ethics council of the Swedish Union of Journalists
(YEN) – Journalistförbundets yrkesetiska nämnd

Project Metropolitan Archive – Metropolitarkivet

Redress Inquiry – Upprättelseutredningen

SIFO, Sifo Research International – Svenska institutet för opinions-
undersökningar

Social Democratic Party – Socialdemokratiska Arbetar Partiet (SAP).

Statistics Sweden – Statistiska centralbyrån (SCB)

Stockholm regional ethical review board – Stockholms regionala
etikprövningsnämnd

The Swedish Abstaining Motorists' Association – Motorförarnas
Helnykterhetsförbund (MHF)

Swedish Association for Mental Health – Svenska föreningen för
psykisk hälsovård

Stockholm Association of Midwives – Stockholms
barnmorskesällskap

Swedish Agency for Public Management – Statskontoret

Swedish Association of the Pharmaceutical Industry
(LIF) – Läkemedelsindustriföreningen

Swedish Association for Remedial Teaching – Svenska Förbundet för
Specialundervisning

Swedish Confederation of Professional Employees – Statstjänste-
männens Centralorganisation (TCO)

Swedish Conservatives – Moderaterna

Swedish Council for Social Science Research – Statens råd för
samhällsforskning

Swedish Data Protection Authority (DPA) – Datainspektionen

Swedish Liberal Party – Folkpartiet

Swedish Medical Research Council – Statens Medicinska
Forskningsråd

Swedish National Archive – Riksarkivet

Swedish National Council for Crime Prevention –
Brottsförebyggande Rådet (BRÅ)

Swedish Police Authority – Rikspolisstyrelsen
Swedish Press and Broadcasting Authority – Myndigheten för Radio
och TV
Swedish Research Council – Vetenskapsrådet
Swedish Security Service – Säkerhetspolisen (SÄPO)
Swedish Social Welfare Association – Svenska Socialvårdsförbundet
Swedish Sociological Association – Svenska Sociologförbundet
Swedish Supreme Commander – Överbefälhavaren
Swedish Teachers' Union – Sveriges Lärarförbund

List of illustrations

Cover image: Photographer: Unknown/DN/TT Nyhetsbyrån. Copyright: DN/TT Nyhetsbyrån, License: CC-BY-NC-ND.

1. The Norwegian historian and sociologist Kaare Svalastoga, who took the initiative for Project Metropolitan. Photographer: W. Månsson/ Nordfoto/NTB/TT Nyhetsbyrån. Copyright: Photographer: W. Månsson/ Nordfoto/NTB/TT Nyhetsbyrån, License: CC-BY-NC-ND. 2

2. Professor Gösta Carlsson. Photographer: Unknown/Sydsvenskan. Copyright: Sydsvenskan, Sydsvenskan, License: CC-BY-NC-ND. 4

3. Professor Gunnar Boalt. Photographer: Unknown/Department of Sociology at Stockholm University. Copyright: Department of Sociology at Stockholm Universit, License: CC-BY-NC-ND. 5

4. Professor Carl-Gunnar Janson. Photographer: Bo Präntare. Copyright: Bo Präntare, License: CC-BY-NC-ND. 6

5. Kaare Svalastoga was interned in the Grini prison camp between 1944 and the end of the war. Here we see the prisoners lined up for the final time in May 1945, waiting to be taken home on the buses that can be seen in the background. Photographer: Unknown/ Nordfoto/NTB/TT Nyhetsbyrån. Copyright: Nordfoto/NTB/TT Nyhetsbyrån, License: CC-BY-NC-ND. 8

6. Professor Kaare Svalastoga in 1969, pushing through the student barricades at the Department of Sociology, University of Copenhagen. Photographer: Erik Gleie/ STELLA pictures Stockholm/Oslo. Copyright: Erik Gleie/ STELLA pictures Stockholm/Oslo, License: CC-BY-NC-ND. 15

7. Stockholm schoolchildren born in 1953. Photographer: Unknown Copyright: Unknown, License: CC-BY-NC-ND. 19

8. The Data Protection Authority's Director General, Jan Freese, 1985. Photographer: Kent Hult/Sydsvenskan. Copyright: Kent Hult/ Sydsvenskan, License: CC-BY-NC-ND. 26

9. The TV-show "Magasinet", February 1986. Photographer: Jan Wirén/Sydsvenskan. Copyright: Jan Wirén/Sydsvenskan, License: CC-BY-NC-ND. 42

10. Sten-Åke Stenberg and Denny Vågerö applied for permission to update the old Metropolitan data set in 2003. When the update process had been completed, the project was given a new name. It is now known as "The Stockholm Birth Cohort.". Photographer: Reidar Österman. Copyright: Reidar Österman, License: CC-BY-NC-ND. 62

11. Sergels torg, Stockholm. Photographer: Sten-Åke Stenberg. Copyright: Sten-Åke Stenberg, License: CC-BY-NC-ND. 70

12. Photographer: Arne Sohlström. Copyright: Arne Sohlström, License: CC-BY-NC-ND. 86

13. When the Project Metropolitan children were born, there were only test broadcasts of Swedish television. When the radio stores showed these broadcasts, spectators flocked around. Photographer: Tore Falk/ TT Nyhetsbyrån. Copyright: Tore Falk/TT Nyhetsbyrån, License: CC-BY-NC-ND. 90

14. Photographer: Björn Henriksson's Malmö collection/ Sydsvenska Medicinhistoriska Sällskapet, Lund. Copyright: Björn Henriksson's Malmö collection/ Sydsvenska Medicinhistoriska Sällskapet, Lund, License: BY-NC-SA. 98

15. A girl is getting dressed, children's home in Örby/Stockholm. Photographer: Unknown/Pressens bild/TT Nyhetsbyrån. Copyright: Pressens bild/TT Nyhetsbyrån, License: BY-NC-ND. 116

16. A girl draws a picture of her mother, children's home in Örby/ Stockholm. Photographer: Unknown/Pressens bild/TT Nyhetsbyrån. Copyright: Pressens bild/TT Nyhetsbyrån, License: BY-NC-ND. 121

17. Subway station. Photographer: Sten-Åke Stenberg. Copyright: Sten-Åke Stenberg, License: BY-NC-ND. 126

18. Child in Stockholm 1954. Photographer: Alma Stenberg. Copyright: Sten-Åke Stenberg, License: BY-NC-ND. 134

19. Single child, middle child, big brother or little sister? What impact does birth order have on incomes as adult? Photographer: Arne Sohlström. Copyright: Arne Sohlström, License: CC-BY-NC-ND. 142

Acknowledgements

A book such as this is not a one-man project, and I would like to take this opportunity to thank those who have not only supported me in this endeavour, but without whose efforts the book would never have come about – neither in the Swedish nor in the English version.

The original Swedish version "Född 1953 – Folkhemsbarn i forskarfokus" was published in 2013 and was intended to be The Story about a remarkable project and dataset, and a Swedish post-war cohort. Finalizing that book was a long process based on the work and assistance from many people at many different stages.

However, none of this would have been possible without the initial and tireless efforts of the late professor Carl-Gunnar Janson who led Project Metropolitan for several decades.

Without good housekeeping, the work of professor Janson and his team would not have come to proper use. I must therefore also mention the invaluable work of Kerstin Nelander (who very sadly passed away in 2017 at a far too early age), Amir Sariaslan and Karina Schiøtt Jensen for bringing order to the Metropolitan Archive during the mid 2000s.

Many other colleagues and friends have provided constructive feedback or helped in a number of ways, primarily in connection with the finalization of the original Swedish version. I would like to thank the following persons – in alphabetical order – for their work and support: Susanne Alm, Ylva B. Almquist, Jan Andersson, Sven-Åke Aulin, Karin Helmersson Bergmark, Olof Bäckman, Christofer Edling, Stefan Englund, Robert Erikson, Felipe Estrada, Tommy Ferrarini, Joanna Stjernschantz Forsberg, Bjørn E. Holstein, Inger Höglund, Ann-Marie Janson, Walter Korpi, Marie Thorstensson Levander, Matthew J. Lindquist, Anders Nilsson, Cecilia von Otter, Therese Reitan, Yerko Rojas, Ann-Mari Sellerberg, Kristina Sonmark,

Magnus Stenbeck, Emil Stensson, Anders Tengström, Denny Vågerö, Marja Walldén, and Reidar Österman.

The journey from a Swedish version to an English one turned out to be quite strenuous and challenging. Apart from the obvious need for substantial updates due to e.g. legal amendments and new publications based on the Metropolitan data, translation is so much more than exchanging one language with another. I am, then, profoundly indebted to David Shannon, who has worked tirelessly not only translating the text but also transforming it into something comprehensible to Swedes and non-Swedes alike. Based on her life-long experience of the English language, Barbara Roterud provided a vital link in this conversion from text to meaning – thank you both!

Last, but not least, I wish to thank Åke Wibergs stiftelse for their contribution to the publishing costs, and the reviewers for useful comments and suggestions.

Special thanks

I would like to say a special thank-you to my cohort colleagues whom we contacted in various ways and who agreed to be interviewed. Ulla Abelin, who grew up in the Östermalm district and in Vällingby, scientist and teacher; Gerd Svensson from Högdalen, nurse; Margareta Kempe Allansson, who grew up in the Östermalm district and Lidingö, formerly a dancer, now an administrator; Jan Andersson, who grew up in Hagsätra, criminologist, Ph.D.; Bo Östlund, who grew up in Kärrtorp, psychoanalyst; and Weje Sandén, who grew up in Gubbängen, journalist and consultant. Three of those interviewed were also cited by the newspapers in 1986: Manni Thofte, who grew up in Solna and in the Östermalm district, explorer and footballer, and now marketing director, who shook his fist at Project Metropolitan in the newspaper *Expressen*; Agneta Wolffelt, salesperson, who grew up in Vasastan and who stated in *Dagens Nyheter* that she knew nothing about the project, and the journalist Lotta Samuelsson Aschberg, who grew up in Södra Ängby, and who stated in *Expressen* that Project Metropolitan had stolen her life.

The interviews were conducted by Ulla Kindenberg and without her, this book would not have been possible. Apart from her skills as an interviewer, I particularly appreciated the way she questioned my social science jargon and her efforts to improve the flavour of the text with unrelenting patience and enthusiasm.

My sincere thanks to you all!

www.ingramcontent.com/pod-product-compliance
Lightning Source LLC
Chambersburg PA
CBHW050241290326
41930CB00044B/3333